Guidelines for Drafting and Editing Legislation

Guidelines for Drafting and Editing Legislation

by

Bryan A. Garner

in conjunction with

The Uniform Law Commission

Foreword by Harriet Lansing
President, The Uniform Law Commission

Distributed as a Public Service by the Uniform Law Commission and LawProse Inc.
Published by RosePen Books

Bryan A. Garner, author and lexicographer, has written more than 20 books on legal language, advocacy, business writing, English grammar, and more, including *Garner's Dictionary of Legal Usage*, *Garner's Modern English Usage*, and two books with Justice Antonin Scalia: *Making Your Case: The Art of Persuading Judges* and *Reading Law: The Interpretation of Legal Texts*. Garner is the editor in chief of *Black's Law Dictionary* and Distinguished Research Professor of Law at Southern Methodist University. He founded LawProse Inc., a Dallas-based training and consulting company, in 1990. Through LawProse, he teaches continuing-legal-education seminars on many subjects, including legal drafting.

The Uniform Law Commission is a nonprofit, nonpartisan organization of volunteers promoting uniformity of laws throughout the United States. Founded in 1892, the ULC has drafted and promoted more than 300 statutes and codes, including (in cooperation with the American Law Institute) the Uniform Commercial Code. Also called the National Conference of Commissioners on Uniform State Laws, the ULC comprises about 350 commissioners appointed by states, the District of Columbia, the U.S. Virgin Islands, and Puerto Rico. Its work simplifies people's lives and helps business transactions by providing consistent rules and procedures from state to state. Every day, when a person conducts business, enters a contract, buys or sells property, or tends to a family matter, it's likely that a ULC law applies.

ROSEPEN

RosePen Books, Dallas, Texas 75254
 Published 2016.
Printed in the United States of America.

ISBN 978-0-9979770-0-4

To the memory of eight great legislative drafters

Justinian I
(ca. A.D. 482–565)

Edward III
(1327–1377)

Gouverneur Morris
(1752–1816)

Jean-Jacques Régis de Cambacérès
(1753–1824)

James Fitzjames Stephen
(1829–1894)

Karl Llewellyn
(1893–1962)

Reed Dickerson
(1909–1991)

Charles Alan Wright
(1927–2000)

Other Books Written or Edited by Bryan A. Garner

Black's Law Dictionary
(Thomson Reuters, 10th ed. 2014)

Garner's Dictionary of Legal Usage
(Oxford Univ. Press, 3d ed. 2011)

Garner's Modern English Usage
(Oxford Univ. Press, 4th ed. 2016)

Reading Law: The Interpretation of Legal Texts
with Justice Antonin Scalia (Thomson/West, 2012)

Making Your Case: The Art of Persuading Judges
with Justice Antonin Scalia (Thomson/West, 2008)

The Winning Brief
(Oxford Univ. Press, 3d ed. 2014)

The Redbook: A Manual on Legal Style
(West, 3d ed. 2013)

Garner on Language and Writing
with foreword by Justice Ruth Bader Ginsburg (ABA, 2009)

Legal Writing in Plain English
(Univ. of Chicago Press, 2d ed. 2013)

The Elements of Legal Style
(Oxford Univ. Press, 2d ed. 2002)

The Law of Judicial Precedent
with 12 appellate-judge coauthors (Thomson Reuters, 2016)

The Chicago Guide to Grammar, Usage, and Punctuation
(Univ. of Chicago Press, 2016)

The Winning Oral Argument
(West, 2009)

Ethical Communications for Lawyers
(LawProse, 2009)

The Chicago Manual of Style, ch. 5, "Grammar and Usage"
(Univ. of Chicago Press, 16th ed. 2010)

HBR Guide to Better Business Writing
(Harvard Business Review Press, 2013)

Securities Disclosure in Plain English
(CCH, 1999)

The Rules of Golf in Plain English
with Jeffrey Kuhn (Univ. of Chicago Press, 4th ed. 2016)

Quack This Way: David Foster Wallace and Bryan A. Garner Talk Language and Writing
(RosePen, 2013)

A New Miscellany-at-Law
by Sir Robert Megarry (Hart, 2005)

Texas, Our Texas: Remembrances of the University
(Eakin Press, 1984)

Basic Law Terms
(West Group, 1999)

Criminal Law Terms
(West Group, 2000)

Family Law Terms
(West Group, 2001)

Business Law Terms
(West Group, 1999)

Bertie Gets It Right: Good Grammar for Kids and Their Parents
(RosePen, 2016)

Contents

Foreword vii

Preface ix

1. Basic Principles 1

1.1 Clarity and readability. 1
- (A) Plain English. 1
- (B) Reasonable sentence length. 5
- (C) Avoiding jargon. 10
- (D) Consistent usage. 13
- (E) Preventing error, misstatement, and ambiguity. 14
- (F) Abundant headings. 19

1.2 Conciseness. 28
- (A) Generally. 28
- (B) Clauses into phrases. 32
- (C) Phrases into words. 33
- (D) Doublets and triplets. 34
- (E) Eliminating zombie nouns. 37

1.3 Format with hanging indents. 38
- (A) Cascading from the left. 38
- (B) Format as integral to the statute. 42

2. General Conventions 43

2.1 Obligations and prohibitions generally. 43
- (A) Definitions for words of authority. 43
- (B) Elimination of *shall.* 43
- (C) Straightforward wordings for powers and duties. 47
- (D) Alternative meaning for *shall.* 48
- (E) Elimination of *may not.* 48

2.2 Criminal prohibitions. 49

2.3 Degree of detail. 55
- (A) Avoiding detail when unnecessary. 55
- (B) Using general terms when clear. 55

2.4 Grammatical number: preference for singular. 56

2.5 Tense. 57
- (A) General preference for present. 57
- (B) For conditions precedent, default to present perfect. 57

2.6 Voice. 58
- (A) Preferring active voice. 58
- (B) Replacing passive voice with adjective. 59
- (C) When to use passive voice. 59

2.7 Positives and negatives. 60
- (A) Preference for positives. 60
- (B) Negatives when necessary. 62

2.8 Gender neutrality. 63
- (A) The goal of invisibility. 63
- (B) Enumeration of nonsexist methods. 64

2.9 Handling numbers, percentages, and currency. 65
- (A) Preference for numerals. 65
- (B) No word–numeral doublets. 65
- (C) Preference for percent sign (%) and section sign (§). 68
- (D) No ".00" for round dollar amounts. 69

2.10 Calculations, diagrams, charts, and other graphics. 70

3. Structure 73

3.1 Organization. 73
- (A) Logical arrangement. 73
- (B) Grouping related items together. 76

3.2 Structural divisions. 78
- (A) The parts. 78
- (B) Two-part requirement. 79
- (C) References to structural divisions. 79

3.3 Numbering of subparts. 81
- (A) Default recommendation. 81
- (B) Consistency. 82
- (C) Avoiding gaps. 83
- (D) Avoiding romanettes except as a last resort. 83

3.4 Enumerations. 85
- (A) Setting off enumerated items. 85
- (B) Appositive for foreshadowing. 90
- (C) Parallel requirements in parallel form. 91
- (D) Economy of parallelism. 92
- (E) Unnumbered "dangling" flush text. 96
- (F) Bullets. 98
- (G) Capitalization. 99
- (H) Avoiding unhelpful enumeration, or "splintering." 102

3.5 **Key Terms and Their Definitions.** 103
- (A) Sparing use of definitions. 103
- (B) Placement. 104
- (C) Glossary. 106
- (D) Precise terminology. 106
- (E) No counterintuitive definitions. 106

4. Syntax 107

4.1 **Kernel sentence parts together.** 107

4.2 **Principle of end weight.** 109

4.3 **Conditions—in general.** 110
- (A) Short condition. 110
- (B) Long condition and short main clause. 110
- (C) Long condition and long main clause. 112
- (D) Hidden conditions. 113

4.4 **Exceptions.** 115
- (A) When to state first. 115
- (B) When to state last. 115

4.5 **Provisos.** 116
- (A) *Provided that.* 116
- (B) *Provided, however, that.* 117

4.6 **Interruptive phrases.** 118
- (A) Avoiding subject–verb and verb–object separation. 118
- (B) Adverbial interruptive phrases. 119
- (C) Other interruptive phrases. 120

4.7 **Modifiers.** 121
- (A) Putting related words together. 121
- (B) When to rephrase. 121

4.8 **Prepositional phrases.** 123
- (A) Minimizing *of*-phrases. 123
- (B) Changing to adjective. 124
- (C) Changing to possessive. 125

4.9 **Punctuation.** 126
- (A) Colon before indented enumerations. 126
- (B) Semicolon at end of nonterminal parts. 126
- (C) Comma after introductory phrase. 127
- (D) Serial comma and semicolon. 127
- (E) Double-dash construction for important interpolations. 127
- (F) No hyphen for most prefixed terms. 128
- (G) Hyphenating phrasal adjectives. 129

5. Words and Phrases 131

5.1 **Pronouns and their antecedents.** 131
- (A) Preference for pronouns when unambiguous. 131
- (B) Necessity of an antecedent. 131
- (C) Avoiding cataphora. 131
- (D) Agreement in number. 132

5.2 **Relative pronouns.** 133
- (A) *That* vs. *which.* 133
- (B) Nonrestrictive *which.* 134
- (C) Remote relatives. 134

5.3 **Conjunctions.** 136
- (A) Conjunctive and disjunctive subparts. 136
- (B) *But* vs. *and.* 136
- (C) Preference for *But* over *However* as a sentence-starter. 137
- (D) Avoiding comma splices with *however.* 137

5.4 **Specific words and forms to avoid.** 138

5.5 **Other wordings requiring attention.** 165

5.6 **Matters not covered here.** 168

Appendix A: A Note on Prohibitions, Pains, and Penalties 169

Appendix B: Two Model Acts Using These Guidelines 179

Appendix C: A Typical Statute in Need of an Overhaul, with Annotations 191

Select Bibliography 199

Index 205

Foreword

When the Uniform Law Commission was created in 1892, its specific mission was to achieve "greater unanimity of law throughout the country" and to eliminate "perplexity, uncertainty and confusion" caused by unnecessarily "variant and conflicting laws."[1] Known during most of our 123 years by our formal title, the National Conference of Commissioners on Uniform State Laws, the Commission has promulgated more than 250 uniform and model acts that have been adopted throughout the United States. During these years the Commission has earned accolades for its historic work in law reform. Justice Ruth Bader Ginsburg attributes the ULC's production of legislative drafts of "uncommon excellence" to the Commission's "tireless attention to detail," the devotion of a collection of "fine minds," and its cumulative years of professional expertise.[2]

From the beginning, our goal at the Commission has been to produce crisp, accurate, and readable statutes that will stand the test of time and serve the purposes of our states and their citizens while maintaining the vitality of our federal system. The statutes should also be as comprehensible as possible to as many people as possible. The casual observer might have little idea just how much attention every sentence in a uniform or model act receives from all across North America. Our members immerse themselves in the content and language of every act, reading and rereading to make the entire act practical and workable, all for the sake of benefiting the law and society.

We bring experts from every state to our drafting task. The ULC has always included the principal administrative officer of each state's legislative reference bureau or reviser's office. Since the legendary struggles for careful crafting and formulation of the Uniform Commercial Code, the ULC has worked with professional reporters on every act. We have created a Style Committee that has functioned as a standing committee since 1938, and we have charged that committee with helping the Executive Committee by periodically reviewing and making recommendations for improvements in the Conference's drafting rules. Throughout our work, we have adhered to our basic ULC rule that the Commission will not finally approve an act unless it has been read line by line and considered section by section at a minimum of two annual meetings. This degree of scrutiny brings many subtle issues to the forefront.

In 2014, I asked the renowned lexicographer and legal drafter Bryan A. Garner to work with the Commission on drafting issues, and together we devised a plan for *Guidelines on Drafting and Editing Legislation*. The idea was for Bryan to assess the literature on legal drafting, isolate the most important principles

1 The State Boards of Commissioners for Promoting Uniformity of Law in the U.S., *Report of Proceedings of the First Conference* 3 (1892); Walter P. Armstrong Jr., *A Century of Service: A Centennial History of the National Conference of Commissioners on Uniform Laws* 20 (1991).

2 *National Conference of Commissioners on Uniform State Laws and Proceedings of the 112th Annual Conference* 81 (2003).

(including reformative principles), and illustrate their workability by having him apply them to existing statutes throughout the United States. We wanted the *Guidelines* to have more illustration than lengthy commentary. Working with Bryan has been an exciting and fast-moving process.

In our world of legislative drafting, we are keenly aware of the need for a concrete, focused, and easily accessible guide to drafting laws. The structure, content, and examples of palpable improvement throughout *Guidelines for Drafting and Editing Legislation* accomplish this mission. Using the techniques brings an unprecedented degree of precision to the literature of legal drafting. Many Uniform Law Commissioners brought their expertise and enthusiasm to these *Guidelines* by carefully reviewing Bryan's advice and revisions and making suggestions.

Because the *Guidelines* are intended not to ratify current practices but to improve them, we were not surprised to find that Bryan's reforms in many instances extend beyond our own conventions in several ways. He has exceeded and sometimes contradicted what we now require in the Uniform Law Commission's Drafting Rules. In doing so, he has provided highly useful material that will serve universally as a reference guide for our commissioners who are working through drafting and editing challenges, as well as for ULC reporters who are stuck on a problem or a passage and do not know where to go for a ready and reliable answer. But many of his precepts jibe beautifully with our Drafting Rules, serving as excellent illustrations of them. Bryan has tactfully suggested ways in which our Style Committee and Executive Committee might go through future rounds of amending our Drafting Rules.

The most exhilarating aspect of these *Guidelines for Drafting and Editing Legislation* is that they will be available to the larger world of legislative drafters and legislatures. With these *Guidelines*—and with his earlier booklet on court rules[3]—Bryan Garner has made an incomparable contribution to clarity and coherence in the halls of our legislatures, the pages of our statute books, and the everyday world of all people as we try to plan our lives and predict legal consequences. So we are particularly pleased to be associated with this landmark publication.

Harriet Lansing
President
Uniform Law Commission
Saint Paul, Minnesota
July 2015

3 Available for free download at <http://www.lawprose.org/bryan-garner/books-by-bryan-garner/guidelines-drafting-editing-court-rules/>.

Preface

Legislative drafting is a peculiar genre of writing. It's a subset of expository prose that (1) imposes duties and liabilities, grants entitlements, supplies remedies, and confers statuses—all with the authority of government; (2) deals almost exclusively with events that have not yet occurred but that are thought to be foreseeable; (3) is predictably subject to hostile, bad-faith misreadings by those wishing not to be bound by its dictates; and (4) constitutes the primary work of legislators, who officially exercise their law-making function exclusively through the provisions they pass.

Statutes are subject to different schools of interpretation—especially today any of three. The textualist school seeks to accord the words enacted their fair meaning and is concerned more with what the legislature has actually said than with what its members might have subjectively intended.[1] The purposivist school considers the words of the statute as enacted only one of many factors to be accounted for in statutory interpretation, others being the putative intent of the legislators collectively (whether expressed or not) and the judge's conception of the statute's broad purposes.[2] The consequentialist school assesses primarily not the words of the statute but instead the judge's own sense of the desirability of the outcome.[3] The textualists interpret statutes not "strictly" but "fairly," applying recognized canons of construction, most of which have developed over centuries; the purposivists and consequentialists interpret statutes "loosely," according to their sense of what the legislature must have been driving at—or should have been.

Despite the competing theories—and whatever their relative merits may be—legislative drafters work best when they write for the textualists. Not only are textualist judges the only ones who will care much about legislative drafters' handiwork, but they are also the only ones who are likely to appreciate it. If a judge who applies a statute ignores its words, or goes around or behind them, then there is simply no help for it. To that degree the words of the statute are beside the point. But most judges of all political backgrounds closely heed legislative words: they seek meaning from what appears on the printed page, not according to what is in their own heads and hearts. They gather meaning from punctuation, the placement of modifiers, the structure of provisions, the implications of consistent or inconsistent terminology, the import of statutory definitions, and the accepted understandings of words. They are mostly of a textualist bent.

1 *See generally* Antonin Scalia & Bryan A. Garner, *Reading Law: The Interpretation of Legal Texts* (2012).

2 *See generally* Henry M. Hart & Albert M. Sacks, *The Legal Process: Basic Problems in the Making and Application of Law* (William N. Eskridge & Philip P. Frickey eds., 1994).

3 *See, e.g.*, Richard A. Posner, *Judicial Opinions and Appellate Advocacy in Federal Courts—One Judge's Views*, 51 Duq. L. Rev. 3, 16–17 (2013).

Hence drafters should approach their work with an unusual degree of linguistic and syntactic rigor.[4] Their sentences have an effect not usual for most compositions: they govern civil society as we know it. They prescribe the conditions under which a citizen may be deprived of liberty and sometimes life itself, the situations in which taxes may be assessed and property confiscated, and the other facets of the intricate network of rules by which our polity operates.

Although nobody—nobody—can aspire to comprehend all the statutory law that governs his or her life, legislative drafters do well to espouse the fiction that anybody should be able to read and understand enacted statutes. People ought to be able to consult the law and feel enlightened, not baffled. That's the goal. It's not always achievable. But if drafters will keep the ordinary reader always in mind, then statutes won't be any more complex than they absolutely must be.

This book is about avoiding undue complexity. It is rich in before-and-after examples, all of them real. It focuses on aspects of legislative drafting that are common to all English-speaking jurisdictions. Yet many of its precepts apply equally to other languages. I hope it will help you achieve the noblest goal that any drafter can pursue: clarity.

❧ ❧ ❧

These guidelines are a natural extension of several of my earlier projects. Since the late 1980s, I have often been retained by federal and state entities to revise statutes, rules, and regulations—and to teach legislative drafting to staff counsel. The most ambitious of these undertakings were wholesale rewrites of the Federal Rules of Civil Procedure, the Federal Rules of Appellate Procedure, and the Federal Rules of Criminal Procedure—for each of which I had the initial and the laboring oar (though *many* others were involved, including Joseph Spaniol on all the rules and Joseph Kimble on the Civil Rules). When the revised versions were enacted from 1997 to 2008, the Standing Committee on Rules of Practice and Procedure had achieved something historic: a massive quantity of rules streamlined for readability and clarity. The style was now equal to the content—as it never had been before.

In my editing and teaching, I have tried to discover the most refined principles of legal drafting. That effort has required a good deal of selectivity within the copious literature on legislative drafting. It has also required the development of new techniques, especially regarding stances on words of authority, enumerations, numbering, placement of modifiers, and page layout.

When President Harriet Lansing of the Uniform Law Commission asked me how I might help the Commission improve its already high standards of drafting, I suggested preparing this book. It is loosely modeled on my *Guidelines for Drafting and Editing Court Rules*, first published in 1996 by the Administrative Office of the United States Courts.

Examples appear from all the states—and Guam as well. I probably owe an apology to two states: Texas and Wisconsin. They are overrepresented not because their statutes are particularly poor but instead for another reason: my

---

4 *See* Jeremy Bentham, "Of the Style of the Laws," in 3 *The Works of Jeremy Bentham* 207, 208 (John Bowring ed., 1843) ("[I]t behooves the legislator either to be or to employ a consummate grammarian." [updating the spelling *behoves* to *behooves*]).

library contains all the statutory law from those two states. The volumes were conveniently nearby, and I took full advantage of that fact.

The extensive array of examples serves three main purposes. First, it demonstrates the consistent workability of the principles to a broad range of statutory subjects—from state and federal statutes to restatements of the law. Second, it reveals a fair sampling of the work produced by American legislative bodies. Third, it lends a variety that is highly desirable in a book that might be expected to be dry as dust. Many of the illustrative statutes are inherently interesting—for example, the one about the official pronunciation of "Arkansas" (see p. 3).

Poor legislative drafting used to be a closely kept secret. Nobody knew except a few lawyers. But the Internet has changed things: nowadays anybody can find any statute without having to trek to the law library to pull dusty tomes off the shelves. More and more people consult legislation and witness the embarrassments that have long lain hidden in the statute books. They might not know it, but there is no repeal by disuse: a statute is repealed only by explicit abrogation or flat-out contradiction by a later statute.[5] So we're governed by lots of old statutes as well as lots of new statutes written as if they were 250 years old.

To the extent that legislatures throughout the world were to adopt the principles of clear legislative drafting, their work would be better and more reliable—and less susceptible to needless litigation. The new techniques might slow drafters down at first, but once drafters become adept at the techniques they'll become more efficient than ever.

Some legislatures work in more than one language. If you're multilingual, consider how much easier it is to translate the righthand columns in this book than their counterparts in the lefthand columns. That point as much as any other clinches the argument for the revisions.

The casual reader might think of facile ways of improving the revisions still further. On the second example on page 86, for example, you might think that *residence* includes *usual place of abode* and that the suggested improvement therefore still contains five unnecessary words (*or usual place of abode*). But if a lawyer takes a moment to reflect about the legal meaning of *residence*, it will immediately become clear why the extra words are necessary as a matter of legal meaning. You're welcome to play the "Gotcha!" game with the righthand versions. Please just do it with a modicum of humility and appropriate self-doubt.

While reviewing these *Guidelines*, keep in mind that they're intended for both drafting and editing. The idea is to improve the drafting to the extent possible at whatever stage—whether before a bill is introduced, when it is reported out of a legislative committee, when it is being circulated at a legislative session, when it is being "engrossed" for final approval by a legislature, when it is being "enrolled" for approval by the executive, or years later when it is being amended or codified. The earlier clarity can come, the better. But clarity arrived at late is better than no clarity at all. To the extent that session laws as well as codified versions reflect these *Guidelines*, everyone affected by the statute stands to benefit.

Throughout the book you'll find shaded boxes at the bottom of some pages. The quotations there serve three purposes. First, they make an argument: you can assess it as you go. Second, they demonstrate age-old wisdom about legislative drafting: consider their years of publication. Third, they lend visual variety

5 *See Reading Law*, *supra* n.1. at 336–39.

and perhaps some aesthetic pleasure. One hopes that sages past might applaud the efforts of the Uniform Law Commissioners to bring their vision to fruition.

Besides Judge Lansing, many Uniform Law Commissioners have played important roles in developing the *Guidelines*: Jerry L. Bassett, Deborah E. Behr, Marion Benfield, David D. Biklen, Carl S. Bjerre, Diane F. Boyer-Vine, James M. Concannon, Vincent C. DeLiberato Jr., Jessica D. French, Debra H. Lehrmann, James C. McKay Jr., Thomas Morris, Louise Nadeau, Joanne M. Pepperl, Rebecca Rockwell, Nathaniel Sterling, John Stieff, Kyle Thiessen, Michele L. Timmons, and Lee Yeakel. Also helping to review the drafts were the ULC's deputy legislative director, Katie Robinson, and staff counsel Ben Orzeske, Garrett Heilman, and Lindsay Beaver. The professional staff of the Minnesota Office of the Revisor of Statutes lent a hand indexing and proofreading the manuscript: Amber Anderson, Sally Ash, Nate Bergin, Julie Campbell, Robert Chenier, Maryann Corbett, Dan Israel, and Ian Lewenstein.

Some friends who are internationally renowned as legal drafters commented on early drafts. I'm grateful to Mark Adler of Dorking, U.K.; Peter Butt of Sydney, Australia; Martin Cutts of Whaley Bridge, U.K.; and Joseph Kimble of Lansing, Michigan.

Dean Ward Farnsworth of the University of Texas and Professor Robert Weisberg of Stanford University generously read and commented on my "Note on Prohibitions, Pains, and Penalties" (Appendix A). They helped me sharpen the essay.

My colleagues at LawProse Inc. in Dallas provided an invaluable service in gathering examples and helping edit them. My heartfelt thanks to John S. Adams, Karolyne H.C. Garner, Christina Gigliotti, Tiger Jackson, Becky R. McDaniel, and Jeff Newman—outstanding lawyers and editors all. Our paralegal and staff editor, Ryden McComas Anderson, proved essential as well. Jeff Newman typeset the book with his usual virtuosity.

To my students at Southern Methodist University and the University of Texas—both cohorts in the spring of 2015—I'm grateful for the suggestions about statutes to be rewritten. Locating the exemplars was no small chore. Of particular help were my excellent research assistants known as Garner Law Scholars at Southern Methodist University: Brittaney N. Davis, Katherine Gnadinger, Ryan C. Hale, Jessica L. Kirk, William K. Knisley, and Victoria L. Spickler. For months on end, they supplied me with a steady diet of statutes to be rewritten. I'm also grateful to my interns from Texas Tech University School of Law: Jeryn R. Crabb, Abigail Drake, Elizabeth Nanez, Aaron Powell, and Petrus J. Wassdorf. Their keen editing polished the final version.

Bryan A. Garner
Dallas, Texas
January 2016

1. Basic Principles

1.1 Clarity and readability.

(A) Plain English.

Use the simplest, most straightforward words and sentences you can. Your goal is to stay, as much as possible, within the bounds of ordinary idiom. Write natural-sounding sentences, but always with an eye to eradicating imprecision. Whenever your tone becomes stiff and artificial, you're bound to be drafting poorly—and probably imprecisely.

The left-hand versions throughout § 1.1(A) exhibit many faults addressed throughout this book. All these faults can make a passage "not plain English."

NOT THIS:	BUT THIS:
The issuance of such bonds, the maturities and other details thereof, the rights of the holders thereof and the rights, duties and obligations of the corporation in respect to the same shall be governed by the provisions of this article inso-far as the same may be applicable. **Ala. Code § 9-10-37(c).**	This article governs the bonds' issuance, maturities, and other details; the bondholders' rights; and the corporation's rights and duties under the bonds.
No action shall be brought in any court in any of the following cases, unless the promise or agreement upon which such action shall be brought, or some memorandum thereof, shall be in writing and signed by the party to be charged therewith or by some person by him thereunto lawfully authorized . . . . **Tex. Rev. Civ. Stat. art. 3995 (repealed in 2013).**	To sue in any of the following types of cases, the complaining party must base the lawsuit on a written promise or agreement—or a memorandum of it—signed by the party to be charged or by that party's lawful agent . . . .
Every individual who enters the property of another to hunt or fish without first having obtained permission from an authorized person in control of hunting and fishing rights or his agent is under a duty to look for posted notices. In the apparent absence of such notices, the individual intending to enter is nevertheless under a duty to determine if practicable whether the property is registered under the terms of this Article. **N.C. Gen. Stat. § 113-284.**	A person must look for posted notices before entering another's property to hunt or fish without permission from an authorized person or agent. If no notices are visible, the person must still determine if practicable whether the property is registered under this Article.
(a) **Interagency Process.**—The Director of the Office of Science and Technology Policy, in consultation with the Administrator, the Administrator of the National Oceanic and Atmospheric Administration, and other relevant stakeholders, shall develop a process to transition, when appropriate, Administration Earth science and space weather missions or sensors into operational status. The process shall include coordination of annual agency budget requests as required to execute the transitions. **51 U.S.C. § 60502(a).**	(A) **Interagency process.** The Director of the Office of Science and Technology Policy—in consultation with the Administrator, the Administrator of the National Oceanic and Atmospheric Administration, and other relevant stakeholders—must develop plans for Earth-science and space-weather missions and sensors. The plans must coordinate annual agency budget requests to make these missions and sensors operational.

NOT THIS:	BUT THIS:
When such river, stream or bay is navigable, the company shall, for the safety of persons navigating the same, maintain a red light at each outer side and a white light at each inner side of said draws, which shall be kept lighted between sunset and daylight. The company shall also keep a suitable person at each bridge or viaduct to open the draws for the free passage of all vessels with standing masts or pipes. For each neglect to keep such light and to open the draws when necessary, the company shall forfeit one hundred dollars, to be recovered with costs in any court having jurisdiction thereof by any person suing for the same within six months after the time of such neglect. **N.J. Stat § 48:12-42.**	(A) **Drawbridge lighting and staffing.** Between sunset and sunrise, the company must maintain a red light at each outer side and a white light at each inner side of a drawbridge on navigable waters. The company must at all times keep a qualified person at each bridge or viaduct to allow all vessels with standing masts or pipes to pass. (B) **Penalty for violation.** Each violation of (A) is punishable by a $100 fine plus court costs recoverable by an injured party. A claim must be brought within 6 months after the violation.
187.01. Religious societies. **(1) How formed.** The members, over 18 years of age, not less than three in number, of any church or society of any religious sect or denomination which shall have been organized in this state and which, at the time, maintains regular public worship may, after due public notice given at some stated meeting of such church, sect or denomination, and any five or more persons of like age, not members of any religious congregation, desirous of organizing a corporation in connection with a church of their own peculiar tenets to be associated therewith, may organize a corporation for religious, charitable or educational purposes in the manner hereinafter provided. **Wis. Stat. § 187.01(1).**	**187.01 Religious societies.** (A) **Existing organization.** The members of a church or religious sect may organize a corporation for religious, charitable, or educational purposes if: (1) at least 3 members are 18 years of age or older; (2) the group maintains regular public worship; and (3) public notice is given at a stated meeting of the group. (B) **New organization.** Persons who are not members of an existing church or religious sect may organize a corporation for religious, charitable, or educational purposes if at least 5 of them who are 18 years of age or older want to establish a church or religious sect with its own tenets.

This provision entailed one of the most challenging revisions in this book. The prose is almost impenetrable.

> "The style of good legal composition (for it has a style of its own) is free from all colour, from all emotion, from all rhetoric. It is impersonal, as if the voice not of any man, but of the law, dealing with the necessary facts. It disdains emphasis and all other artifices. It uses no metaphors or figures of speech. It is always consistent and never contradicts itself. It never hesitates or doubts. It says in the plainest language, with the simplest, fewest, and fittest words, precisely what it means."
>
> —J.G. Mackay, *Introduction to an Essay on the Art of Legal Composition Commonly Called Drafting*, 3 L.Q. Rev. 326, 326 (1887).

NOT THIS:	BUT THIS:
Whereas, confusion of practice has arisen in the pronunciation of the name of our state and it is deemed important that the true pronunciation should be determined for use in oral official proceedings. And, whereas, the matter has been thoroughly investigated by the State Historical Society and the Eclectic Society of Little Rock, which have agreed upon the correct pronunciation as derived from history and the early usage of the American immigrants. Be it therefore resolved by both houses of the General Assembly, that the only true pronunciation of the name of the state, in the opinion of this body, is that received by the French from the native Indians and committed to writing in the French word representing the sound. It should be pronounced in three (3) syllables, with the final "s" silent, the "a" in each syllable with the Italian sound, and the accent on the first and last syllables. The pronunciation with the accent on the second syllable with the sound of "a" in "man" and the sounding of the terminal "s" is an innovation to be discouraged. **Ark. Code § 1-4-105.**	(A) **Purpose.** This Act resolves the issue of how to pronounce "Arkansas" during official proceedings. (B) **Official pronunciation of "Arkansas."** "Arkansas" has 3 syllables: /**ahr**-kən-saw/. Everyone should discourage the incorrect pronunciation that stresses the second syllable (making it rhyme with "man") and sounds the last "s."
Before a hearing before the Commission, and during a hearing upon reasonable cause shown, the Commission shall issue subpoenas and subpoenas duces tecum at the request of a party. All witnesses appearing pursuant to subpoena, other than parties, officers or employees of the State of Nevada or any political subdivision thereof, are entitled to receive fees and mileage in the same amounts and under the same circumstances as provided by law for witnesses in civil actions in the district courts. Witnesses entitled to fees or mileage who attend hearings at points so far removed from their residences as to prohibit return thereto from day to day are entitled, in addition to witness fees and in lieu of mileage, to the per diem compensation for subsistence and transportation authorized for state officers and employees for each day of actual attendance and for each day necessarily occupied in traveling to and from the hearings. Fees, subsistence and transportation expenses must be paid by the party at whose request the witness is subpoenaed. The Commission may award as costs the amount of all such expenses to the prevailing party. **Nev. Rev. Stat. § 463.3125(1).**	(A) **Witness expenses.** If a party so requests before a Commission hearing and shows reasonable cause, the Commission must issue a subpoena or subpoena duces tecum. For each day spent attending a hearing or traveling to or from it, a subpoenaed witness is entitled to the same fee and mileage compensation as a witness in a civil lawsuit in district court. In addition to fees but instead of mileage, a subpoenaed witness who, in the Commission's opinion, cannot commute each day is entitled to the same compensation for travel, meals, and lodging as is authorized for State officers and employees. The party that requested the subpoena must pay the witness's compensation unless the Commission awards it as a cost to the prevailing party. (B) **Exception.** A subpoenaed witness who is either a party or an officer or employee of the State or of a State political subdivision is not entitled to any compensation.

NOT THIS:	BUT THIS:
§ 1821 Transportation of dentures. Whoever transports by mail or otherwise to or within the District of Columbia or any Possession of the United States or uses the mails or any instrumentality of interstate commerce for the purpose of sending or bringing into any State or Territory any set of artificial teeth or prosthetic dental appliance or other denture, constructed from any cast or impression made by any person other than, or without the authorization or prescription of, a person licensed to practice dentistry under the laws of the place into which such denture is sent or brought, where such laws prohibit; (1) the taking of impressions or casts of the human mouth or teeth by a person not licensed under such laws to practice dentistry; (2) the construction or supply of dentures by a person other than, or without the authorization or prescription of, a person licensed under such laws to practice dentistry; or (3) the construction or supply of dentures from impressions or casts made by a person not licensed under such laws to practice dentistry - Shall be fined under this title or imprisoned not more than one year, or both. **18 U.S.C. § 1821.**	**§ 1821 Transportation of dentures.** Only a person licensed to practice dentistry or authorized by a licensed dentistry professional may transport a set of artificial teeth, a prosthetic dental appliance, or other denture by mail or other method of interstate commerce into any State, Territory, or United States Possession, including the District of Columbia. The person must be licensed or authorized in the state or other jurisdiction into which the item is brought. Violation of this provision is punishable by fine under this title or imprisonment of up to 1 year, or both, if the laws of the jurisdiction into which the item is brought prohibit: (A) taking an impression or cast of the human mouth or teeth by a nonlicensed person; (B) constructing or supplying a denture from an impression or cast made by a nonlicensed person; or (C) constructing or supplying a denture by a person not licensed to practice dentistry or without authorization from a licensed professional.

"Legislative drafting requires more definite, more exacting qualities of language, and demands greater skill in composition than other writing. There is no language of sonorous phrases or rhetorical flourishes; it is the language of the exact words and clear sentences, driven home with swift, direct, accurate, inescapable, incisive strokes. Simple English, but exact simple English; certain English, but powerful or delicate as the occasion requires; common words, but precise common words; brevity, but the brevity of completeness, definiteness, and clarity. Bill drafting must have the accuracy of engineering, for it is law engineering; it must have the detail and consistency of architecture, for it is law architecture."

—Duncan L. Kennedy, *Drafting Bills for the Minnesota Legislature* 7 (1946).

(B) Reasonable sentence length.

Break long compound sentences into two or more sentences. But when doing this, show some linguistic savvy: no choppy, ungainly sentences—just smooth exposition. Aim for an average sentence length of no more than 30 words. (A 20-word maximum is recommended for general expository prose in law.*) One way to achieve this goal is to subenumerate: every separately indented subpart counts as a separate sentence, even if it begins with a lowercase letter and ends with a semicolon.

For counting purposes, "sentence" includes a chunk of text that can be read by itself or by reference to an introductory line shared with other items in a list. Hence you should count a subpart set off in a hanging indent as a separate sentence. The rationale is that when the introductory material is stored separately in memory, each item in the list can be considered by itself. Although it must be taken with what precedes or follows to make up a full sentence in the traditional grammarian's sense, each chunk of text is read independently.

NOT THIS:	BUT THIS:
The board of county visitors each year shall prepare a full report of their proceedings during the year, with such recommendations as they may deem advisable, and shall file the same with the presiding judge of the circuit court, sheriff, and county commission. [Sentence length: 43 words.] **Mo. Rev. Stat. § 221.350.**	The board of county visitors must prepare a full annual report of its proceedings during the year. The report must contain the board's recommended actions. The board must file the report with the presiding judge of the circuit court, the sheriff, and the county commission. [Avg. sentence length: 16 words.]
Any person who shall represent, as an inducement to the sale of any course of study, that that person or the school offering such course will, upon the purchaser's completion of such course, place such purchaser in employment unless there is a written contract between such school and an employer whereby the latter is bound to furnish such employment as represented, is guilty of a misdemeanor. [Sentence length: 66 words.] **Wis. Stat. § 241.025.**	No person may represent, as an inducement to sell a school's course of study, that the purchaser will be placed in employment upon completion of the course—unless the school has a written contract with an employer that has agreed to furnish employment as represented. Violation of this provision is a misdemeanor. [Avg. sentence length: 26 words.]
With respect to a consumer credit sale, an assignee of the rights of the seller is subject to all defenses of the buyer against the seller arising out of the credit sale, but the assignee's liability under this section may not exceed the amount owing to the assignee at the time the defense is asserted against the assignee, and the rights of the buyer may only be asserted as a matter of defense to or setoff against a claim by the assignee. [Sentence length: 82 words.] **Utah Code § 70C-2-205.**	In a consumer-credit sale, an assignee of the seller's rights is subject to all the buyer's defenses against the seller arising out of the sale. The assignee's liability under this section cannot exceed the amount owed to the assignee when the buyer asserts the defense. The buyer's rights may be asserted only as a defense to or as a setoff against an assignee's claim. [Avg. sentence length: 22 words.]

*Bryan A. Garner, *Legal Writing in Plain English* § 6, at 27–31 (2d ed. 2013).

NOT THIS:	BUT THIS:
(2) **Nonbank financial companies supervised by the Board.** Any nonbank financial company supervised by the Board that engages in proprietary trading or takes or retains any equity, partnership, or other ownership interest in or sponsors a hedge fund or a private equity fund shall be subject, by rule, as provided in subsection (b)(2), to additional capital requirements for and additional quantitative limits with regards to such proprietary trading and taking or retaining any equity, partnership, or other ownership interest in or sponsorship of a hedge fund or a private equity fund, except that permitted activities as described in subsection (d) shall not be subject to the additional capital and additional quantitative limits except as provided in subsection (d)(3), as if the nonbank financial company supervised by the Board were a banking entity. [Sentence length: 124 words.] **12 U.S.C. § 1851(a)(2).**	(2) **Nonbank financial companies supervised by the Board.** Any Board-supervised nonbank financial company that engages in proprietary trading is subject to additional capital requirements and quantitative limits under (B)(2). These requirements and limits also apply to companies that take or retain an equity, partnership, or other ownership interest in a hedge or private-equity fund. An activity permitted under (D) is not subject to the additional limits unless authorized under (D)(3), as if the company were a banking entity. [Avg. sentence length: 24 words.]
The Congress,* recognizing the profound impact of man's activity on the interrelations of all components of the natural environment, particularly the profound influences of population growth, high-density urbanization, industrial expansion, resource exploitation, and new and expanding technological advances and recognizing further the critical importance of restoring and maintaining environmental quality to the overall welfare and development of man, declares that it is the continuing policy of the Federal Government, in cooperation with State and local governments, and other concerned public and private organizations, to use all practicable means and measures, including financial and technical assistance, in a manner calculated to foster and promote the general welfare, to create and maintain conditions under which man and nature can exist in productive harmony, and fulfill the social, economic, and other requirements of present and future generations of Americans. [Sentence length: 136 words.] **42 U.S.C. § 4331(a).**	Congress recognizes the significant effects of human activity on the natural environment. These include the substantial influences of population growth, the expansion of urbanization and industry, and modern technological advances. In light of these effects, the federal government must use all feasible methods, including financial and technical assistance, to promote the general welfare, to create and maintain conditions under which humans and nature may coexist harmoniously, and to help fulfill the social, economic, and other needs of present and future generations of Americans. In these endeavors, the federal government will cooperate with state and local governments and other concerned organizations. [Avg. sentence length: 25 words.]

*On the preference for *Congress* over *the Congress*, see *Garner's Dictionary of Legal Usage* 203 (3d ed. 2011).

NOT THIS:	BUT THIS:
Whoever, being of the crew of a vessel of the United States, on the high seas, or on any other waters within the admiralty and maritime jurisdiction of the United States, endeavors to make a revolt or mutiny on board such vessel, or combines, conspires, or confederate with any other person on board to make such revolt or mutiny, or solicits, incites, or stirs up any other of the crew to disobey or resist the lawful orders of the master or other officer of such vessel, or to refuse or neglect his proper duty on board thereof, or to betray his proper trust, or assembles with others in a tumultuous and mutinous manner, or makes a riot on board thereof, or unlawfully confines the master or other commanding officer thereof, shall be fined under this title or imprisoned not more than five years, or both. [Sentence length: 145 words.] **18 U.S.C. § 2192.**	(A) **Inciting seamen to revolt or mutiny is prohibited.** It is unlawful for a crew member of a U.S. vessel on the high seas or any other waters within the admiralty and maritime jurisdiction of the United States to: (1) attempt to conspire to cause or join a revolt or mutiny aboard a U.S. vessel; (2) solicit, encourage, or incite other crew members to disobey or resist an officer's lawful orders; or (3) neglect a duty, betray the proper trust, or confine a commanding officer. (B) **Penalties.** Violation of (A) is punishable by fine or imprisonment for up to 5 years, or both. [Avg. sentence length: 18 words.]
§ 213. Occupancy 1. The dwelling units in any existing multiple dwelling aided by a loan pursuant to this article shall be available solely for persons or families of low income during the period in which any part of such loan remains unpaid and for a period of at least ten years from the occupancy date. 2. In the event that after any person or family included within the provisions of paragraph a of subdivision three of section two hundred eleven of this chapter, but not included within the provisions of paragraph b of such subdivision three, begins occupancy of any dwelling unit in any multiple dwelling aided by a loan pursuant to this article, and during the period while such dwelling unit is subject to a maximum rent prescribed by the agency pursuant to this article, the income of such person or family increases so as to exceed the applicable maximum prescribed by such paragraph a by more than fifty per centum, such person shall be required to move from such dwelling. [Avg. sentence length: 85 words.] **N.Y. Pub. Hous. Law § 213(1), (2).**	**§ 213. Occupancy.** (A) **Restriction to low-income persons or families.** A dwelling unit in a multifamily dwelling financed under this article may be rented only to a low-income family or person until the financing is repaid or 10 years after the date of the original occupancy, whichever is later. (B) **Later increase in income.** If a multifamily dwelling subject to (A) is occupied by a person or family whose income later exceeds the maximum in § 211(3)(a) by more than 50%, the person or family must vacate the dwelling. (C) **Exception.** Subsection (B) does not apply to a person or family included under § 211(3)(b). [Avg. sentence length: 30 words.]

The entire provision here counts as five sentences because of the indented enumerations in (A). See text at § 1.1(B).

> "Brevity is not the sole virtue. But when what is to be said can be said, and said clearly, in few words rather than many, it is better said in those few words."
> —Sir William Dale, *Legislative Drafting: A New Approach* 55 (1977).

NOT THIS:	BUT THIS:
After September 30, 1985, no part of any appropriation (except trust funds) to the Bureau of Indian Affairs may be used directly or by contract for general or other welfare assistance (except child welfare assistance) payments (1) for other than essential needs (specifically identified in regulations of the Secretary or in regulations of the State public welfare agency pursuant to the Social Security Act [42 U.S.C. 301 et seq.] adopted by reference in the Secretary's regulations) which could not be reasonably expected to be met from financial resources or income (including funds held in trust) available to the recipient individual which are not exempted under law from consideration in determining eligibility for or the amount of Federal financial assistance or (2) for individuals who are eligible for general public welfare assistance available from a State except to the extent the Secretary of the Interior determines that such payments are required under sections 6(b)(2), 6(i), and 9(b) of the Maine Indian Claims Settlement Act of 1980 (94 Stat. 1793, 1794, 1796; 25 U.S.C. 1725(b)(2), 1725(i), 1728(b)). [Sentence length: 175 words.] **25 U.S.C. § 13d.**	After September 1985, no part of an appropriation to the Bureau of Indian Affairs (except trust funds) may be used directly or indirectly for a welfare-assistance payment to a person eligible for governmental welfare assistance. This provision does not preclude a payment for child welfare assistance or an essential need specifically identified in regulations published by the Secretary or a state welfare agency under the Social Security Act. An essential need is eligible for payment if it cannot be met from a source considered nonexempt in determining either the eligibility for federal assistance or its amount. The Secretary may authorize an exception if payment is required under §§ 6(b)(2), 6(i), and 9(b) of the Maine Indian Claims Settlement Act of 1980. [Avg. sentence length: 30 words.]

NOT THIS:	BUT THIS:
(a) Sale or delivery after sale of unregistered securities Unless a registration statement is in effect as to a security, it shall be unlawful for any person, directly or indirectly— (1) to make use of any means or instruments of transportation or communication in interstate commerce or of the mails to sell such security through the use or medium of any prospectus or otherwise; or (2) to carry or cause to be carried through the mails or in interstate commerce, by any means or instruments of transportation, any such security for the purpose of sale or for delivery after sale. **(b) Necessity of prospectus meeting requirements of section 77j of this title** It shall be unlawful for any person, directly or indirectly— (1) to make use of any means or instruments of transportation or communication in interstate commerce or of the mails to carry or transmit any prospectus relating to any security with respect to which a registration statement has been filed under this subchapter, unless such prospectus meets the requirements of section 77j of this title; or (2) to carry or cause to be carried through the mails or in interstate commerce any such security for the purpose of sale or for delivery after sale, unless accompanied or preceded by a prospectus that meets the requirements of subsection (a) of section 77j of this title. **(c) Necessity of filing registration statement** It shall be unlawful for any person, directly or indirectly, to make use of any means or instruments of transportation or communication in interstate commerce or of the mails to offer to sell or offer to buy through the use or medium of any prospectus or otherwise any security, unless a registration statement has been filed as to such security, or while the registration statement is the subject of a refusal order or stop order or (prior to the effective date of the registration statement) any public proceeding or examination under section 77h of this title. [Avg. sentence length: 33 words.] **15 U.S.C. § 77e.**	(A) **Sale or delivery after sale of unregistered securities.** The following prohibitions apply if a person uses any means or instrument of transportation or communication in interstate commerce or by mail. (1) ***Prefiling period.*** It is unlawful to offer to sell or buy a security, or to deliver one as part of a sale, until a registration statement has been filed for that security. (2) ***Waiting period.*** It is unlawful to: (a) disseminate a prospectus after a registration statement has been filed, unless the prospectus satisfies § 10; (b) sell or deliver a security without an accompanying § 10(a) prospectus; or (c) offer to sell or buy a security whose registration statement is the subject of a refusal order, stop order, or—before the registration statement is effective—any public proceeding or examination under § 77h. (3) ***Posteffective period.*** It is unlawful to conclude the sale of a security or to deliver it after sale until its registration statement has been declared effective. [Avg. sentence length: 20 words.]

Under principles of computing average sentence length, (A)(2) counts as four sentences. See text at § 1.1(B).

> "Complexity is primarily, but not exclusively, a mechanical failure. It results from not keeping the relationship between words, phrases, and clauses simple and logical. It usually comes about when we pack too many facts and ideas into a single sentence; when we thread together too many related objects or effects."
> —John O'Hayre, *Gobbledygook Has Gotta Go* 30 (1966).

(C) Avoiding jargon.

Use the simplest possible words to express the idea clearly. Whenever language is simplifiable without a loss in meaning, the style is poor.

NOT THIS:	BUT THIS:
(a) IN GENERAL.—Copyright in a work created on or after January 1, 1978, subsists from its creation and, except as provided by the following subsections, endures for a term consisting of the life of the author and 70 years after the author's death. **17 U.S.C. § 302.**	(A) **In general.** For a work created after December 31, 1977, copyright begins at creation and lasts for 70 years after the author's death, unless (B)–(E) provide otherwise.
If in the agreement provision be made for a method of naming or appointing an arbitrator or arbitrators or an umpire, such method shall be followed; but if no method be provided therein, or if a method be provided and any party thereto shall fail to avail himself of such method, or if for any other reason there shall be a lapse in the naming of an arbitrator or arbitrators or umpire, or in filling a vacancy, then upon the application of either party to the controversy the court shall designate and appoint an arbitrator or arbitrators or umpire, as the case may require, who shall act under the said agreement with the same force and effect as if he or they had been specifically named therein; and unless otherwise provided in the agreement the arbitration shall be by a single arbitrator. **9 U.S.C. § 5.**	If the agreement prescribes a method for naming or appointing 1 or more arbitrators or an umpire, the parties must follow that method. If the agreement does not prescribe a method, if a party fails to use a prescribed method, or if there is a lapse in naming an arbitrator or umpire or in filling a vacancy, the court must appoint one upon application by either party. The appointee may act with the same effect as if named in the agreement. Unless the agreement provides otherwise, arbitration is by a single arbitrator.
1. A child heretofore or hereafter born of parents who prior or subsequent to the birth of such child shall have entered into a civil or religious marriage, or shall have consummated a common-law marriage where such marriage is recognized as valid, in the manner authorized by the law of the place where such marriage takes place, is the legitimate child of both birth parents notwithstanding that such marriage is void or voidable or has been or shall hereafter be annulled or judicially declared void. 2. Nothing herein contained shall be deemed to affect the construction of any will or other instrument executed before the time this act shall take effect or any right or interest in property or right of action vested or accrued before the time this act shall take effect, or to limit the operation of any judicial determination heretofore made containing express provision with respect to the legitimacy, maintenance or custody of any child, or to affect any adoption proceeding heretofore commenced, or limit the effect of any order or orders entered in such adoption proceeding. **N.Y. Dom. Rel. Law § 24.**	(A) **Legitimate child of legally recognized marriage.** A child is considered the legitimate child of both parents of a legally recognized marriage, regardless of whether the parents marry before or after the child's birth. A legally recognized marriage includes a civil marriage, a religious marriage, and a common-law marriage authorized by law where it becomes effective. (B) **Exceptions to retroactivity.** This statute does not apply retroactively to affect: (1) an adoption proceeding already filed; (2) an order entered in an adoption proceeding; (3) the interpretation of a will, deed, or contract; (4) a vested property interest; (5) an accrued right of action; or (6) a judicial determination expressly addressing the legitimacy, maintenance, or custody of a child.

NOT THIS:	BUT THIS:
725.01 Promise to pay another's debt, etc. No action shall be brought whereby to charge any executor or administrator upon any special promise to answer or pay any debt or damages out of her or his own estate, or whereby to charge the defendant upon any special promise to answer for the debt, default or miscarriage of another person or to charge any person upon any agreement made upon consideration of marriage, or upon any contract for the sale of lands, tenements or hereditaments, or of any uncertain interest in or concerning them, or for any lease thereof for a period longer than 1 year, or upon any agreement that is not to be performed within the space of 1 year from the making thereof, or whereby to charge any health care provider upon any guarantee, warranty, or assurance as to the results of any medical, surgical, or diagnostic procedure performed by any physician licensed under chapter 458, osteopathic physician licensed under chapter 459, chiropractic physician licensed under chapter 460, podiatric physician licensed under chapter 461, or dentist licensed under chapter 466, unless the agreement or promise upon which such action shall be brought, or some note or memorandum thereof shall be in writing and signed by the party to be charged therewith or by some other person by her or him thereunto lawfully authorized. **Fla. Stat. § 725.01.**	**725.01 Agreement or promise to pay.** In the absence of an agreement or promise, or a note or memorandum of it, signed by the party to be charged or someone lawfully authorized to sign for that party, no person may bring a lawsuit that charges: (A) an executor or administrator on a promise to answer or pay any debt or damages from his or her own estate; (B) a defendant on a promise to answer for another's debt, default, or miscarriage; (C) a person on an agreement made on consideration of marriage; (D) a person on either a contract for the sale of an interest in real estate or a real-estate lease for a period longer than 1 year; (E) a person on any agreement that is not to be performed within 1 year of its making; or (F) a healthcare* provider on a guarantee, warranty, or assurance of the results of a medical, surgical, or diagnostic procedure performed by a physician, osteopath, chiropractor, podiatrist, or dentist licensed under chapters 459–461 and 466.

*The better practice is to make *healthcare* solid as both a noun and an adjective. *See Black's Law Dictionary* 835 (10th ed. 2014). If the noun is two words, then the phrasal adjective (as in the left column) would need to be hyphenated (hence *health care* as a noun phrase but *health-care provider*). The solid form avoids this punctuation dilemma—which eludes many legal writers. See § 4.9(G).

> "A draftsman seldom dares to think about how he would write the law if he had a free hand. He adopts the style in which earlier laws have been written, lest the words should fail to sound like the words of a legislature. This practice ensures that laws will be written in a style as ancient as the draftsman's learning permits. It is like the habit which made lawyers write pleadings in French and Latin long after these languages had ceased to be current."
>
> —Alfred F. Conard, *New Ways to Write Laws*, 56 Yale L.J. 458, 459–60 (1947).

NOT THIS:	BUT THIS:
§ 2522 Charitable and similar gifts. **(a) Citizens or residents** In computing taxable gifts for the calendar year, there shall be allowed as a deduction in the case of a citizen or resident the amount of all gifts made during such year to or for the use of— (1) the United States, any State, or any political subdivision thereof, or the District of Columbia, for exclusively public purposes; (2) a corporation, or trust, or community chest, fund, or foundation, organized and operated exclusively for religious, charitable, scientific, literary, or educational purposes, or to foster national or international amateur sports competition (but only if no part of its activities involve the provision of athletic facilities or equipment), including the encouragement of art and the prevention of cruelty to children or animals, no part of the net earnings of which inures to the benefit of any private shareholder or individual, which is not disqualified for tax exemption under section 501(c)(3) by reason of attempting to influence legislation, and which does not participate in, or intervene in (including the publishing or distributing of statements), any political campaign on behalf of (or in opposition to) any candidate for public office; (3) a fraternal society, order, or association, operating under the lodge system, but only if such gifts are to be used exclusively for religious, charitable, scientific, literary, or educational purposes, including the encouragement of art and the prevention of cruelty to children or animals; (4) posts or organizations of war veterans, or auxiliary units or societies of any such posts or organizations, if such posts, organizations, units, or societies are organized in the United States or any of its possessions, and if no part of their net earnings inures to the benefit of any private shareholder or individual. **26 U.S.C. § 2522(a).**	**§ 2522 Charitable and similar gifts.** **2522.1 Citizens or residents.** Each calendar year, a citizen or resident may deduct from taxable income the amount donated that year to: (A) the United States, any state or its political subdivisions, or the District of Columbia, for exclusively public purposes; (B) a corporation, trust, community chest, fund, or foundation that: (1) is organized and operated exclusively: (a) for religious, charitable, scientific, literary, or educational purposes; (b) to foster national or international sports competition, unless it provides athletic facilities or equipment; (c) to encourage the arts; or (d) to prevent cruelty to children or animals; and (2) does not: (a) have any net earnings inuring to the benefit of private shareholders or individuals; (b) have a disqualification for tax exemption under § 501(c)(3) because it attempts to influence legislation; or (c) actively involve itself in a political campaign, including publishing or distributing statements; (C) a fraternal society, order, or association operating under the lodge system exclusively for religious, charitable, scientific, literary, or educational purposes, including promotion of the arts and the prevention of cruelty to children or animals; or (D) a veterans' organization or post, including an auxiliary unit or society organized in the United States or its possessions, if no part of the entity's net earnings benefit private shareholders or individuals.

(D) Consistent usage.

Use a word or phrase consistently to express a single idea. Don't vary your terminology for the sake of "elegant variation." Under the canon of construction known as presumption of consistent usage, courts presume that a change in wording indicates a change of meaning.

This variation in teminology violates the presumption of consistent usage.

NOT THIS:	BUT THIS:
A person who commits the offense of possession of altered property or its component parts which exceed one hundred dollars in value, shall be guilty of a class A misdemeanor. In the event that more than one item of personal property is defaced, erased, or otherwise altered or unlawfully possessed, as specified in sections 12.1-23-08.2 and 12.1-23-08.3, by an individual, then an offense is determined to be committed under this section if the aggregate of the value of the property so defaced, erased, or otherwise altered or unlawfully possessed is in excess of one hundred dollars. **N.D. Cent. Code § 12.1-23-08.2(2).**	It is unlawful for a person to possess altered property or its component parts worth over $100, or to deface, erase, or otherwise alter or unlawfully possess—as specified in §§ 12.1-23-08.2 and 12.1-23-08.3—multiple items of personal property cumulatively worth over $100. Violation of this provision is a class A misdemeanor.

"What is essential is that the writer should really want his readers to understand what is commanded and what is forbidden by the law."
—Alfred F. Conard, *New Ways to Write Laws*, 56 Yale L.J. 458, 469 (1947).

(E) Preventing error, misstatement, and ambiguity.

Read drafts critically—even hypercritically. Be sure you've actually said what you mean to say. Identify and cure instances of substantive error, ambiguity, and curable vagueness.

Understand that ambiguity is *always* a disease of legislative drafting. Think of the signs placed all around the streets of a major city: "Fine for parking." What are the drivers to think? That it's okay, or that they'll be fined?

Although some vagueness is purposeful and desirable (*within a reasonable time*), you should sharpen the wording when you can (*within 30 days* or *within 24 hours*).

Any football stadium? Changing the name of a high-school stadium requires permission of a professional team? That's literally what this provision says. Note that this is a stand-alone, separately numbered provision—not a follow-on sentence plucked from a paragraph about professional football stadiums.

Those who die at the university hospital must be moved to the state psychiatric hospital to be prepared for shipping?

This common-law definition derives from *Black's Law Dictionary*.

This provision also spells out the common-law doctrine—as explained in *Black's Law Dictionary*. The idea is to be explicit in the drafting—not to rely on vague references to the common law.

NOT THIS:	BUT THIS:
The name of a football stadium may not be changed without the written consent of the municipality in which it is located and the professional football team described in s. 229.823. **Wis. Stat. § 229.8245(1).**	The name of a stadium used for professional football cannot be changed without the written consent of the municipality in which it is located and the professional football team described in § 229.823.
In the event that a committed public patient or a voluntary public patient or a committed private patient should die while at the state psychiatric hospital or at the university hospital, the state psychiatric hospital shall have the body prepared for shipment in accordance with the rules prescribed by the state board of health for shipping such bodies; . . . **Iowa Code § 225.33.**	If a committed or voluntary public patient or a committed private patient dies at a state psychiatric hospital or the university hospital, the hospital must have the body prepared for shipment according to the rules of the state board of health for shipping bodies. . . .
"Fresh pursuit" shall include fresh pursuit as defined by the common law, and also the pursuit of a person who has committed a felony or who is reasonably suspected of having committed a felony. It shall also include the pursuit of a person suspected of having committed a supposed felony, though no felony has actually been committed, if there is reasonable ground for believing that a felony has been committed. Fresh pursuit as used herein shall not necessarily imply instant pursuit, but pursuit without unreasonable delay. **N.J. Stat. 2A:155-2.**	"Fresh pursuit" is not necessarily instant but is pursuit without unreasonable delay. It includes: (A) a police officer's warrantless search of a fleeing suspect or pursuit across jurisdictional lines to arrest or capture a fleeing suspect, as allowed by the common law; (B) the pursuit of a person who has committed a felony or who is reasonably suspected of having committed a felony; and (C) the pursuit of a person suspected of having committed a felony, though no felony has actually been committed, if there is reasonable ground for believing that a felony has been committed.

Margin note	NOT THIS:	BUT THIS:
This can't be right: you get a hearing only if the discharge was unjust? This prejudges the question. Also, the statute suggests that the counsel might be provided at the state's expense.	(a) The teachers, officers, and employees shall perform such other duties as the Superintendent of the Arkansas School for the Deaf may direct, and, when their services are not needed, they shall be discharged. (b) However, if the teachers, officers, and employees are unjustly discharged, they shall be entitled to a fair and impartial hearing before the Board of Trustees of the Arkansas School for the Deaf and to be represented by counsel if they desire. **Ark. Code § 6-43-306.**	(A) **Responsibilities.** A teacher, officer, or employee must perform other duties as the Superintendent of the Arkansas School for the Deaf reasonably directs. When that person's services are not needed, he or she will be discharged. (B) **Hearing upon discharge.** A teacher, officer, or employee who is discharged is entitled to: (1) a fair hearing before the Board of Trustees of the Arkansas School for the Deaf to determine whether the discharge was proper; and (2) representation by legal counsel.
The provisions *are to apply so far as applicable thereto*? Circular.	**§ 20-230. Application to convictions prior to act.** Provisions of this act so far as applicable thereto are to apply to all convicted persons now serving time in the state penitentiary to the end that at all times the same provisions relating to sentences, imprisonment, and paroles of prisoners shall apply to the inmate thereof. **Idaho Code § 20-230.**	**§ 20-230. Application to convictions before act.** This Act applies to all inmates of the state penitentiary so that the same provisions relating to sentences, imprisonment, and paroles of prisoners always apply to all inmates.
Is the *owner* the old owner (the seller) or the new one (the buyer)?	Whenever title or interest in a vehicle registered under the provisions of this section is transferred or assigned, the owner may transfer the special plates to another vehicle upon payment of the required transfer fees. The owner may only display the plates on another vehicle upon receipt of the new registration from the department. **Idaho Code § 49-415E(3).**	**Transferability.** When title or an interest in a vehicle registered under this section is sold or otherwise assigned, the seller or assignor may move the special plates to the other vehicle after paying the required transfer fees. The seller or assignor may display the plates on another vehicle after receiving the new registration from the department.
This provision seems to empower authorities to construct only crosswalks that can never be used.	(a) Local authorities, by ordinance or resolution, may establish crosswalks between intersections. (b) Local authorities may install signs at or adjacent to an intersection directing that pedestrians shall not cross in a crosswalk indicated at the intersection. It is unlawful for any pedestrian to cross at the crosswalk prohibited by a sign. **Cal. Veh. Code § 21106.**	(A) **Crosswalks.** By ordinance or resolution, local authorities may establish a crosswalk between intersections. (B) **Signage.** A sign may be installed, at or adjacent to the intersection, directing pedestrians when to cross and not to cross the intersection. (C) **Unlawful crossing.** It is unlawful for a pedestrian to cross in violation of a sign installed under (B).

> "We need a campaign for intelligible laws, and for intelligible interpretation of this law. Codification of existing law and judicial decisions in statutes couched in intelligible language appears to be the only solution."
>
> —B. Ifor Evans, *The Use of English* 16–17 (1949).

NOT THIS:	BUT THIS:
§ 102503 - Authority of Secretary (d) **Exchanges.**— The Secretary may make exchanges by accepting museum objects and other personal property and by granting in exchange for the museum objects or other personal property museum property under the administrative jurisdiction of the Secretary that no longer is needed or that may be held in duplicate among the museum properties administered by the Secretary. Exchanges shall be consummated on a basis that the Secretary considers to be equitable and in the public interest. **54 U.S.C. § 102503(d).**	(D) **Exchanges.** The Secretary may accept on the museum's behalf objects and other personal property in exchange for museum property under the Secretary's administrative jurisdiction if: (1) the museum property is no longer needed or is held in duplicate among the museum properties administered by the Secretary; and (2) the exchange is consummated on an equitable basis and in the public interest, as determined by the Secretary.
(b) **Cooperation.** Subject to sections 1003(e), 1007(a), and 1008(b) and (d) of this title, a manufacturer of telecommunications transmission or switching equipment and a provider of telecommunications support services shall, on a reasonably timely basis and at a reasonable charge, make available to the telecommunications carriers using its equipment, facilities, or services such features or modifications as are necessary to permit such carriers to comply with the capability requirements of section 1002 of this title and the capacity requirements identified by the Attorney General under section 1003 of this title. **47 U.S.C. § 1005(b).**	(B) **Cooperation on compliance updates.** A manufacturer of telecommunications transmission or switching equipment and a provider of telecommunications support services must each make available—on a reasonably timely basis and at a reasonable charge—features or modifications necessary to allow telecommunications carriers using its equipment, facilities, or services to comply with the capability requirements of § 1002 and the capacity requirements identified by the Attorney General under § 1003.
If a combination of cities and/or counties establishes a joint riverport authority, the mayors and/or county judges/executive involved shall jointly choose six (6) members to the terms as provided in subsection (2) of this section, and shall jointly choose successors and may upon agreement appoint a mayor or a member of a city legislative body and a county judge/executive or a member of a fiscal court as two (2) additional members of the authority for terms of two (2) years, provided that such persons may not serve on the authority after the expiration of their terms as an elected official. **Ky. Rev. Stat. § 65.540(1)(d).**	If any combination of cities or counties establishes a joint riverport authority, the mayors, county judges, and county executives involved must jointly choose both the 6 members whose terms are provided for under (2) and their successors. They may agree to appoint 2 additional members for 2-year terms. An additional member must be a mayor, a member of a city legislative body, a county judge, a county executive, or a member of a fiscal court. No additional member may serve on the riverport authority after his or her term as an elected official expires.

A Secretary might argue that this allows him or her personally to accept property.

Does this refer only to a manufacturer who is also a provider of support services? Or is this the obligation on both manufacturers and support-service providers? The revised version assumes the latter.

It's hard if not impossible to know who gets to choose. The *and/or* creates a problem: see § 5.4 at 139–40.

Behold: this provision is a mess.

NOT THIS:	BUT THIS:
222.03 Survey at instance of dissatisfied creditor. If the creditor in any execution or process sought to be levied is dissatisfied with the quantity of land selected and set apart, and shall himself or herself, or by his or her agent or attorney, notify the officer levying, the officer shall at the creditor's request cause the same to be surveyed, and when the homestead is not within the corporate limits of any town or city, the person claiming said exemption shall have the right to set apart that portion of land belonging to him or her which includes the residence, or not, at the person's option, and if the first tract or parcel does not contain 160 acres, the said officer shall set apart the remainder from any other tract or tracts claimed by the debtor, but in every case taking all the land lying contiguous until the whole quantity of 160 acres is made up. The person claiming the exemption shall not be forced to take as his or her homestead any tract or portion of a tract, if any defect exists in the title, except at the person's option. The expense of such survey shall be chargeable on the execution as costs; but if it shall appear that the person claiming such exemption does not own more than 160 acres in the state, the expenses of said survey shall be paid by the person directing the same to be made. **Fla. Stat. § 222.03.**	**222.03 Survey at request of dissatisfied creditor.** (A) **Notice and requirements.** If upon levy or execution a creditor is dissatisfied with the amount of land claimed as a debtor's homestead, the creditor may notify the levying officer, who must then order a survey of the land. If the land is outside the limits of a municipality, the debtor may set apart up to 160 acres. If one parcel contains less than 160 acres, the officer may set apart more of the debtor's land until 160 acres is claimed—using contiguous parcels first. At the debtor's option, the parcel claimed may include a residence. A debtor may refuse to take as homestead a parcel of land with defective title. (B) **Paying for the survey.** The survey expense under (A) is chargeable as a cost of execution. But if the survey report concludes that the homestead claimant owns less than 160 acres in Florida, the person who requested the survey must pay the expense.

> "The art of drafting is an individual talent. As elements of the art of drafting, sensitivity and wisdom are personal traits that can be developed only through experience; and the first step toward one's developing his own sensitivity and wisdom is recognition that, in terms of structure and language, most legal drafting, legislative or otherwise, is not well done."
>
> —Maurice B. Kirk, *Legal Drafting: Curing Unexpressive Language*, 3 Tex. Tech. L. Rev. 23, 24 (1971).

NOT THIS:	BUT THIS:
(a) PUBLICATION OF NOTICE.—If, after considering the report of a convener or conducting its own assessment, an agency decides to establish a negotiated rulemaking committee, the agency shall publish in the Federal Register and, as appropriate, in trade or other specialized publications, a notice which shall include— (1) an announcement that the agency intends to establish a negotiated rulemaking committee to negotiate and develop a proposed rule; (2) a description of the subject and scope of the rule to be developed, and the issues to be considered; (3) a list of the interests which are likely to be significantly affected by the rule; (4) a list of the persons proposed to represent such interests and the person or persons proposed to represent the agency; (5) a proposed agenda and schedule for completing the work of the committee, including a target date for publication by the agency of a proposed rule for notice and comment; (6) a description of administrative support for the committee to be provided by the agency, including technical assistance; (7) a solicitation for comments on the proposal to establish the committee, and the proposed membership of the negotiated rulemaking committee; and (8) an explanation of how a person may apply or nominate another person for membership on the committee, as provided under subsection (b). **5 U.S.C. § 564(a).**	(A) **Publication of notice.** Before promulgating a new rule, an agency must publish notice of its intent to do so in the Federal Register and other appropriate specialty publications. The notice must include: (1) an announcement that the agency intends to establish a committee to develop the new rule; (2) a description of the rule's subject and scope; (3) a list of interests the rule is likely to affect significantly; (4) a list of people who represent those interests; (5) a list of people who represent the agency's interests; (6) a proposed committee schedule for public notice and comment, including a target date of rule publication; (7) a description of administrative and technical support that the agency will provide to the committee; (8) a solicitation of comments on the establishment of the committee and its proposed membership; and (9) an explanation of how to request changes to committee membership, as provided in (B).

The initial paragraph of the APA notice requirement is misleading or else circumlocutory: agencies do not publish notice of their intent to establish a committee to talk about a new rule—they publish their intent to promulgate a new rule. The subsections cover establishing the committee.

> "Ludicrous instances of confused expression occasionally enliven the pages of the statute book. Thus among the things which might have been expressed differently, an instance is to be found in the fifty-second of Geo. III. c. 146—penalties under this Act were to be given half to the informer and half to the poor of the parish; but the only penalty imposed by the statute was transportation for fourteen years."
>
> —Lord Thring, *Practical Legislation* 3 (2d ed. 1902).

(F) Abundant headings.

Make your principles of organization overt. Use subparts with headings to enhance readability and reinforce meaning. Generally, any subpart that contains at least one full sentence should be introduced by a heading.

This requirement contradicts the prevailing practice in many English-speaking jurisdictions. That contradiction is purposeful: it is among the most desirable reforms to be made in legislative drafting. Headings help readers get their bearings. They focus attention that would otherwise drain away from the reader's mind. The many examples in this book illustrate how this requirement should be carried out. Study them. Mimic them.

In some states, the headings contained in bills are not printed in the statute books. One way or another, this practice should be changed.

In other states, headings are by statute not to be considered part of the official legislation. Such a rule is understandable and possibly commendable, since it is notoriously difficult to devise headings that adequately disclose everything dealt with in a given provision. That is a rule that should be known to all lawyers and judges within a state where the rule applies. It could even be printed in boldface on the endpapers of the statute book to alert all readers—or perhaps as a running footer on every righthand page. But it should not affect the imperative to use headings for every subpart that contains at least one full sentence.

Headings help not only readers but also drafters, who will organize their work more logically if they are required to use headings more liberally than has traditionally been done in the past.

NOT THIS:	BUT THIS:
Except where permitted pursuant to the provisions of Chapter 4 (commencing with Section 13200) of Division 7 of the Water Code, any person that intentionally or negligently causes or permits any oil to be deposited in the water of this state, including but not limited to navigable waters, shall be liable civilly in an amount not exceeding six thousand dollars ($6,000) and, in addition, shall be liable to any governmental agency charged with the responsibility for cleaning up or abating any such oil for all actual damages, in addition to the reasonable costs actually incurred in abating or cleaning up the oil deposit in such waters. The amount of the civil penalty which is assessed pursuant to this section shall be based upon the amount of discharge and the likelihood of permanent injury and shall be recoverable in a civil action by, and paid to, such governmental agency. If more than one such agency has responsibility for the waters in question, the agency which conducts the cleaning or abating activities shall be the agency authorized to proceed under this section. **Cal. Harb. & Nav. Code § 151.**	(A) **Oil-deposits violation.** Unless permitted under Chapter 4 (§§ 13200–13292) of Division 7 of the Water Code, a person who intentionally or negligently causes or permits oil to be deposited in California water, including navigable waters, is liable under (1) or (2), or both. (1) ***Civil liability.*** A person is civilly liable for an amount up to $6,000, based on: (a) the amount of oil discharged; and (b) the likelihood of permanent injury. (2) ***Governmental liability.*** A liable person must pay a governmental agency for all actual damages and for all reasonable abatement and cleanup costs. (B) **Agency's standing.** To bring a civil claim under this section, the government agency must be: (1) an agency responsible for cleaning up or abating the oil; or (2) the agency that conducts the cleanup or abatement activities.

NOT THIS:	BUT THIS:
§ 61-2-26. Doors to be removed from abandoned refrigerators, freezers and other appliances; penalties. No person shall abandon any refrigerator or food freezer appliance or other airtight appliance having a height or length greater than two feet without first removing all entry doors therefrom. Any person violating the provisions of this section shall be guilty of a misdemeanor, and, upon conviction thereof, shall be fined not more than two hundred dollars, or imprisoned in the county jail not more than six months, or both fined and imprisoned. Justices of the peace shall have jurisdiction of cases arising hereunder concurrent with courts of record. **W. Va. Code § 61-2-26.**	**§ 61-2-26. Remove doors on abandoned appliances; penalties; jurisdiction.** (A) **Removal of doors on airtight appliances.** It is unlawful to abandon a refrigerator, food freezer, or other airtight appliance over 2 feet in height or length without first removing all its entry doors. (B) **Penalties.** Violation of (A) is a misdemeanor punishable by a fine up to $200 or imprisonment in county jail for up to 6 months, or both. (C) **Jurisdiction.** For a case brought under this section, a justice of the peace has concurrent jurisdiction with a court of record.
§ 2900. Assessment limitations If the report on the proposed acquisition or improvement shows that the estimated amount proposed to be assessed upon any parcel for the proposed acquisition or improvement will exceed one-half of the true value of the parcel as set forth in the report, or shows that the total estimated cost of the proposed improvement or acquisition, less any amount to be paid towards the cost from any source other than special assessments upon the parcels benefited by the acquisition or improvement, when added to the aggregate totals of all unpaid assessments and estimated assessments, as the totals are stated in the report, will exceed in total amount one-half of the true value of all the parcels proposed to be assessed, the proposed proceeding shall be abandoned or modified so that the amount to be specially assessed for the cost of the acquisition or improvement will be less than the limits hereby established, unless the excess of the cost and indebtedness over one-half of the true value shall be paid from some source other than by special assessment on the parcels, or unless the limitation is overruled. **Cal. Sts. & High. Code § 2900.**	**§ 2900. Assessment limit.** (A) **General rule.** Except as provided otherwise in (B), a proposed proceeding must be abandoned or modified so that the amount specially assessed for the acquisition or improvement's cost is less than the established limit if the report on the proposed acquisition or improvement shows that: (1) the proposed assessment on any parcel exceeds half the parcel's true value as stated in the report; or (2) the proposed improvement or acquisition's total estimated cost, less any amount to be paid from a source other than a benefited parcel's special assessment, when added to the totals of all unpaid assessments and estimated assessments in the report, exceeds half the assessed parcel's true value. (B) **Exceptions.** This section does not apply if: (1) any excess cost and indebtedness, over half the parcel's true value, will not be paid from the parcel's special assessment; or (2) the limit is overruled.

NOT THIS:	BUT THIS:
The Director of the United States Geological Survey is authorized and directed, on the approval of the Secretary of the Interior, to dispose of the topographic and geologic maps and atlases of the United States, made and published by the United States Geological Survey, at such prices and under such regulations as may from time to time be fixed by him and approved by the Secretary of the Interior; and a number of copies of each map or atlas, not exceeding five hundred, shall be distributed gratuitously among foreign governments and departments of our own Government to literary and scientific associations, and to such educational institutions or libraries as may be designated by the Director of the Survey and approved by the Secretary of the Interior. On and after June 7, 1924, the distribution of geological publications to libraries designated as special depositaries of such publications shall be discontinued. **43 U.S.C. § 42.**	(A) **Disposition.** Subject to the Secretary of the Interior's approval, the Director of the United States Geological Survey must establish prices and regulations for disposing of United States topographic and geological maps and atlases made and published by the Geological Survey. (B) **Distribution.** Subject to the Secretary's approval, the Director may distribute without charge up to 500 copies of each map or atlas among foreign governments, federal departments, literary and scientific associations, educational institutions, and libraries. (C) **Discontinuation to special depositories.** Beginning June 7, 1924, the Geological Survey will not distribute maps or atlases to libraries designated as special depositories of geological publications.

Note the inconsistent usage: *geologic* first but later *geological.*

"It would be Utopian to believe that all Acts could be written and structured in a way that every adult of average intelligence would readily be able to understand. (This should still be the goal, however.) But legislators and parliamentary counsel ought to do much more to keep the language and ideas as straightforward as possible, given that citizens sometimes need to read and make sense of Acts in order to take knowledge into their own hands rather than have it filtered for them by professionals."

—Martin Cutts, *Lucid Law* § 5.8, at 16 (1994).

Notice how the romanettes in midparagraph worsen the style: see § 3.3(D).

NOT THIS:	BUT THIS:
§ 159-137. Lost, stolen, defaced, or destroyed bonds or notes (a) If lost, stolen, or completely destroyed, any bond, note, or coupon may be reissued in the same form and tenor upon the owner's furnishing to the satisfaction of the secretary and the issuing unit: (i) proof of ownership, (ii) proof of loss or destruction, (iii) a surety bond in twice the face amount of the bond or note and coupons, and (iv) payment of the cost of preparing and issuing the new bond, note, or coupons. (b) If defaced or partially destroyed, any bond, note, or coupon may be reissued in the same form and tenor to the bearer or registered holder, at his expense, upon surrender of the defaced or partially destroyed bond, note, or coupon and on such other conditions as the Commission may prescribe. The Commission may also provide for authentication of defaced or partially destroyed bonds, notes, or coupons instead of reissuing them. (c) Each new bond, note, or coupon issued under this section shall be signed by the officers of the issuing unit who are in office at the time, or by the State Treasurer if the unit no longer exists, and shall contain a recital to the effect that it is issued in exchange for or replacement of a certain bond, note, or coupon (describing it sufficiently to identify it) and is to be deemed a part of the same issue as the original bond, note, or coupon. **N.C. Gen. Stat. § 159-137.**	**§ 159-137. Lost, stolen, defaced, or destroyed bond, note, or coupon.** (A) **Requirements for reissue if lost, stolen, or completely destroyed.** A bond, note, or coupon that has been lost, stolen, or completely destroyed may be reissued in the same form and tenor upon the owner's furnishing to the secretary's satisfaction and the issuing unit: (1) proof of ownership; (2) proof of loss or destruction; (3) a surety bond in twice the bond's, note's, or coupon's face amount; and (4) payment of costs of preparing and issuing the new bond, note, or coupon. (B) **Requirements for reissue if defaced or partly destroyed.** A bond, note, or coupon that has been defaced or partly destroyed may be reissued in the same form and tenor to the bearer or registered holder, at his or her expense, on surrender of the defaced or partly destroyed bond, note, or coupon and on any other conditions the Commission prescribes. The Commission may authenticate a defaced or partly destroyed bond, note, or coupon instead of reissuing it. (C) **Requirements for newly issued bond, note, or coupon.** A new bond, note, or coupon issued under this section: (1) must be signed by the current officers of the issuing unit, or by the State Treasurer if the unit no longer exists; (2) must contain a recital that it is issued in exchange for or as a replacement of a certain bond, note, or coupon and describe it sufficiently to identify it; and (3) is considered a part of the same issue as the original bond, note, or coupon.

> "For all the awkwardness in expression that they produce, traditional drafting practices have been defended on the grounds that they produce legally accurate statements. While plain English documents are subjected to the closest scrutiny by opponents, the same rigour is not applied to traditional documents. When it is, the sweeping claims that are made for them do not hold up. Errors, inadequacies, ambiguities, and uncertainties are regularly found."
>
> —Robert D. Eagleson, "Efficiency in Legal Drafting," in *Essays on Legislative Drafting in Honour of J.Q. Ewens* 13, 25–26 (David St. Leger Kelly ed., 1988).

This sounds as if the Department of Roads must work jointly with local authorities. If that is so, *and* is appropriate. But *or* may in fact be the intended meaning, as the revision assumes.

NOT THIS:	BUT THIS:
No-passing zones; exception. (1) The Department of Roads and local authorities may determine those portions of any highway under their respective jurisdictions where overtaking and passing or driving to the left of the center of the roadway would be especially hazardous and may by appropriate signs or markings on the roadway indicate the beginning and end of such zones. When such signs or markings are in place and clearly visible to an ordinarily observant person, every driver of a vehicle shall obey such indications. (2) Where signs or markings are in place to define a no-passing zone, no driver shall at any time drive on the left side of the roadway within such no-passing zone or on the left side of any pavement striping designed to mark such no-passing zone throughout its length. (3) This section shall not apply (a) under the conditions described in subdivision (1)(b) of section 60-6,131 or (b) to the driver of a vehicle turning left into or from an alley, private road, or driveway unless otherwise prohibited by signs. **Neb. Rev. Stat. § 60-6,137.**	**No-passing zones; exceptions.** (A) **Designation.** The Department of Roads or the appropriate local authority may determine specific zones of highways in its jurisdiction where passing or driving to the left of center on the roadway is especially hazardous. Signs or markings may indicate the beginning and end of a no-passing zone. (B) **Signs or markings.** Signs or markings clearly visible to an ordinarily observant driver must be obeyed. Where signs or markings define a no-passing zone, no driver may drive on the left side of the roadway or pavement striping where: (1) a sign or marking defines a no-passing zone; and (2) the sign or marking is clearly visible to an ordinarily observant driver. (C) **Exceptions.** This section does not apply to: (1) conditions described in § 60-6,131(1)(b); or (2) a driver who turns left into or from an alley, private road, or driveway, unless a sign prohibits the turn.
§ 8.055. Amount of Maintenance (a) A court may not order maintenance that requires an obligor to pay monthly more than the lesser of: (1) $5,000; or (2) 20 percent of the spouse's average monthly gross income. (b) The court shall set the amount that an obligor is required to pay in a maintenance order to provide for the minimum reasonable needs of the obligee, considering employment or property received in the dissolution of the marriage or otherwise owned by the obligee that contributes to the minimum reasonable needs of the obligee. (c) Department of Veterans Affairs service-connected disability compensation, social security benefits and disability benefits, and workers' compensation benefits are excluded from maintenance. (d) For the purposes of this chapter, "gross income" means resources as defined in Sections 154.062(b) and (c), disregarding any deductions listed in Section 154.062(d) and disregarding those benefits excluded under Subsection (c) of this section. **Tex. Fam. Code § 8.055 (subsections (b)–(d) repealed in 2011).**	**§ 8.055. Amount of maintenance.** (A) **Payment amount.** A court may order the obligor-spouse to pay monthly maintenance up to the lesser of: (1) $5,000; or (2) 20% of the obligor-spouse's average monthly gross income. (B) **Definition of "gross income."** In (A), "gross income" means resources defined in §§ 154.062(B) and (C), disregarding deductions listed in § 154.062(D) and disregarding benefits excluded under § 8.055(D). (C) **Considerations for calculating.** The court must specify the amount the obligor-spouse is to pay in a maintenance order, after considering the obligee-spouse's minimum reasonable needs, the property received in the divorce, the property otherwise owned by the obligee-spouse, and employment. (D) **Benefits excluded.** In calculating the obligor-spouse's average monthly gross income, a court must not include Department of Veterans Affairs service-connected disability compensation, social-security benefits, disability benefits, and workers'-compensation benefits.

Logicians would want *and* here. Idiomatically, *or* is more natural for 90% of readers. *See Garner's Dictionary of Legal Usage* 517 (3d ed. 2011) (s.v. "later of [date] or [date]; later of [date] and [date]").

Notice how daunting the left-hand side is without headings.

NOT THIS:	BUT THIS:
(a) A special events permit authorizes the holder to sell or dispense beer or wine for consumption at designated premises for a specific occasion and limited period of time. Only nonprofit fraternal, civic, or patriotic organizations active for a period of at least two years before application and incorporated under AS 10.20 are eligible for a special events permit, and only if all profits derived from the sale of beer or wine are paid to the organization and not to an individual. (b) An application for a special events permit must be received in the main office of the board at least 10 days before the date for which the permit is requested. The application must be signed by both the president and secretary of the organization applying for the permit. A sworn affidavit showing the length of time the organization has been in existence must accompany the application, together with a certified copy of the resolution of the board of directors authorizing the application. The written approval of the law enforcement agency having jurisdiction over the designated premises of the occasion for which the permit is sought must also be obtained and accompany the application. (c) The special events permit must be surrendered to the board, its agent, or the law enforcement agency approving the permit, within 48 hours of its expiration time. Failure to surrender the permit is cause, in the discretion of the board, for denial of applications for permits made in the future by the organization. No more than five special events permits may be granted to an organization, including its auxiliary, in any one calendar year. (d) A special events permit may not be transferred or renewed. (e) The fee for a special events permit is $50 a day. **Alaska Stat. § 04.11.240.**	(A) **Scope of special-events permit.** A special-events permit-holder may sell or dispense beer and wine for consumption at designated premises for a limited period at a specific event. (B) **Organization eligibility.** A fraternal, civic, or patriotic organization that is nonprofit is eligible for a special-events permit if: (1) the organization has been active for at least 2 years before applying; (2) the organization is incorporated under § 10.20; and (3) all profits from beer and wine sales are paid only to the organization. (C) **Application.** The board's main office must receive a permit application at least 10 days before the permit's requested date. The organization's president and secretary must both sign the application. The application must include the following: (1) a sworn affidavit stating how long the organization has existed; (2) a certified copy of the board of directors' resolution authorizing the application; and (3) written approval of the law-enforcement agency having jurisdiction over the premises where the event will take place. (D) **Fee.** The permit fee is $50 per day payable at the time of application. (E) **Allowable permits.** An organization, including its auxiliary, cannot be granted more than 5 special-events permits in a calendar year. (F) **Surrender; penalties.** A permit must be surrendered to the board, its agent, or the approving law-enforcement agency within 48 hours after it expires. Failure to surrender is cause for denying the organization's future permit applications. (G) **Transfer and renewal prohibition.** A permit is neither transferable nor renewable.

Note that this phrasing—*payable at the time of application*—is new. The original is undesirably vague on this important point.

"Most of the rules and principles that you should follow in drafting . . . would be self-evident to any good writer, and many others would become evident upon a little reflection, simply as a matter of common sense. But good drafting also involves the application of specialized rules, unique to that form, which would not be likely to occur to a nondrafter spontaneously; and it is important that you understand what they are and why they matter."

—Lawrence E. Filson, *The Legislative Drafter's Desk Reference* § 1.2, at 4 (1992).

What is a "recast fiscal year"? The phrase is unclear in the original, and I've kept it in the revision. But it needs clarification.

NOT THIS:

107.034 Determination of appropriation limitations.

(A)(1) The governor, in determining the state appropriation limitation for fiscal year 2008, shall use estimates regarding the aggregate general revenue fund appropriations for fiscal year 2007. For the first fiscal year of any biennium, the governor shall use the most recent published data available regarding the rates of inflation and population change. For the second fiscal year of any biennium, the governor shall use estimated rates of inflation and population change.

(2) When determining the state appropriation limitations for each fiscal biennium after the 2008-2009 biennium that does not begin with a recast fiscal year, the governor shall update the rates of inflation and population change used in the determination of the state appropriation limitation for the second fiscal year of the previous biennium to reflect the most recent published data, shall recalculate that second fiscal year's limitation based on the update, and shall use the recalculated limitation for determining the state appropriation limitations for the ensuing biennium to be included in the budget submitted under section 107.03 of the Revised Code.

(3) When determining the state appropriation limitations for each fiscal biennium after the 2008-2009 biennium that begins with a recast fiscal year, the governor shall update the rates of inflation and population change used in the determination of the state appropriation limitation for the second fiscal year of the previous biennium to reflect the most recent published data, and also shall update the aggregate general revenue fund appropriations amount for the second fiscal year of the previous biennium. The governor then shall recalculate that second fiscal year's limitation based on the updates and shall use the recalculated limitation for determining the state appropriation limitations for the ensuing biennium to be included in the budget submitted under section 107.03 of the Revised Code.

(B) The governor may designate the director of budget and management to perform the governor's duties under this section.

Ohio Rev. Code § 107.034.

BUT THIS:

§ 107.034 Setting limits on appropriations.

(A) **Governor's duties.**

(1) ***Using estimates.*** In determining the state appropriation limit for fiscal year 2008, the governor must use estimates regarding the aggregate general revenue fund appropriations for fiscal year 2007. For the first fiscal year of any biennium, the governor must use the most recently published inflation rate and population change. For the second fiscal year of any biennium, the governor must use an estimated inflation rate and population change.

(2) ***If biennium does not begin with recast fiscal year.*** When determining the state appropriation limit for each fiscal biennium after the 2008–2009 biennium that does not begin with a recast fiscal year, the governor must:

(a) update the inflation rate and population change used to determine the state appropriation limit for the previous biennium's second fiscal year so that it reflects the most recent published data;

(b) recalculate the second fiscal year's limit based on that update; and

(c) use the recalculated limit to determine the state appropriation limit for the following biennium and include it in the budget submitted under § 107.03.

(3) ***If biennium begins with recast fiscal year.*** When determining the state appropriation limit for each fiscal biennium after the 2008–2009 biennium that begins with a recast fiscal year, the governor must:

(a) update the inflation rate and population change used to determine the state appropriation limit for the previous biennium's second fiscal year so that it reflects the most recent published data;

(b) update the aggregate general-revenue-fund appropriation amount for the previous biennium's second fiscal year;

(c) recalculate the second fiscal year's limit based on those updates; and

(d) use the recalculated limit to determine the state appropriation limit for the following biennium and include it in the budget submitted under § 107.03.

(B) **Director of budget and management.** The governor may designate the director of budget and management to perform the governor's duties under this section.

> The word *kill* seems to be missing here. See the "threaten" phrase just below.

> The ordinary word *vaccine* is preferable to the faux precision of the technical noun *vaccinate* (/**vak**-si-nət/). Ordinary readers would read *vaccinates* not as a noun but as a third-person singular verb.

NOT THIS:	BUT THIS:
Sec. 531. Bank, safe and vault robbery—Any person who, with intent to commit the crime of larceny, or any felony, shall confine, maim, injure or wound, or attempt, or threaten to confine, kill, maim, injure or wound, or shall put in fear any person for the purpose of stealing from any building, bank, safe or other depository of money, bond or other valuables, or shall by intimidation, fear or threats compel, or attempt to compel any person to disclose or surrender the means of opening any building, bank, safe, vault or other depository of money, bonds, or other valuables, or shall attempt to break, burn, blow up or otherwise injure or destroy any safe, vault or other depository of money, bonds or other valuables in any building or place, shall, whether he succeeds or fails in the perpetration of such larceny or felony, be guilty of a felony, punishable by imprisonment in the state prison for life or any term of years. **Mich. Comp. Laws § 750.531.**	**§ 531. Bank, safe, and vault robbery.** (A) **Prohibition.** It is unlawful for a person with the intent to commit larceny or any felony—regardless of whether the person succeeds or fails in the larceny or felony—to do any of the following: (1) confine, kill, maim, injure, wound, or frighten another, or attempt or threaten any of these, for the purpose of stealing from a building, bank, safe, or other depository of money, bond, or other valuables; (2) compel someone by intimidation, fear, or threat to disclose or surrender the means of opening any building, bank, safe, vault, or other depository of money, bonds, or other valuables; or (3) attempt to break, burn, blow up, injure, or otherwise destroy a building, bank, safe, vault, or other depository of money, bonds, or other valuables. (B) **Penalty.** Violation of (A) is a felony punishable by imprisonment in state prison for a term of years up to life.
(1) No indemnity for brucellosis shall be paid: (a) On steers. (b) On any animal unless reactor tagged and permanently marked as required by department regulation and unless the claim is accompanied by such proof, as the department may require, of (1) slaughter within the time limited, (2) actual salvage and (3) cleaning and disinfection of the premises. (c) On any animal vaccinated against brucellosis, other than official vaccinates, unless it can be established that such animal, subsequent to vaccination, returned to a negative status as established by a negative test conducted not less than 30 days prior to the test on which the claim is based but more than 30 days after vaccination. **Wis. Stat. § 95.48(1)(a)-(c).**	(A) **Exemptions for brucellosis indemnity.** No indemnity for brucellosis may be paid on the following: (1) steers; (2) any animal unless: (a) the animal is reactor-tagged and permanently marked as the department's regulation requires; and (b) the claim is accompanied by any proof the department requires of slaughter within the time limited, actual salvage, and cleaning and disinfection of the premises; or (3) an animal vaccinated against brucellosis with an unofficial vaccine unless there is proof the animal returned to a negative status as shown by a negative test made: (a) more than 30 days after vaccination; and (b) at least 30 days before the test on which the claim is based.

NOT THIS:	BUT THIS:
§ 67-1-7. Applicability of chapter, generally; exceptions; qualified resort areas. (1) Except as otherwise provided in Section 67-9-1 for the transportation and possession of limited amounts of alcoholic beverages for the use of an alcohol processing permittee, and subject to all of the provisions and restrictions contained in this chapter, the manufacture, sale, distribution, possession and transportation of alcoholic beverages shall be lawful, subject to the restrictions hereinafter imposed, in those counties and municipalities of this state in which, at a local option election called and held for that purpose under the provisions of this chapter, a majority of the qualified electors voting in such election shall vote in favor thereof. Except as otherwise provided in Section 67-1-51 for holders of a caterer's permit, the manufacture, sale and distribution of alcoholic beverages shall not be permissible or lawful in counties except in (a) incorporated municipalities located within such counties, (b) qualified resort areas within such counties approved as such by the State Tax Commission, or (c) clubs within such counties, whether within a municipality or not. The manufacture, sale, distribution and possession of native wines shall be lawful in any location within any such county except those locations where the manufacture, sale or distribution is prohibited by law other than this section or by regulations of the commission. **Miss. Code § 67-1-7(1).**	**§ 67-1-7(1) Applicability of Mississippi Alcoholic Beverage Code** (A) **Where alcohol is allowed.** It is legal to manufacture, sell, distribute, transport, or possess alcohol in any county or municipality that, by election of the voters, allows the activity, as long as it occurs in one of the following places within that county: (1) an incorporated municipality; (2) a qualified resort area approved by the State Tax Commission; or (3) a club. (B) **Exceptions.** (1) ***Alcohol-processing permittees.*** An alcohol-processing permittee may possess and transport alcohol in all counties, even if that county does not allow transporting or possessing alcohol. (2) ***Caterer-permittees.*** A caterer-permittee may sell alcohol at any location in a county that has elected to allow alcohol sales. (3) ***Native wines.*** Native wines may be sold, manufactured, possessed, or distributed at any location in a county that has elected to allow alcohol, except where prohibited by law or Commission regulation.

Note that part of the problem in the original is the use of a run-in enumeration, without hanging indents: see § 1.3(A).

> "Is readability by the layman a fair test of a statute? Since every citizen is required to obey the law, and since, if he has failed to do so and finds himself in trouble, he cannot excuse himself on the ground that he did not know what the law was, it is scarcely disputable that statutes ought, if possible, to be written in terms comprehensible to the nonlawyer. It is moreover harmful to the general cause of respect for the law if the people of a country are under the impression . . . that the enacted laws cannot be understood by them."
>
> —Sir William Dale, *Legislative Drafting: A New Approach* 11 (1977).

1.2 Conciseness.

(A) Generally.

Verbosity is a scourge to all prose. Every unnecessary word weighs down a sentence, and the cumulative effect is to burden the reader—especially one who is (to use the psychologists' term) cognitively busy. Tighten wordings as much as is consistent with natural idiom. Under the surplusage canon of construction, courts try to give effect to every word in legislation; they tend to assume that no word in a statute is idle or needless.

In the following examples, my collaborators and I satisfied ourselves that no reasonable reader could say that the right-hand revisions omitted any significant meaning. That's not to say that nobody could find a quibble. But the revisions do illustrate the capital importance of concise wording. We think you'll find its advantages self-evident.

This statement could be read, mistakenly, as *requiring* the board to approve each agreement—as if it didn't have discretion to disapprove one.

NOT THIS:	BUT THIS:
The finance board shall approve each agreement before it is executed by the director and the director may not execute any agreement not approved by the finance board. [Word count: 28.] **W. Va. Code § 5-16C-4(b).**	The director must not sign any agreement until the finance board approves it. [Word count: 13—a 54% reduction.]
In the event that a land occupier or person proposes to develop a new point of withdrawal, and the new point is a high-capacity well, the land occupier or person shall notify the District before construction of the well begins. [Word count: 41.] **525 Ill. Comp. Stat. 45/5.**	A person who proposes to develop a new point of withdrawal with a high-capacity well must notify the District before the well's construction begins. [Word count: 25—a 39% reduction.]
The Mayor shall instruct the Office of Management and Budget Systems to coordinate with the Commission the establishment of a bookkeeping and accounting system to allow for swift transference of grant monies from the District government to a recipient, and shall instruct that Office, in concert with the Commission, to establish a voucher system which would also allow for the swift transference of funds from the District government to grant recipients. [Word count: 71.] **D.C. Code § 39-206(a).**	The Office of Management and Budget Systems must coordinate with the Commission to establish both a bookkeeping-and-accounting system and a voucher system that allow the District to transfer grant money swiftly to recipients. The mayor must ensure that this coordination takes place. [Word count: 44—a 38% reduction.]

This provision is fulfilled by mere instruction, not by implementation. The revision more effectively states the requirement.

> "[T]he shorter the distance between the beginning and ending of each sentence, the more numerous the points of repose for the mind."
>
> —Jeremy Bentham, "A General View of a Complete Code of Laws," in 3 *The Works of Jeremy Bentham* 155, 208 (John Bowring ed., 1843).

NOT THIS:	BUT THIS:
The term "border crossing identification card" means a document of identity bearing that designation issued to an alien who is lawfully admitted for permanent residence, or to an alien who is a resident in foreign contiguous territory, by a consular officer or an immigration officer for the purpose of crossing over the borders between the United States and foreign contiguous territory in accordance with such conditions for its issuance and use as may be prescribed by regulations. Such regulations shall provide that (A) each such document include a biometric identifier (such as the fingerprint or handprint of the alien) that is machine readable and (B) an alien presenting a border crossing identification card is not permitted to cross over the border into the United States unless the biometric identifier contained on the card matches the appropriate biometric characteristic of the alien. [Word count: 141.] **8 U.S.C. § 1101(a)(6).**	"Border-crossing identification card" means any document so designated by a consular or immigration office and issued to an alien to identify the alien when crossing the border between the United States and a foreign territory. The document and its use must comply with regulations requiring a machine-readable biometric identifier. To cross into the United States, an alien must match the data contained in the card. [Word count: 67—a 52% reduction.]
Every year, in rapidly increasing numbers, the inhabitants of the state of West Virginia and nonresidents are enjoying the recreational value of West Virginia rivers and streams. The tourist trade is of vital importance to the state of West Virginia and the services offered by commercial whitewater outfitters and commercial whitewater guides significantly contribute to the economy of the state of West Virginia. The Legislature recognizes that there are inherent risks in the recreational activities provided by commercial whitewater outfitters and commercial whitewater guides which should be understood by each participant. It is essentially impossible for commercial whitewater outfitters and commercial whitewater guides to eliminate these risks. It is the purpose of this article to define those areas of responsibility and affirmative acts for which commercial whitewater outfitters and commercial whitewater guides are liable for loss, damage or injury. [Word count: 139.] **W. Va. Code § 20-3B-1.**	Each year, more and more West Virginians and nonresidents enjoy recreation in the state's waters. Tourism is vital to West Virginia, and the commercial whitewater industry contributes significantly to the state's economy. Commercial whitewater rafting poses inherent, unavoidable risks to participants. This article defines the areas of responsibility and affirmative acts for which commercial whitewater outfitters and guides are liable for loss, damage, or injury. [Word count: 71—a 49% reduction.]

Some readers might wonder why this provision is within a statute. It is a purpose clause that appears at the outset. The point of the illustration is that the 139-word version at left is terribly verbose.

> "Edmund Burke observed that bad laws are the worst form of tyranny. But, equally, well-intentioned laws that are badly drafted or not readily accessible are also a form of tyranny."
>
> —Rt. Hon. Lord Oliver of Aylmerton, *A Judicial View of Modern Legislation*, 14 Statute L. Rev. 1, 2 (1993).

In this section, as in most, you're also witnessing the advantages of using more headings: see § 1.1(F).

NOT THIS:	BUT THIS:
§ 1256. Rescission of adjustment of status; effect upon naturalized citizen. (a) If, at any time within five years after the status of a person has been otherwise adjusted under the provisions of section 1255 or 1259 of this title or any other provision of law to that of an alien lawfully admitted for permanent residence, it shall appear to the satisfaction of the Attorney General that the person was not in fact eligible for such adjustment of status, the Attorney General shall rescind the action taken granting an adjustment of status to such person and cancelling removal in the case of such person if that occurred and the person shall thereupon be subject to all provisions of this chapter to the same extent as if the adjustment of status had not been made. Nothing in this subsection shall require the Attorney General to rescind the alien's status prior to commencement of procedures to remove the alien under section 1229a of this title, and an order of removal issued by an immigration judge shall be sufficient to rescind the alien's status. (b) Any person who has become a naturalized citizen of the United States upon the basis of a record of a lawful admission for permanent residence, created as a result of an adjustment of status for which such person was not in fact eligible, and which is subsequently rescinded under subsection (a) of this section, shall be subject to the provisions of section 1451 of this title as a person whose naturalization was procured by concealment of a material fact or by willful misrepresentation. [Word count: 254.] **8 U.S.C. § 1256.**	**§ 1256. Rescinding adjustment of status; effects.** (A) **Rescission.** The Attorney General must rescind the grant of an adjustment of status to legal permanent residency under § 1255 or § 1259 if, within 5 years after the adjustment, the Attorney General determines that the person was not actually eligible to adjust. The person then becomes subject to the Immigration and Naturalization Act as if the adjustment had never occurred. The Attorney General need not rescind the status before initiating procedures to remove the alien under § 1229a. An immigration judge's removal order also rescinds an alien's status. (B) **Misrepresenting material fact.** A person who gains citizenship based on a record that results in rescission under (A) is subject to a revocation of naturalization for concealing or willfully misrepresenting a material fact. [Word count: 115—a 55% reduction.]

"When and when not to use particular language is the lawyer's daily decision. If some reason requires special language, the choice is made. If there is no reason for departure from the language of common understanding, the special usage is suspect. If, in addition, a special usage works evil, it should be abandoned, and quickly."

—David Mellinkoff, *The Language of the Law* vii (1963).

NOT THIS:	BUT THIS:
(a) Design Requirements.— (1) In general.—The design of the coins minted under this Act shall be emblematic of the centennial of America's involvement in World War I. (2) Designation and inscriptions.—On each coin minted under this Act, there shall be— (A) a designation of the value of the coin; (B) an inscription of the year "2018"; and (C) inscriptions of the words "Liberty", "In God We Trust", "United States of America", and "E Pluribus Unum". (b) Selection.—The design for the coins minted under this Act shall be selected by the Secretary based on the winning design from a juried, compensated design competition described under subsection (c). (c) Design Competition.—The Secretary shall hold a competition and provide compensation for its winner to design the obverse and reverse of the coins minted under this Act. The competition shall be held in the following manner: (1) The competition shall be judged by an expert jury chaired by the Secretary and consisting of 3 members from the Citizens Coinage Advisory Committee who shall be elected by such Committee and 3 members from the Commission of Fine Arts who shall be elected by such Commission. (2) The Secretary shall determine compensation for the winning design, which shall be not less than $5,000. (3) The Secretary may not accept a design for the competition unless a plaster model accompanies the design. [Word count: 229.] **World War I American Veterans Centennial Commemorative Coin Act, Pub. L. No. 113-212, § 4, 128 Stat. 2082, 2083.**	(A) **Design requirements.** (1) ***Generally.*** The centennial coin's design must commemorate America's involvement in World War I. (2) ***Designation and inscriptions.*** Each centennial coin must contain: (a) the coin's designated value; and (b) the inscriptions: "2018," "Liberty," "In God We Trust," "United States of America," and "E Pluribus Unum." (B) **Selection.** The centennial coin's design will be based on a winning design selected by the Secretary from the competition described in (C). (C) **Design competition.** The Secretary must hold a competition to select the centennial coin's design, obverse and reverse, and must compensate the winning designer. The following conditions apply: (1) the competition will be judged by 7 panelists: the Secretary (as chair), 3 peer-elected members of the Citizens Coinage Advisory Committee, and 3 peer-elected members of the Commission of Fine Arts; (2) at least $5,000 must be awarded for the winning design; and (3) a plaster model must be submitted with the design. [Word count: 156—a 32% reduction.]

> "You can find mistakes and flaws in plain drafting. But anyone who enjoys that pursuit would have much more fun with old-style drafting, where ambiguities, inconsistencies, and uncertainties flourish in all the verbosity and disorder."
>
> —Joseph Kimble, *Wrong—Again—About Plain Language*, Mich. B.J., July 2013, at 44, 45.

(B) Clauses into phrases.

Collapse clauses into phrases when possible. Instead of *case to be tried without a jury*, use *nonjury trial* or *nonjury case.*

Notice the remote relative. See § 5.2(C).

NOT THIS:	BUT THIS:
(1) The amount of the withdrawal is income to the individual that is subject to taxation under IC 6-3-2-18(e). **Ind. Code 6-8-11-17(c)(1).**	(1) The amount withdrawn is taxable as income to the employee under IC 6-3-2-18(e).
Except as otherwise provided in this part or as otherwise ordered by the court, a supervised personal representative has the same duties and powers as a personal representative who is not supervised. **Mich. Comp. Laws § 700.3501(3).**	Unless this part provides otherwise or a court orders otherwise, a supervised personal representative has the same duties and powers as an unsupervised one.
An application which is incomplete will be closed after one year of inactivity. At the end of this period, any application which is not completed will be considered abandoned and closed by the board and fees paid to the board will not be refunded. Should the applicant reapply after his incomplete application is closed, he shall be required to begin the process anew, including the payment of the application fee to the board. **La. Admin. Code tit. 46, pt. LIV, § 151(N).**	After 1 year of inactivity, an incomplete application will be considered abandoned, and the board may close it. Fees paid to the board will not be refunded. An applicant who reapplies after an incomplete application has been closed must begin the process anew, with a new application fee.

(C) Phrases into words.

Avoid circumlocutions. When you can, collapse phrases into single words. For example, never use *person who seeks election to public office through a political campaign* when you can write *political candidate* or just *candidate.*

NOT THIS:	BUT THIS:
(b) Peer review panel To assist the Secretary in evaluating applications under section 6514 of this title, the Secretary may establish a panel of not less than three persons who have expertise in organic farming and handling methods, to evaluate the State governing official or private person that is seeking accreditation as a certifying agent under such section. Not less than two members of such panel shall be persons who are not employees of the Department of Agriculture or of the applicable State government. **7 U.S.C. § 6516(b).**	(B) **Peer-review panel.** To help the Secretary evaluate applications under § 6514, the Secretary may establish a panel of at least 3 experts in organic-farming and handling methods to evaluate the State official or private person who seeks accreditation as a certifying agent. At least 2 members of the panel must be nonemployees of the Department of Agriculture or of the applicable State agency.
Every electrical corporation furnishing electricity to an agricultural producer shall, in addition to its regular service, prepare and file tariffs providing, where economically and technologically feasible, for optional alternative interruptible service to any agricultural producer upon reasonable notice to the agricultural producer consistent with safety of operations by the agricultural producer and providing for limits upon the frequency and duration of interruption of service which the commission finds are reasonable in relation to the needs of the electrical corporation for reductions in load to meet system peak requirements and the burdens imposed upon the agricultural producer of reducing its operations during periods of interruption of electrical service. **Calif. Pub. Util. Code § 744(b).**	When economically and technologically feasible, an electrical corporation that provides electricity to an agricultural producer must prepare and file tariffs providing for optional, alternative, interruptible service, with reasonable limits on the frequency and duration of outages. To promote safety, the agricultural producer must be given reasonable notice of an outage. The commission will determine what is a reasonable limit based on the electrical corporation's need to reduce the load to meet system-peak requirements and the burden imposed on the agricultural producer to reduce operations during outages.

NOT THIS:	BUT THIS:
The hunting license of any person convicted under section fifty-seven, article two, chapter twenty of the Code of West Virginia, one thousand nine hundred thirty-one, as amended, shall be revoked, and such person shall not be issued any other hunting license for a period of five years: Provided, that any person heretofore or hereafter convicted of any offense under section eleven, article seven, chapter sixty-one, or under section fifty-seven, article two, chapter twenty, other than a negligent shooting which has resulted in the killing of a human being, after the expiration of two years may petition the director for reinstatement of all hunting license privileges and if the director upon a hearing and full investigation finds that the applicant has paid and satisfied all claims against him, if any, and the circumstances at the time and the nature of the offense indicate that he is not likely again to commit a like or similar offense and that the public good does not require that the applicant's hunting privileges remain revoked or suspended, the director may enter an order restoring full hunting privileges to the applicant. **W. Va. Code, § 20-2-38.**	A person convicted under § 57, art. 2, ch. 20, of the Code of West Virginia, 1939, as amended, cannot be issued a hunting license for 5 years. If the person has a hunting license, it is revoked. After 2 years, a person convicted of any offense under § 11, art. 7, ch. 61, or § 57, art. 2, ch. 20, other than a negligent shooting that resulted in a homicide, may petition the director for reinstatement of all hunting-license privileges. After a full investigation and hearing, the director may restore the applicant's full hunting privileges if the director finds that: (A) the applicant has paid and satisfied all claims against him or her; (B) the nature of the offense and the circumstances at the time of the offense show that it is unlikely the applicant will commit the same or a similar offense; and (C) the public good does not require that the applicant's hunting privileges remain revoked or suspended.

(D) Doublets and triplets.

Try to find just the right word—the one that most accurately conveys the meaning. Avoid doublets, triplets, and synonym strings. Be sure that if you add a near-synonym, you're actually adding meaning. For a full list and extended discussion of the subject, see "Doublets, Triplets, and Synonym-Strings" in *Garner's Dictionary of Legal Usage* 294–97 (3d ed. 2011).

NOT THIS:	BUT THIS:
Powers not limited. The powers conferred by sections 23-11-31 to 23-11-35 are in addition and supplemental to the powers conferred by any other law, and nothing contained herein may be construed as limiting any other powers of a housing authority. **N.D. Cent. Code § 23-11-36.**	**Powers not limited.** The powers conferred by §§ 23-11-31 to 23-11-35 supplement the powers conferred by other laws. Nothing in this statute limits any other housing-authority powers.
Any applicant who is granted the use of vacant public land for gardening, agricultural purposes or agricultural restoration purposes shall indemnify and save harmless the state and all of its officers, agents and employees against suits and claims of liability of each name and nature arising out of, or in consequence of the use of vacant public land. **Conn. Gen. Stat. § 22-6e(a).**	An applicant who is granted the use of vacant public land for gardening, agricultural purposes, or agricultural-restoration purposes indemnifies the state and its officers, agents, and employees against all claims of liability resulting from the applicant's use of the land.

Related to would be even broader than *resulting from*. It's a policy choice.

NOT THIS:	BUT THIS:
No action or proceeding to set aside, vacate, cancel or annul any assessment or tax for a local improvement shall be maintained, except for total want of jurisdiction to levy and assess the same on the part of the officers, board or body authorized by law to make such levy or assessment or to order the improvement on account of which the levy or assessment was made. **N.Y. S.C.C. Law § 164.**	**Subject-matter jurisdiction.** A lawsuit or proceeding to cancel an assessment or tax for a local improvement may be brought only if the officers, board, or body authorized by law to order the improvement on account for which the levy or assessment was made, or to make the levy or assessment, lacked jurisdiction to act.
In the event of neglect, refusal or failure on the part of any partnership to pay the annual tax to be paid hereunder on or before the first day of June in any year, such partnership shall pay the sum of $200 to be recovered by adding that amount to the annual tax, and such additional sum shall become a part of the tax and shall be collected in the same manner and subject to the same penalties. **Del. Code tit. 6, § 15-1208(d).**	**Failure to pay.** If a partnership does not pay the required annual tax by June 1 in any year, the partnership must pay $200. That amount will be added to and become part of the annual tax due and will be collected in the same manner and subject to the same penalties.
In order to be informed and to determine the status of boards of pharmacy of other jurisdictions which desire to effect arrangements for reciprocal registration of pharmacists, and in order to also be advised regarding fitness of applicants, and of the progress and changes in pharmacy throughout the country, the board may annually select one (1) of its members to meet with like representatives from other jurisdictions, and may join in creating and maintaining an association for such mutual ends, and in its discretion the board may contribute such information as it possesses which is useful to such aims and objects. **Wyo. Stat. 1977 § 33-24-133.**	(A) **Cooperation with other jurisdictions.** The board may annually select one of its members to meet with representatives from other jurisdictions to: (1) stay informed of and determine the status of boards of pharmacy of other jurisdictions that want to arrange for reciprocal registration of pharmacists, and (2) keep advised about the fitness of applicants and of the progress and changes in pharmacy throughout the country. (B) **Associations.** The selected member may join, create, and maintain an association for these purposes. In its discretion, the board may contribute information it possesses that is useful for these purposes.
All licenses granted under the provisions of this chapter shall remain in effect for a period of fifty years from and after the date of granting thereof. From and after the expiration of such terms of fifty years the licensee, its successors and assigns, shall hold the property and rights acquired under the authority of this chapter under an indeterminate license, which shall continue until such property and rights have been purchased by the Commonwealth, or until the same have been acquired by the Commonwealth by due process of law; provided that the right of the Commonwealth to take over, maintain and operate any development licensed under this chapter at any time by condemnation proceedings, upon payment of just compensation, is hereby expressly reserved. **Va. Code § 62.1-94.**	**Term; effect of expiration.** A license granted under this chapter is in effect for 50 years after the date of the grant. After the 50 years expire, the licensee, together with its successors and assigns, hold the property and rights acquired under the authority of this chapter under an indeterminate license, which continues until the Commonwealth purchases the property and rights or acquires them by due process of law. The Commonwealth reserves the right to use condemnation proceedings to take over, maintain, and operate any development licensed under this chapter, upon payment of just compensation.

NOT THIS:	BUT THIS:
(e) 3609(e). If the deceased member of the police department leaves a surviving widow and no children under the age of eighteen years, the widow shall, until she remarries, receive one hundred percent of the benefits to which he was entitled as hereinabove provided, and in the event that the deceased member leaves minor children under the age of eighteen years and no widow, the minor child or children shall be entitled to receive one hundred percent of the benefits until the child or children of the deceased member are eighteen years of age or are in an accredited institution of higher learning and age twenty-one, whichever is applicable. If the child or children are not living with the deceased member at the time of his death, then and in that event, the children shall not be entitled to any benefits payable under the provisions of this Subpart unless it is affirmatively shown that the children were dependent upon said deceased member for support and the percentage of said dependency. Then and in that event, the board shall have the exclusive right to consider all facts and to determine whether or not the children shall be entitled to benefits hereinabove provided and to determine from time to time whether the benefits should be continued or discontinued, all of which shall be entirely discretionary with the board. **La. Rev. Stat. 11:3609(e).**	**(E) Survivor benefits.** If a deceased police officer leaves a surviving spouse and no children under the age of 18, the spouse will, until remarrying, receive 100% of the benefits to which the officer was entitled. If the officer leaves a child under the age of 18 and no spouse, each minor child will share 100% of the benefits equally until the child reaches 18 or, if in an accredited institution of higher learning, reaches 21. If the child is not living with the deceased officer when he or she dies, then the child is not entitled to any benefits payable under this Subpart unless it is affirmatively shown that the child was dependent on the officer for support and for what percentage of the child's dependency. Then the board has the exclusive right and sole discretion to: (A) consider all facts; (B) determine whether the child is entitled to benefits; and (C) determine from time to time whether the benefits should be continued or discontinued.

Notice the ill-advised plural. See § 2.4.

If there is more than one child, the benefits would probably be shared evenly. But possibly each child is to receive an amount equal to 100%. The original isn't at all clear.

"It is only the cumulative effect of a large number of minor changes that can bring about a major improvement. In this respect, the analogy to streamlining is close. In the process of streamlining a locomotive, probably the removal of no single protuberance or angle would produce a perceptible difference in the operation of the train. The removal of fifty does."

—David Cavers, *The Simplification of Government Regulations*, 8 Fed. B.J. 339, 345 (1947).

(E) Eliminating zombie nouns.

Uncover so-called "zombie nouns"—i.e., abstract nouns usually ending in the suffixes *-tion*, *-sion*, *-ment*, *-ence*, *-ance*, *-ity*—and make them into verbs. Doing so has several advantages:

- it saves words by eliminating prepositional phrases;
- it increases readability by forcing the writer to be explicit about implied actors; and
- it makes the style more lively by substituting action verbs in place of stagnant *be*-verbs.

NOT THIS:	BUT THIS:
The dissolution court may make a reasonable allocation of an undifferentiated award between its marital and separate-property components. **Principles of the Law of Family Dissolution: Analysis and Recommendations § 4.08(2)(a) (Tentative Draft No. 1, 1995).**	The dissolution court may reasonably allocate an undifferentiated award between its marital- and separate-property components.
§ 4203. Statement of policy It is the policy of the United States— (1) to assist in the conservation and protection of the African elephant by supporting the conservation programs of African countries and the CITES Secretariat; and (2) to provide financial resources for those programs. **16 U.S.C. § 4203.**	**§ 4203. Statement of policy.** To help conserve and protect the African elephant, the United States will: (A) support the conservation programs of African countries and the CITES Secretariat; and (B) provide financial resources for those programs.
Unless applicable law otherwise provides, a third person may give notification to a client, in a matter in which the client is represented by a lawyer, by . . . . **Restatement (Third) of the Law Governing Lawyers § 40(2) (Tentative Draft No. 5, 1992).**	Unless applicable law provides otherwise, in a matter in which a lawyer represents a given client, a third person may notify that client by . . . .

1.3 Format with hanging indents.

(A) Cascading from the left.

Indenting should progress from the left margin, starting there—not with a first-line indent, as in a letter. The first character of the second line of a subpart should line up precisely with the first character of the subpart's first line. See the markings below.

Although many official printers go margin-to-margin to cut down the number of pages, the result is counterproductive. It makes all the statutes look as if they're "fine print," and readers are inevitably repelled by the monolithic look of the page.

NOT THIS:	BUT THIS:
Attendance in adjoining state. Upon a determination by the State Board of Education and of the regional superintendent of schools of the region in which a high school student or an eighth grade graduate resides that no high school of this State is readily accessible to the pupil or graduate, but that a high school in an adjoining state providing a course of two or more years of work approved by the State Board of Education of this State is readily accessible to him, the pupil or graduate may attend such high school in an adjoining state and the board of education of the high school district or of the non-high school district in which he resides shall pay his tuition. **105 Ill. Comp. Stat. 5/12-21.**	(A) **Attendance in adjoining state.** A high-school student or an eighth-grade graduate may attend a high school in an adjoining state if the State Board of Education and the regional superintendent of the schools in the region where the student or graduate resides determine that: (1) no Illinois public high school is readily accessible to the student or graduate; (2) the out-of-state high school provides 2 or more years of coursework approved by the Illinois Board of Education; and (3) the out-of-state high school is readily accessible to the student or graduate. (B) **Tuition.** The board of education of the school district in which that student or graduate resides will pay tuition for attendance at the out-of-state high school.
153.67. Unpaid fees to constitute lien In the event that the fees, rates or charges for the services and facilities of any water or sewer system shall not be paid as and when due, any unpaid balance thereof and all interest accruing thereon shall be a lien on any parcel or property affected thereby. Such liens shall be superior and paramount to the interest on such parcel or property of any owner, lessee, tenant, mortgagee or other person except the lien of county taxes and shall be on a parity with the lien of any such county taxes. In the event that any such service charge shall not be paid as and when due and shall be in default for thirty days or more the unpaid balance thereof and all interest accrued thereon, together with attorneys fees and costs, may be recovered by the district in a civil action, and any such lien and accrued interest may be foreclosed or otherwise enforced by the district by action or suit in equity as for the foreclosure of a mortgage on real property. **Fla. Stat. § 153.67.**	**§ 153.67. Unpaid fees are a lien.** (A) **Unpaid fees become lien.** If the fees, rates, or charges for water- or sewer-system service and facilities are not paid as they become due, the unpaid balance and all accrued interest become a lien on the affected property. (B) **Priority of liens.** A lien under (A) is superior to the interest on the property of any owner, lessee, tenant, mortgagee, or other person. A lien under (A) is equal to a county tax lien on the property. (C) **Recovery in civil lawsuit.** If a service charge under (A) is in default for 30 days or more, the district may recover in a civil lawsuit the unpaid balance, accrued interest, attorney's fees, and court costs. (D) **Recovery by foreclosure.** The district may foreclose or otherwise enforce a lien and collect accrued interest in a foreclosure lawsuit.

NOT THIS:	BUT THIS:
§ 1738-68. Time roads are to be taken over; exceptions. The township roads hereinbefore described shall be taken over by the Commonwealth, through the Department of Highways, not later than the fifteenth day of August, one thousand nine hundred thirty-one, subject, however, to the following exceptions: (a) No township road, or part thereof, described in the foregoing sections of this act, shall be taken over by the Commonwealth, if an order or decree for the improvement thereof has been issued, until there has been full compliance with the terms of such order or decree. (b) No township road, or part thereof, described in the foregoing sections of this act, shall be taken over by the Commonwealth, if a contract for the improvement thereof has been entered into between a contractor and the Commonwealth or the local authorities, or both, until the contract has been completed. (c) No township road, or part thereof, described in the foregoing sections of this act, shall be taken over by the Commonwealth, if an agreement has been entered into between the local authorities and the Commonwealth for the maintenance or construction of such road, even though no formal contract has been executed pursuant to such agreement and no work has been done, until the terms of the agreement have been fulfilled or the agreement has been cancelled by the local authorities. **36 Pa. Cons. Stat. § 1738-68.**	**§ 1738-68. When township roads will be taken over; exceptions.** (A) **General rule.** Township roads must be taken over by the Commonwealth, through the Department of Highways, no later than August 15, 1931. (B) **Exceptions.** A township road must not be taken over by the Commonwealth, in full or in part, until: (1) there has been full compliance with the terms of any order or decree for the road's improvement; (2) any road-improvement contract between a contractor and the Commonwealth, local authorities, or both, has been completed; and (3) the terms of any agreement for building or maintaining the road made between the local authorities and the Commonwealth or any other party have been fulfilled or canceled, even if no formal contract has been executed under that agreement and no work has been done.

> "Choosing more familiar words doesn't mean that the drafter must choose friendly over precise. A word that is too narrow in scope for a particular purpose or would result in ambiguity in the statute would not be appropriate under present drafting standards or under the plain language banner."
>
> —Susan Krongold, *Writing Laws: Making Them Easier to Understand*, 24 Ottawa L. Rev. 495, 528 (1992).

Note that the reference isn't entirely clear. It would be better to write that §§ 741–750 must be followed.

NOT THIS:	BUT THIS:
§ 736. Issuance of summons. (1) On the filing of a petition under this article, the court may cause a copy of the petition and a summons to be issued, requiring the respondent and his parent or other person legally responsible for his care, or with whom he is domiciled, to appear at the court at a time and place named to answer the petition. The summons shall be signed by the court or by the clerk or deputy clerk of the court. If those on whom a summons must be served are before the court at the time of the filing of a petition, the provisions of part four of this article shall be followed. (2) In proceedings originated pursuant to subdivision (b) of section seven hundred thirty-three of this article, the court shall cause a copy of the petition and notice of the time and place to be heard to be served upon any parent of the respondent or other person legally responsible for the respondent's care who has not signed the petition, provided that the address of such parent or other person legally responsible is known to the court or is ascertainable by the court. Such petition shall include a notice that, upon placement of the child in the care and custody of the department of social services or any other agency, said parent may be named as a respondent in a child support proceeding brought pursuant to article four of this act. Service shall be made by the clerk of the court by mailing such notice and petition by ordinary first class mail to such parent or other person legally responsible at such person's last known residence. (3) In proceedings originated pursuant to subdivision (a), (c), (d) or (e) of section seven hundred thirty-three of this article, the court shall cause a copy of the petition and notice of the time and place to be heard to be served upon each parent of the respondent or other person legally responsible for the respondent's care, provided that the address of such parent or other person legally responsible is known to the court or is ascertainable by the court. Service shall be made by the clerk of the court by mailing such notice and petition by ordinary first class mail to such parent or other person legally responsible at such person's last known residence. **N.Y. Family Court Act § 736.**	**§ 736. Issuing summons.** (A) **Requirements.** When a petition is filed under this article, the court may demand that a copy of the petition and a summons, signed by the court or a court clerk, be issued requiring the respondent and the respondent's legal guardian or other person who is legally responsible for the respondent's care, or with whom the respondent lives, to appear at the court to answer the petition at a time and place named. If the parties served are before the court when a petition is filed, §§ 741–750 must be followed. (B) **Notice served in matters under § 733.** In a matter originating under § 733, if the court knows the legal guardian's or responsible person's address or can obtain it: (1) the court may demand that a copy of the petition and notice of the hearing's time and place be served on any legal guardian or responsible person who has not signed the petition; and (2) the petition must include a notice that, upon the child's placement with a governmental agency, the legal guardian or responsible person may be named as a respondent in a child-support case under article 4. (C) **Notice served in matters under § 733(a), (c), (d), or (e).** In a matter originating under § 733(a), (c), (d), or (e), the court may demand that a copy of the petition and notice of the hearing's time and place be served on each legal guardian or responsible person if the court knows the legal guardian's or responsible person's address or can obtain it. (D) **Notice by mail.** For (B) and (C), the clerk of court must make service by mailing the notice and petition first class to the legal guardian's or responsible person's last known residence.

A paragraph treating disparate topics all run together is a nightmare for readers. Note the mental tidiness signaled by headings: see § 1.1(F).

NOT THIS:	BUT THIS:
§ 240-B Order of Support by Parent. When the court makes an order of support pursuant to section two hundred forty of this article, and where permitted under federal law and where the record of the proceedings contains such information, the court shall require the social security number of such parent to be affixed to such order; provided, however, that no such order shall be invalid because of the omission of such number. Where the record of the proceedings contains such information, such order shall also include on its face the name and address of the employer, if any, of the person chargeable with support provided, however, that failure to comply with this requirement shall not invalidate such order. Where the order of child support or combined child and spouse support is made on behalf of persons in receipt of public assistance or in receipt of services pursuant to section one hundred eleven-g of the social services law, the court shall require each party to provide, and update upon any change, the following information to the court by reporting such change to the support collection unit designated by the appropriate social services district: social security number, residential and mailing addresses, telephone number, driver's license number; and name, address and telephone number of the parties' employers. Due process requirements for notice and service of process for subsequent hearings are met, with respect to such party, upon sending written notice by first class mail to the most recent residential address on record with the support collection unit; or by sending by first class mail written notice to the most recent employer address on record with the support collection unit, if a true copy thereof also is sent by first class mail to the most recent residential address on record with the support collection unit. Any such order issued on or after the first day of October, nineteen hundred ninety-nine shall also include, where available, the social security number of each child on whose behalf support has been ordered. **N.Y. Dom. Rel. Law § 240-B.**	**§ 240-B Support orders.** When the court enters a support order under § 240, the following requirements apply: (A) **Requisite information.** The court must affix the following information to an order of support if available in the record and permitted by federal law (but failing to do so does not invalidate the order): (1) the ordered party's social-security number; (2) the ordered party's employer's name and address on the front of the order, if applicable; and (3) the social-security number for the child named in the order, if the order was issued on or after October 1, 1999. (B) **Updating child-support information.** If the beneficiary of a child-support order or combined child-spouse-support order receives public-assistance services or services under Social Services Law § 111-G, the court must require each party to provide and update the following information with the support-collection unit designated by the appropriate social-services district: (1) social-security number; (2) residential address; (3) mailing address; (4) telephone number; (5) driver's-license number; and (6) name, address, and telephone number of the party's employer. (C) **Adequacy of notice.** Due process for notice and service-of-process requirements regarding subsequent hearings is met when written notice is sent to the ordered party by first-class mail to the most recent residential or employer address on record with the support-collection unit.

(B) Format as integral to the statute.

As part of the official format, use hanging indents to reveal structure cleanly as they cascade in from the left margin—leaving the division indicator (the number or letter) isolated to the left so as to provide a clear signpost for readers. If possible, enact a provision that states: "The format of this Act is integral to its official form. No printed version of this Act is official unless it reflects the hanging indents set forth in the version signed into law." Alert the printers to this provision.

As for online versions, legislatures concerned with the readability of their work must provide for a person minimally competent in typography to lay out statutes in an acceptable form that complies with this guideline. The task can be accomplished relatively inexpensively once a good template is in place.

NOT THIS:	BUT THIS:
§ 323.159 Applying homestead exemption to nonprofit corporation that owns and operates housing cooperatives. . . . (B) Not later than the first day of May of each year, any nonprofit corporation that owns and operates a housing cooperative shall determine the amount of property taxes it paid for the housing cooperative for the preceding tax year and shall attribute to each homestead in the housing cooperative a portion of the total property taxes as if the homestead's occupant paid the taxes. The taxes attributed to each homestead shall be based on square footage of the housing cooperative and on other reasonable factors that reflect the value of the homestead. Not later than the fifteenth day of May each year, the corporation shall file this information with the county auditor, along with any applications submitted to it under division (A) of section 323.153 of the Revised Code. No nonprofit corporation that owns and operates a housing cooperative shall fail to file with the county auditor the information required by this division and division (A) of section 323.153 of the Revised Code. **Ohio Rev. Code § 323.159(B).**	**§ 323.159 Reduction in taxes for housing cooperatives.** . . . (B) **Application.** (1) ***Tax determination.*** No later than May 1 of each year, a nonprofit corporation that owns and operates a housing cooperative must determine the amount of property taxes it paid in the preceding tax year for the housing cooperative. A proportion of that total must be attributed to each homestead in the housing cooperative, as if the homestead's occupant had paid the taxes. The attributed amount of taxes must be based on: (a) the percentage of the homestead's square footage as compared to the housing cooperative's total square footage;* and (b) other reasonable factors that reflect the homestead's value. (2) ***Filing date.*** No later than May 15 of each year, the nonprofit corporation must file with the county auditor the information required by this section and by § 323.153(A).

*This is almost certainly the meaning of the original—but it's obscure.

2. General Conventions

2.1 Obligations and prohibitions generally.

(A) Definitions for words of authority.

Use the following words of authority as your basic vocabulary for establishing duties, rights, powers, entitlements, and disentitlements:

must = is required to
must not = is required not to
may = is permitted to, has discretion to, has a right to, is authorized to [+ *verb*]
is entitled to = has a right to [+ *noun*]
will = (expresses a policy or a future contingency in the manner of normal English)
can = is legally or physically capable
cannot = is legally or physically incapable

(B) Elimination of *shall*.

Replace *shall* with *must* or some other, more appropriate term. *Shall* is infamous for the ambiguities it causes* and is best dropped from modern legislative drafting. Its multifarious meanings should be allocated among *must*, *will*, *is*, and *may*. This substitution alone would result in the single greatest improvement to modern legislative drafting.

This shift will require many experienced legislative drafters to adjust their practices. Many will resist at first because they've grown fond of *shall* and believe (mistakenly, on close inspection) that they've been using *shall* precisely and consistently. With a little patience and humility, these drafters will almost uniformly come to see the wisdom of jettisoning *shall*. The issue is a huge one because it affects almost every legislative sentence.

NOT THIS:	BUT THIS:
There shall be fire extinguishers of adequate size, type and amounts in locations as recommended by the National Fire Protection Association. **Me. Rev. Stat. tit. 6, § 102(3)(B).**	Fire extinguishers of adequate size, type, and amount must be located where the National Fire Protection Association recommends.
The city council shall have the power to remove any officer for incompetency, corruption, misconduct or malfeasance in office, after due notice and an opportunity to be heard in his defense. **Tex. Rev. Civ. Stat. art. 1006 (repealed in 1987).**	The city council may remove any officer for incompetence, corruption, misconduct, or malfeasance in office. The council must first give the officer notice and an opportunity to be heard.

*See *Garner's Dictionary of Legal Usage* 952–53 (3d ed. 2011) (s.v. "Words of Authority").

> "To want to retain 'shall' in its obligatory sense when the rest of the world has changed and when there is a suitable alternative is perverse — and doubly so when we acknowledge the inaccurate ways in which lawyers handle 'shall'."
> —Robert D. Eagleson & Michele Asprey, *Must We Continue with "Shall"?* 63 Austl. L.J. 75, 78 (1989).

NOT THIS:	BUT THIS:
§ 31-21-17. Motorcycle parking privileges. (a) Whenever the proprietor of any shopping center including a shopping mall shall provide for parking spaces designated for use by motorcycles only, then no person shall park any vehicle other than a properly registered motorcycle in the space. **R.I. Gen. Laws § 31-21-17(a).**	**§ 31-21-17. Motorcycle parking privileges.** (A) **Shopping center or mall.** If the proprietor of a shopping center or a shopping mall provides parking spaces designated for use by motorcycles only, no person may park any vehicle there other than a properly registered motorcycle.
Subject to such limitations as the court may prescribe, a debtor in possession shall have all the rights, other than the right to compensation under section 330 [11 U.S.C.S. § 330], and powers, and shall perform all the functions and duties, except the duties specified in paragraphs (3) and (4) of section 1106(a) [11 U.S.C.S. § 1106(a)], of a trustee serving in a case under chapter 11, including operating the debtor's farm or commercial fishing operation. **11 U.S.C. § 1203.**	Subject to limits the court prescribes, a debtor in possession has all the rights and powers, and may perform all the functions and duties, of a Chapter 11 trustee, including operating the debtor's farm or commercial-fishing operation. A debtor does not have the right to compensation under § 330 and cannot perform the duties specified in paragraphs (3) and (4) of § 1106(a).
§ 2103. Officers (a) The Archivist of the United States shall be appointed by the President by and with the advice and consent of the Senate. The Archivist shall be appointed without regard to political affiliations and solely on the basis of the professional qualifications required to perform the duties and responsibilities of the office of Archivist. The Archivist may be removed from office by the President. The President shall communicate the reasons for any such removal to each House of the Congress. **44 U.S.C. § 2103(a).**	**§ 2103. Officers.** (A) **Archivist.** The Archivist of the United States is appointed by the President with the Senate's advice and consent. The President must make the appointment without regard to political affiliations and solely on the basis of the professional qualifications required to perform the duties and responsibilities of the office. The President may remove the Archivist from office. The President must communicate the reasons for removal to each House of the Congress.
§ 203. Jurisdiction; amount in controversy An action or proceeding falling under the Convention shall be deemed to arise under the laws and treaties of the United States. The district courts of the United States (including the courts enumerated in section 460 of title 28) shall have original jurisdiction over such an action or proceeding, regardless of the amount in controversy. **9 U.S.C. § 203.**	**§ 203. Jurisdiction under the Convention granted to U.S. district courts.** A lawsuit or proceeding falling under the Convention arises under the laws and treaties of the United States, whose district courts (including the courts stated in 28 U.S.C. § 460) have original jurisdiction over the lawsuit or proceeding regardless of the amount in controversy.

"I warn against *shall* because few writers understand the odd word (suggesting that few readers do either) and because it invites writers to affect an antique, pseudo-legal, and inefficient style generally. Save the word for polite queries such as 'Shall we dance?' or 'Shall I draw your bath, my lord?'"
—Thomas A. Murawski, *Writing Readable Regulations* 70 (1999).

NOT THIS:	BUT THIS:
(a) Upon termination, dissolution, or abandonment of a corporate business, any officer or other person who has control or supervision of or is charged with the responsibility for the filing of returns or the payment of tax, or who is under a duty to act for the corporation in complying with any requirement of this part, shall be personally liable for any unpaid taxes and interest and penalties on those taxes, if that officer or other person willfully fails to pay or to cause to be paid any taxes due from the corporation pursuant to this part. **Cal. Rev. & Tax. Code § 11533(a).**	(A) **Continuing tax liability.** Once a corporate business is terminated, dissolved, or abandoned, an officer or other person who has control or supervision over or responsibility for filing returns or paying taxes, or who is required to act for the corporation to comply with this part, is personally liable for unpaid taxes, interest, and penalties on the taxes if that officer or other person willfully fails to ensure that all taxes due from the corporation under this part are paid.
(a) All administrative remedies shall be exhausted before an agency determination under this section shall be subject to judicial review. Final decisions after hearing shall be subject to judicial review exclusively as provided in s. 227.52, except that any petition for review of department action under this section shall be filed within 15 days after receipt of notice of the final agency determination. **Wis. Stat. § 49.498(19)(a).**	(A) **Exhaustion of administrative remedies.** All administrative remedies must be exhausted before an agency determination under this section is subject to judicial review. A final decision after a hearing is subject to judicial review only as provided in § 227.52. A petition for review of a final decision must be filed within 15 days after the party seeking review receives notice of the decision.
Any person who shall wilfully wear, exhibit, display, print, or use, for any purpose, the badge, motto, button, decoration, charm, emblem, rosette or other insignia, of any such association or organization, herein mentioned, duly registered hereunder, unless he or she shall be entitled to use and wear the same under the constitution and by-laws, rules and regulations of such association and organization, shall be guilty of a misdemeanor, and, upon conviction, shall be punished by a fine not exceeding twenty dollars, and, in default of payment, committed to jail for a period of not to exceed ten days. **W. Va. Code § 35A-1-6.**	**Unlawful display.** It is unlawful to willfully wear, display, print, or use, for any purpose, the emblem, motto, or other insignia of any association or organization duly registered under § 35A, unless the person is entitled to do so under that association's or organization's constitution, bylaws, rules, or regulations. Violation of this provision is punishable by a fine up to $20 or—in default of payment—a jail term up to 10 days.

"There are some simple maxims . . . [that] might be commended to writers of expository prose. First: never use a long word if a short word will do. Second: if you want to make a statement with a great many qualifications, put some of the qualifications in separate sentences."

—Bertrand Russell, "How I Write," in *The Basic Writings of Bertrand Russell* 63, 65 (Robert E. Egner & Lester E. Denonn eds., 1961).

NOT THIS:	BUT THIS:
(a) No person, association, partnership or corporation shall operate or conduct a barbershop or barber school without a valid, unexpired license. Licenses shall be issued by the secretary of the board of barber examiners or the board's designee. The annual license fee shall be set by the board pursuant to W.S. 33-1-201 for each shop or school, payable in advance, but if not paid on or before July 31 of each year, a late fee set by board rule and regulation shall be assessed. The licenses shall be conspicuously displayed at all times, and no license shall be issued until all sanitary regulations required by W.S. 33-7-101 through 33-7-211 or prescribed by the board have been complied with. Applications for new shops or schools or for shops or schools changing locations shall be made in writing on forms furnished by the board, and shall contain information required by the board. An inspection fee for a new shop or school or for a shop or school changing location shall be set by the board pursuant to W.S. 33-1-201. A shop or school license is not transferable. **Wyo. Stat. § 33-7-108(a).**	(A) **Licensing requirement.** To operate a barbershop or barber school, a person, association, partnership, or corporation must have a valid license.* Only the Board of Barber Examiners' secretary or designee may issue licenses. The Board's secretary or designee must not issue a license until the applicant complies with all sanitary regulations required by W.S. 33-7-101 through 33-7-211 or prescribed by the Board. Under W.S. 33-1-201, the Board must set the annual license fee for each shop or school, payable in advance. If the fee is not paid by July 31 of each year, a late fee set by Board rule and regulation must be assessed. The licensee must display the license conspicuously at all times. An application for a new shop or school or for a shop or school changing location must be made in writing on the Board's forms and must contain the information the Board requires. A shop or school license is not transferable. Under W.S. 33-1-201, the Board must set an inspection fee for a new shop or school or for a shop or school changing location.
No person who is required to testify before either house of the legislature or a committee thereof, or joint committee of the 2 houses, and is examined and so testifies, shall be held to answer criminally in any court or be subject to any penalty or forfeiture for any fact or act touching which the person is required to testify and as to which the person has been examined and has testified, and no testimony so given nor any paper, document or record produced by any such person before either house of the legislature or any such committee shall be competent testimony or be used in any trial or criminal proceeding against such person in any court, except upon a prosecution for perjury committed in giving such testimony; and no witness shall be allowed to refuse to testify to any fact, or to produce any papers, documents or records touching which the person examined before either house or any such committee, for the reason that the testimony touching such fact, or the production of such papers, documents or records may tend to disgrace the person or otherwise render the person infamous. **Wis. Stat. § 13.35(1).**	(A) **Immunity.** A person who is required to testify before the legislature (or any subset of it) and does so cannot be held to answer criminally or be penalized in any way, including through forfeiture, for a matter relating to the testimony. No testimony—and no paper, document, or record produced by a witness required to testify—may be used against the witness in any proceeding, unless it is a prosecution for perjury committed in giving the testimony. A witness cannot refuse to testify or to produce a document on grounds that the evidence might incriminate, disgrace, or cause infamy.

*The preference in these Guidelines for a criminal prohibition is *It is unlawful to* (see § 2.2). But note that *No person may* (i.e., "is allowed to") is much preferable to *No person shall* (literally, "is required to"). Note also the gradations of meaning captured throughout this passage by the more specific words used in this revision.

(C) Straightforward wordings for powers and duties.

Avoid creating requirements through circumlocution.

NOT THIS:	BUT THIS:
Suppression of a material fact which a party is under an obligation to communicate constitutes fraud. **Ga. Code Ann., § 23-2-53.**	Suppression of a material fact that a party must communicate constitutes fraud.
An administrator may not administer a plan in the absence of a written agreement between the administrator and a principal. The administrator and principal shall each retain a copy of the written agreement for the duration of the agreement and for 5 years thereafter. **Wis. Stat. § 633.04.**	An administrator may administer a plan only with a written agreement between the administrator and a principal. The administrator and principal must each retain a copy of the agreement for 5 years after it ends.
An applicant is not considered to be named on a previously filed application for purposes of subsection (a)(2) if the applicant has assigned, or is under an obligation by contract or law to assign, all ownership rights in the application as the result of the applicant's previous employment. **35 U.S.C. § 123(b).**	For purposes of subsection (a)(2), an applicant is not considered to be named on a previously filed application if the applicant has assigned, or must assign under contract or law, all ownership rights in the application because of the applicant's previous employment.
A peace officer or probation officer of the court may take a child into custody without a court order if he has reasonable grounds to believe that the child's surroundings are such as to endanger his welfare and immediate removal appears to be necessary for his protection. The peace officer shall have the responsibility to promptly notify and release the child to the department. **La. Stat.—Children's Code Art. 621(A).**	A peace officer or probation officer of the court may take a child into custody without a court order if the officer has reasonable grounds to believe that the child's surroundings endanger the child's welfare and immediate removal appears to be necessary for the child's protection. A peace officer must promptly notify the department and release the child to it.
The state board of land commissioners shall serve as the trustee for the lands granted to the state in public trust by the federal government, lands acquired in lieu thereof, and additional lands held by the board in public trust. The board shall have the duty to manage, control, encumber, and dispose of such lands in accordance with the purposes for which said grants of land were made and section 10 of article IX of the state constitution, and subject to such terms and conditions consistent therewith as may be prescribed by law. **Colo. Rev. Stat. § 36-1-101.5(6)(b).**	The state board of land commissioners is the trustee for the lands granted to the state in public trust by the federal government, lands acquired in place of granted lands, and additional lands held by the board in public trust. The board must manage, control, encumber, and dispose of the lands according to Article 9, § 10 of the state constitution and the purposes for which the land grants were made, subject to any consistent terms and conditions required by law.

(D) Alternative meaning for *shall.*

As an alternative to the convention outlined in 2.1(B), some drafters consider it defensible to use *shall* exclusively to mean "has a duty to." Avoid it when it does not impose a duty on the subject of the clause. [Note: Either the convention in 2.1(B) or this convention in 2.1(D) should appear consistently in one piece of legislation: the two should not be mixed.] The problem with this alternative is that (as shown above) *shall* multiplies with such promiscuity that few legal drafters can think clearly once they use it at all. We recommend strongly against this alternative.

(E) Elimination of *may not.*

Change *may not* to *must not* (if it's a duty not to do something) or *cannot* (if it's a legal inability to do something). Idiomatically, *may not* is traditionally a way of denying permission <No, you may not go to that concert>. Sometimes, though, it functions as a near equivalent of *might not* <I may not be able to go>. It is therefore increasingly viewed as a mild expression in all its uses. The prohibitory *must not* is unequivocal.

NOT THIS:	BUT THIS:
A person may not be a member of the commission or act as the general counsel to the commission if the person is required to register as a lobbyist under Chapter 305 because of the person's activities for compensation on behalf of a profession related to the operation of the commission. **Tex. Gov't Code § 411.0035(c).**	A person required to register as a lobbyist under Chapter 305 because of the person's activities for compensation on behalf of a profession related to the operation of the commission cannot serve as a member of the commission or act as the commissioner's general counsel.
A municipality may not be considered a corporation under a state statute governing corporations unless the statute extends its application to a municipality by express use of the term "municipal corporation," "municipality," "city," "town," or "village." **Tex. Loc. Gov't Code § 5.904(a).**	A municipality cannot be considered a corporation under a state statute governing corporations unless the statute extends its application to municipalities by express use of the term "municipal corporation," "municipality," "city," "town," or "village."

2.2 Criminal prohibitions.

There are many ways of expressing a criminal prohibition—several of them retrograde. The recommendation here is to use the formula "It is unlawful to [actus reus]. Violation of this section is a [level of crime: Class A felony, Class H misdemeanor, etc.]." We also recommend a heading preceding the prohibitory statement: "**X prohibited**"—in boldface.

For a full rationale for the systematic approach adopted in the "But This" columns throughout this section, and elsewhere for criminal pains and penalties, see "A Note on Prohibitions, Pains, and Penalties," Appendix A (pp. 169–75).

NOT THIS:	BUT THIS:
§ 39A. Aiming a laser pointer at an aircraft. (a) **Offense.**—Whoever knowingly aims the beam of a laser pointer at an aircraft in the special aircraft jurisdiction of the United States, or at the flight path of such an aircraft, shall be fined under this title or imprisoned not more than 5 years, or both. **18 U.S.C. § 39A**	**§ 39A. Aiming a laser pointer at aircraft prohibited.** (A) **Offense.** It is unlawful to knowingly aim the beam of a laser pointer at an aircraft, or at the flight path of an aircraft, in the special aircraft jurisdiction of the United States. Violation of this provision is punishable by fine or by imprisonment of up to 5 years, or both.
Every person to whom a child has been confided for nursing, education or any other purpose, who, with intent to deceive a person, guardian or relative of such child, shall substitute or produce to such parent, guardian or relative, another child or person in the place of the child so confided, is guilty of a class B felony and shall be punished by imprisonment in a state correctional facility for not more than ten years. **Wash. Rev. Code § 9.45.020.**	(*). **Deceptive switching of children prohibited.** It is unlawful for a person with custody of a child to cause a substitute child to be produced to anyone (such as the child's parent, guardian, or relative) with intent to deceive. Violation of this provision is a class B felony punishable by up to 10 years' imprisonment in a state correctional facility.
§ 473. Dealing in counterfeit obligations or securities Whoever buys, sells, exchanges, transfers, receives, or delivers any false, forged, counterfeited, or altered obligation or other security of the United States, with the intent that the same be passed, published, or used as true and genuine, shall be fined under this title or imprisoned not more than 20 years, or both. **18 U.S.C. § 473.**	**§ 473. Dealing in counterfeit obligations or securities prohibited.** It is unlawful to buy, sell, exchange, transfer, receive, or deliver any false, forged, counterfeited, or altered obligation or other security of the United States, with the intent to pass, publish, or use as true and genuine. Violation of this provision is punishable by fine or imprisonment of up to 20 years, or both.

Subpart to be numbered appropriately.

> "A criminal statute ought not to be drawn so obscurely that the meaning of one section can only be judged by a subtle argument based on other sections creating different offences. In such circumstances, the principle of strict construction requires an acquittal."
>
> —Glanville Williams, *Criminal Law* 240 (2d ed. 1961).

<table>
<tr><th>NOT THIS:</th><th>BUT THIS:</th></tr>
<tr><td>A person who instigates, promotes, conducts, is employed at, provides a dog for, allows property under the person's ownership or control to be used for, gambles on, or profits from an exhibition featuring the baiting of a dog or the fighting of a dog with another dog or with another animal is guilty of a Class H felony. A lease of property that is used or is intended to be used for an exhibition featuring the baiting of a dog or the fighting of a dog with another dog or with another animal is void, and a lessor who knows this use is made or is intended to be made of the lessor's property is under a duty to evict the lessee immediately.
N.C. Gen. Stat. § 14-362.2(a).</td><td>(A) Dog-baiting & dog fights prohibited. It is unlawful to instigate, promote, conduct, be employed at, provide a dog for, allow property under one's ownership or control to be used for, gamble on, or profit from an exhibition featuring the baiting or fighting of a dog with another dog or other animal. Violation of this provision is a Class H felony.
(B) Leased premises for dog-baiting & dog fights. A lease is void if the property is used or intended to be used for an exhibition featuring the baiting or fighting of a dog with another dog or other animal. The lessor must immediately evict the lessee upon discovering the use or intention.</td></tr>
<tr><td>§ 18-7303. Denial of right to work or accommodations a misdemeanor.
Every person shall be guilty of a misdemeanor who denies to any other person because of race, creed, color, sex, or national origin the right to work: (a) by refusing to hire, (b) by discharging, (c) by barring from employment, or (d) by discriminating against such person in compensation or in other terms or conditions of employment; or who denies to any other person because of race, creed, color, sex, or national origin, the full enjoyment of any of the accommodations, advantages, facilities or privileges of any place of public resort, accommodation, assemblage, or amusement, provided, however, that denial of the right to work on the basis of sex shall be permissible in situations where sex is a bona fide occupational qualification reasonably necessary to the normal operation of the business.
Idaho Code § 18-7303.</td><td>§ 18-7303. Denial of right to work or accommodations prohibited.
(A) Denial of right to work. It is unlawful to deny a person the right to work because of race, creed, color, sex, or national origin, by:
(1) refusing to hire the person;
(2) discharging the person;
(3) barring the person from employment; or
(4) discriminating against the person in compensation or in other terms or conditions of employment.
(B) Exception. It is permissible to deny a person the right to work on the basis of sex in situations where sex is a bona fide occupational qualification reasonably necessary to the business's normal operation.
(C) Denial of accommodations. It is unlawful to deny a person—based on race, creed, color, sex, or national origin—the full enjoyment of any of the accommodations, advantages, facilities or privileges of any place of public resort, accommodation, assemblage, or amusement.
(D) Misdemeanor. Violation of (A) or (C) is a misdemeanor.</td></tr>
</table>

> "Law-writers are usually talking about who shall go to jail, and what epithet shall be applied to him. 'Every person who shall do such and such shall be deemed guilty of a misdemeanor and shall be punishable . . . .' Or else they seem to be engaged in making preposterous predictions like 'No person shall make any agreement . . . .' What the citizen wants to know is not how to get in jail but how to stay out."
>
> —Alfred F. Conard, *New Ways to Write Laws*, 56 Yale L.J. 458, 477 (1947).

NOT THIS:	BUT THIS:
§ 1792. Mutiny and riot prohibited Whoever instigates, connives, willfully attempts to cause, assists, or conspires to cause any mutiny or riot, at any Federal penal, detention, or correctional facility, shall be imprisoned not more than ten years or fined under this title, or both. **18 U.S.C. § 1792.**	**§ 1792. Mutiny and riot prohibited.** It is unlawful to instigate, connive, assist, or attempt or conspire to cause a mutiny or riot at a federal penal, detention, or correctional facility. Violation of this provision is punishable by a fine under this title or imprisonment of up to 10 years, or both.
§ 1910. Nepotism in appointment of receiver or trustee Whoever, being a judge of any court of the United States, appoints as receiver, or trustee, any person related to such judge by consanguinity, or affinity, within the fourth degree-- Shall be fined under this title or imprisoned not more than five years, or both. **18 U.S.C. § 1910.**	**§ 1910. Nepotism in appointment of receiver or trustee prohibited.** A federal judge must not appoint a receiver or trustee who is related to the judge by consanguinity or affinity within the fourth degree. A judge who violates this provision is punishable by a fine under this title or imprisonment up to 5 years, or both.
§ 2382. Misprision of treason Whoever, owing allegiance to the United States and having knowledge of the commission of any treason against them, conceals and does not, as soon as may be, disclose and make known the same to the President or to some judge of the United States, or to the governor or to some judge or justice of a particular State, is guilty of misprision of treason and shall be fined under this title or imprisoned not more than seven years, or both. **18 U.S.C. § 2382.**	**§ 2382. Misprision of treason prohibited.** (A) **Duty to disclose treason.** A person who owes allegiance to the United States and has knowledge of treason against the United States must disclose this knowledge to the President, a federal judge, a state governor, or a state judge. (B) **Prohibition of failing to disclose.** It is unlawful to conceal knowledge of treason against the United States or to fail to disclose this knowledge as soon as possible. (C) **Penalty.** Violation of (A) or (B) is misprision of treason punishable by fine under this title or imprisonment of up to 7 years, or both.
Whoever embezzles, steals, purloins, or knowingly converts to his use or the use of another, or without authority, sells, conveys or disposes of any record, voucher, money, or thing of value of the United States or of any department or agency thereof, or any property made or being made under contract for the United States or any department or agency thereof . . . [s]hall be fined under this title or imprisoned not more than ten years, or both . . . . **18 U.S.C. § 641.**	**§ 641. Theft of public money, property, or records prohibited.** It is unlawful to steal or knowingly convert to one's own use or that of another, or without authority to sell, convey, or dispose of any record, voucher, money, or thing of value of the United States or of any federal department or federal agency, or of any property made or being made under contract for the United States or a federal department or federal agency. . . . Violation of this provision is a felony punishable by fine under this title or imprisonment of up to 10 years, or both.

NOT THIS:	BUT THIS:
§ 876. Mailing threatening communications (a) Whoever knowingly deposits in any post office or authorized depository for mail matter, to be sent or delivered by the Postal Service or knowingly causes to be delivered by the Postal Service according to the direction thereon, any communication, with or without a name or designating mark subscribed thereto, addressed to any other person, and containing any demand or request for ransom or reward for the release of any kidnapped person, shall be fined under this title or imprisoned not more than twenty years, or both. **18 U.S.C. § 876.**	**§ 876. Mailing threatening communications prohibited.** (A) **Kidnapping ransom or reward.** It is unlawful to knowingly deposit in a post office a communication to be sent or delivered by the Postal Service containing a demand or request for ransom or reward for the release of a kidnapped person. "Post office" includes any authorized depository for U.S. mail. "Communication to be sent or delivered by the Postal Service" includes any communication a person knowingly causes to be delivered by the Postal Service according to the direction on the communication. A communication may appear with or without a name or designating mark subscribed to it, and may be addressed to any other person. (B) **Penalty.** Violation of (A) is punishable by fine under this title or imprisonment of up to 20 years, or both.
Hunting, fishing, trapping; disturbance or injury on wildlife refuges. Whoever, except in compliance with rules and regulations promulgated by authority of law, hunts, traps, captures, willfully disturbs or kills any bird, fish, or wild animal of any kind whatever, or takes or destroys the eggs or nest of any such bird or fish, on any lands or waters which are set apart or reserved as sanctuaries, refuges or breeding grounds for such birds, fish, or animals under any law of the United States or willfully injures, molests, or destroys any property of the United States on any such lands or waters, shall be fined under this title or imprisoned not more than six months, or both. **18 U.S.C. § 41.**	**§ 41. Disrupting wild animals prohibited.** In a federally designated sanctuary, refuge, or breeding ground, it is unlawful (unless authorized by another law) to hunt, trap, capture, knowingly disturb, or kill any wild animal, or to take or destroy a fish's or bird's egg or nest, or to knowingly damage or destroy any United States property. Violation of this provision is punishable by a fine under this title or imprisonment of up to 6 months, or both.
§ 2342. Unlawful acts (a) It shall be unlawful for any person knowingly to ship, transport, receive, possess, sell, distribute, or purchase contraband cigarettes or contraband smokeless tobacco. (b) It shall be unlawful for any person knowingly to make any false statement or representation with respect to the information required by this chapter to be kept in the records of any person who ships, sells, or distributes any quantity of cigarettes in excess of 10,000 in a single transaction. **18 U.S.C. § 2342.**	**§ 2342. Unlawful acts prohibited.** (A) **Contraband cigarettes.** It is unlawful to knowingly ship, transport, receive, possess, sell, distribute, or purchase contraband cigarettes or contraband smokeless tobacco. (B) **Required records.** Any person who ships, sells, or distributes more than 10,000 cigarettes in a single transaction must keep records as required by 18 U.S.C. § 2343(a).* It is unlawful to knowingly make any false statement or representation with respect to these records.

*This more specific language was inserted only after further research into the context of the provision.

NOT THIS:	BUT THIS:
§ 1761. Transportation or importation (a) Whoever knowingly transports in interstate commerce or from any foreign country into the United States any goods, wares, or merchandise manufactured, produced, or mined, wholly or in part by convicts or prisoners, except convicts or prisoners on parole, supervised release, or probation, or in any penal or reformatory institution, shall be fined under this title or imprisoned not more than two years, or both. **18 U.S.C. § 1761.**	**§ 1761. Interstate transportation or importation of inmate-produced goods prohibited.** (A) **Goods produced by prisoners.** It is unlawful to knowingly transport in interstate commerce or from any foreign country into the United States any goods produced by a prison inmate. (B) **Definition of "goods."** "Goods" includes any wares or merchandise manufactured, produced, or mined, wholly or in part, by convicts or prisoners. (C) **Exception.** This statute does not apply to goods produced by convicts or prisoners on parole, supervised release, or probation, or in a penal or reformatory institution. (D) **Penalty.** Violation of (A) is punishable by fine under this title or imprisonment of up to 2 years, or both.
(a) **Nonconforming labels.** It shall be unlawful for any person engaged in the packaging or labeling of any consumer commodity (as defined in this Chapter [15 U.S.C. §§ 1451 et seq.]) for distribution in commerce, or for any person (other than a common carrier for hire, a contract carrier for hire, or a freight forwarder for hire) engaged in the distribution in commerce of any packaged or labeled consumer commodity, to distribute or to cause to be distributed in commerce any such commodity if such commodity is contained in a package, or if there is affixed to that commodity a label, which does not conform to the provisions of this Chapter [15 U.S.C. §§ 1451 et seq.] and of regulations promulgated under the authority of this Chapter [15 U.S.C. §§ 1451 et seq.]. **15 U.S.C. § 1452(a).**	(A) **Nonconforming labels prohibited.** It is unlawful for a person engaged in the following activities to distribute or to cause to be distributed in commerce a packaged or labeled commodity that does not conform to this Act and to the regulations promulgated under this Act: (1) the packaging or labeling of a consumer commodity (as defined in this Act) for commercial distribution; or (2) the commercial distribution of a packaged or labeled consumer commodity—except by a common carrier for hire, a contract carrier for hire, or a freight-forwarder for hire.

> "The practice of legislating in too much detail is a main cause of complexity and of some of the obscurity in our statute law."
>
> —*The Preparation of Legislation* ¶ 6.7, at 30 (Lord Renton ed., 1975).

Note the wild subject-verb separation here. See § 4.1.

NOT THIS:	BUT THIS:
§ 1074. Flight to avoid prosecution for damaging or destroying any building or other real or personal property (a) Whoever moves or travels in interstate or foreign commerce with intent either (1) to avoid prosecution, or custody, or confinement after conviction, under the laws of the place from which he flees, for willfully attempting to or damaging or destroying by fire or explosive any building, structure, facility, vehicle, dwelling house, synagogue, church, religious center or educational institution, public or private, or (2) to avoid giving testimony in any criminal proceeding relating to any such offense shall be fined under this title or imprisoned not more than five years, or both. **18 U.S.C. § 1074.**	**§ 1074. Flight to avoid prosecution for damaging or destroying building or other real or personal property prohibited.** (A) **Flight from prosecution.** It is unlawful for a person to travel in interstate or foreign commerce with intent to avoid prosecution, custody, or imprisonment, under the laws of the place from which the person flees, for willfully causing or attempting to cause damage to any building or vehicle with fire or explosives. (B) **Flight to avoid testifying.** It is unlawful to move or travel in interstate or foreign commerce with the intent to avoid testifying in a criminal proceeding relating to an offense listed in (A). (C) **Punishment.** Violation of (A) or (B) is punishable by a fine under this title or imprisonment of up to 5 years, or both.
3-3-33. Vaporized forms of alcoholic beverages; alcohol vaporizing devices; misdemeanor violations. . . . (b) (1) No person shall purchase, offer for sale or use, sell, or use any vaporized form of an alcoholic beverage produced by an alcohol vaporizing device. This paragraph shall not apply to a product that contains alcohol as otherwise lawfully prescribed by a health care practitioner who is licensed under Title 43. (2) No person shall own or possess any alcohol vaporizing device, including but not limited to any machine known as an Alcohol Without Liquid (AWOL) machine. This paragraph shall not apply to any nebulizer or atomizer used to supply a product that contains alcohol as otherwise lawfully prescribed by a health care practitioner who is licensed under Title 43. (c) No operator shall keep or allow to be kept on the licensed premises thereof any vaporized form of an alcoholic beverage produced by an alcohol vaporizing device. (d) Any person convicted of a violation of this Code section shall be guilty of a misdemeanor. Any person convicted of a violation of this Code section involving the offer for sale or use to a person under the age of 21 shall be guilty of a misdemeanor, except that upon the second or subsequent conviction such person so convicted shall be guilty of a misdemeanor of a high and aggravated nature. **Ga. Code § 3-3-33(b)–(d).**	**3-3-33. Vaporized alcoholic beverages and alcohol-vaporizing devices prohibited.** . . . (B) **Unlawful actions regarding vaporized alcoholic beverages.** (1) ***Buying, selling, or using vaporized alcoholic beverages.*** It is unlawful to purchase, sell, or use a vaporized alcoholic beverage produced by an alcohol-vaporizing device. This prohibition does not apply to an alcohol-containing product that has been lawfully prescribed by a healthcare* practitioner licensed under Title 43. (2) ***Owning or possessing an alcohol-vaporizing device.*** It is unlawful to own or possess any alcohol-vaporizing device, including an alcohol-without-liquid machine. This prohibition does not apply to a nebulizer or atomizer used to supply a product that contains alcohol and is otherwise lawfully prescribed by a healthcare practitioner licensed under Title 43. (C) **Licensed operators.** It is unlawful for an operator to keep a vaporized form of an alcoholic beverage on the licensed premises. (D) **Penalty.** (1) ***Generally.*** Violation of this title is a misdemeanor. (2) ***Sale to minor.*** Selling vaporized alcoholic beverages or machines to a person under the age of 21 is a misdemeanor. A second or subsequent conviction is an aggravated misdemeanor.

Notice that the original statute doesn't carry forward the healthcare exceptions of (B)(1) and (B)(2). That may or may not have been a drafting error.

*On the preferred one-word spelling of *healthcare*, see n.* at p. 11.

2.3 Degree of detail.

(A) Avoiding detail when unnecessary.

Use only as much detail as is absolutely necessary. Understand that detail easily accumulates into detritus.

NOT THIS:	BUT THIS:
§ 423. **Diversion from normal flight; careless operation.** (a) An aircraft shall not be diverted from a normal flight nor engage in acrobatic maneuvers nor be so operated as to diminish the stability and safety of the aircraft when the aircraft is over a thickly settled portion of a town, city, or village or over a place where a celebration, game, or contest is being held or over a place where a failure of the aircraft might cause personal injury or damage to property, or under 1,500 feet, unless by special permission of the federal aviation administration and the agency. **Vt. Stat. tit. 5, § 423.**	**§ 423. Diversion from normal flight; careless operation.** (A) **Diversion prohibited.** Unless the Federal Aviation Administration and the agency give special permission, when an aircraft flies under 1,500 feet or is over a thickly settled area, a place where people have congregated, or a place where a failure of the aircraft might cause personal injury or property damage, an aircraft must not: (1) be diverted from a normal flight; (2) engage in acrobatic maneuvers; or (3) be operated in a way that diminishes aircraft stability and safety.

(B) Using general terms when clear.

If you can use general terms to convey the idea with greater clarity, do so.

NOT THIS:	BUT THIS:
Any orphanage or society organized and incorporated under the laws of this state for the care of orphans and needy children . . . is authorized and empowered to take and have, from time to time, the exclusive care, custody, and control of children during their minority . . . . **R.I. Gen. Laws § 14-3-1.**	An organization incorporated under Rhode Island law to care for orphans and needy children . . . may from time to time take and have exclusive care, custody, and control of a minor . . . .

> "This evil [obscurity in legislation] will be still greater, if the laws be written in a language unknown to the people; who, being ignorant of the consequences of their own actions, become necessarily dependent on a few, who are interpreters of the laws, which, instead of being public and general, are thus rendered private and particular. What must we think of mankind when we reflect, that such is the established custom of the greatest part of our polished and enlightened Europe?"
>
> —Cesare Beccaria, *An Essay on Crimes and Punishments* 29 (anon. trans., rev. ed. 1778).

2.4 Grammatical number: preference for singular.

Draft in the singular number unless the sense is undeniably plural, as when the sentence refers to a habitual practice. Remember that the singular always includes the plural—yet (despite legislative protestations to the contrary) the reverse often isn't true.

NOT THIS:	BUT THIS:
On roads, streets, or highways with three or more lanes allowing for movement in the same direction, it shall be unlawful . . . . **Ga. Code § 40-6-53(a).**	On a road, street, or highway with 3 or more lanes moving in the same direction, it is unlawful . . . .
§ 10. Holidays Holidays within the meaning of this code are every Sunday and any other days that are specified or provided for as judicial holidays in Section 135. **Cal. Civ. Proc. Code § 10.**	**§ 10. Holidays.** "Holiday" means a Sunday or a judicial holiday specified or described in § 135.
It shall be lawful for all persons keeping or boarding any animals at livery within the District, under any agreement with the owner thereof, to detain such animals until all charges under such agreement for the care, keep, or board of such animals shall have been paid; provided, however, that before enforcing the lien hereby given notice in writing shall be given to such owner in person or by registered mail at his last-known place of residence of the amount of such charges and the intention to detain such animal or animals until such charges shall be paid. **D.C. Code § 40-101.**	A person who by agreement with the owner keeps or boards an animal at a livery within the District may legally detain the animal there until all charges for the animal's care, keep, or board under the agreement with the owner have been paid. But before this lien can be enforced, the animal's owner must receive written notice, in person or by registered mail at the owner's last known address, of the charges due and the intent to detain the animal until the charges are paid.

For the elimination of this proviso, see § 4.5.

When is the plural justified? When the sense is unavoidably plural—e.g.: "Revenue is to be divided among municipal units." Or: "Wherever the term *rescue squad* appears in this chapter, it refers only to those persons or organizations who are members of a state rescue squad."

> "The plural number is, in a particular degree, liable to be productive of perplexity and misstatement. . . . For remedy, substitute the singular to the plural number where substitutable without impropriety; and by one means or other it may generally be so substituted."
>
> —Jeremy Bentham, "Essay on Language," in 8 *The Works of Jeremy Bentham* 315 (John Bowring ed., 1843).

2.5 Tense.

(A) General preference for present.

Use the present tense unless the past or future tense clarifies the idea. Avoid especially the future perfect (*shall have been served*, etc.).

The *shall* here is known as a "false future."

NOT THIS:	BUT THIS:
The reproduction shall be in lieu of inclusion in the daily journal of the house in which the proposal is introduced. **Wis. Stat. § 13.525(5)(c).**	The reproduction is in lieu of inclusion in the daily journal of the house in which the proposal is introduced.
The motor vehicle repair dealer, mechanic, or apprentice shall give the customer a written estimated price for labor and parts necessary for a specific job prior to commencement of the job. Such written estimated price need not be given if waived in writing by the customer. . . . **Haw. Rev. Stat. § 437B-15(a).**	The motor-vehicle-repair dealer, mechanic, or apprentice must give the customer a written estimated price for labor and parts necessary for a specific job before beginning work. But a written estimated price is not required if the customer waives it in writing. . . .

(B) For conditions precedent, default to present perfect.

When you are saying that something is permitted once something else has been done—write *has been done*—not *is done*. For further guidance on this sequence-of-tenses issue, see *Garner's Modern English Usage* 895–97 (4th ed. 2016) (s.v. "Tenses").

Weirdly, this wording suggests that it's going to happen from time to time. See p. 167.

NOT THIS:	BUT THIS:
Whenever any employee of a school district or of the office of a county superintendent of schools is attacked, assaulted, or physically threatened by any pupil, it shall be the duty of the employee, and the duty of any person under whose direction or supervision the employee is employed in the public school system who has knowledge of the incident, to promptly report the incident to the appropriate law enforcement authorities of the county or city in which the incident occurred. Failure to make the report shall be an infraction punishable by a fine of not more than one thousand dollars ($1,000). **Cal. Educ. Code § 44014(a).**	If a school-district employee or county-superintendent-of-schools employee has been attacked, assaulted, or physically threatened by a pupil, that employee must promptly report the incident to the appropriate county or city law-enforcement authorities. Any other public-school-system employee who directs or supervises that employee and has knowledge of the incident must also report it to the appropriate county or city law-enforcement authorities. Failure to report is punishable by a fine up to $1,000.

> "Negative phrasing is acceptable if your object is to tell people not to do something—or if it is used to allay fears or dispel myths. Otherwise, use positive phrasing."
>
> —Plain Language Institute, *Editorial and Design Stylebook* 10 (1993).

2.6 Voice.

(A) Preferring active voice.

Prefer the active voice over the passive voice. When feasible, rephrase a passive-voice verb by putting it in active voice. Passive voice can be justified (1) when, in a statute dealing with such matters as building and safety codes, human actors don't appear much in requirements relating to things; (2) when it is the most natural, elegant way to achieve gender neutrality; and (3) when the passive voice keeps the focus appropriately on the recipient of the verb's action.

This is a passive construction preceded by what grammarians call a "whiz-deletion." That is, the words *that are* have been deleted before *performed.*

NOT THIS:	BUT THIS:
For acts performed while representing a client, a lawyer is subject to professional discipline . . . . **Restatement (Third) of the Law Governing Lawyers § 42(1) (Tentative Draft No. 5, 1992).**	For an act that a lawyer performs while representing a client, the lawyer is subject to professional discipline . . . .
An interrogatory directed to an individual shall be answered by the individual, and an interrogatory directed to an entity shall be answered by a managerial official. **Tex. Bus. Orgs. Code § 12.002(b).**	A person must answer an interrogatory directed to him or her. A managerial official must answer an interrogatory directed to an entity.
Deposits of any royalty funds derived from the production of oil or gas from, or allocated to, Indian lands shall be made by the Secretary to the appropriate Indian account . . . . **30 U.S.C. § 1714.**	The Secretary must deposit into the appropriate Indian account all royalty funds derived from oil and gas produced from or allocated to Indian lands . . . .
No person in the United States shall, on the ground of blindness or severely impaired vision, be denied admission in any course of study by a recipient of Federal financial assistance for any education program or activity, but nothing herein shall be construed to require any such institution to provide any special services to such person because of his blindness or visual impairment. **20 U.S.C. § 1684.**	An institution that receives federal financial assistance for an education program or activity must not deny a person in the United States admission to a course of study on the ground of blindness or severely impaired vision. This statute does not require the recipient to provide special services to the person because of the blindness or impairment.

"[Active voice] has the advantage of helping to avoid ambiguity by forcing the draftsman to name the person, if identifiable, who has the relevant duty, right, power, or privilege."

—Reed Dickerson, *Materials on Legal Drafting* 185 (1981).

NOT THIS:	BUT THIS:
(a) General rule With respect to alterations of an existing facility or part thereof used in the provision of designated public transportation services that affect or could affect the usability of the facility or part thereof, it shall be considered discrimination, for purposes of section 12132 of this title and section 794 of Title 29, for a public entity to fail to make such alterations (or to ensure that the alterations are made) in such a manner that, to the maximum extent feasible, the altered portions of the facility are readily accessible to and usable by individuals with disabilities, including individuals who use wheelchairs, upon the completion of such alterations. **42 U.S.C. § 12147(a).**	(A) **General rule.** For purposes of § 12132 and 29 U.S.C. § 794, a public entity discriminates if it: (1) alters an existing facility used to provide designated public-transportation services in a manner that might affect the facility's usability or accessibility; and (2) fails to ensure, upon completing the alterations, that people with disabilities—including those who use wheelchairs—have ready access to and may use the altered portions of the facility.

By plain meaning, "altering a facility" includes altering a part of a facility.

(B) Replacing passive voice with adjective.

When feasible, rephrase a passive-voice verb by using an adjective.

NOT THIS:	BUT THIS:
A buyer may cancel a preneed burial contract as to preneed goods not delivered or preneed services not performed if the buyer . . . . **Md. Code, Bus. Reg. § 5-709(a)(1).**	A buyer may cancel a preneed burial contract for undelivered preneed goods or unperformed preneed services if the buyer . . . .
If a class meets more than once per week, part-time faculty should* be paid for all classes that were scheduled for that week. **Cal. Educ. Code § 87482.8(b).**	If a class meets more than once per week, the school must pay part-time faculty for all classes scheduled for that week.

(C) When to use passive voice.

Use passive voice primarily in two circumstances: (1) when naming the actor would unduly narrow the meaning or impede the flow of the sentence; or (2) when changing to active voice would undesirably shift the emphasis from one subject to another.

NOT THIS:	BUT THIS:
Upon the filing of a complaint to abate the drug-, firearm-, or prostitution-related nuisance, the court shall hold a hearing on the motion for a preliminary injunction, within 10 business days of the filing of such action. **D.C. Code § 42-3104(a).**	Within 10 business days after a complaint has been filed to abate a drug-, firearm-, or prostitution-related nuisance, the court must hold a hearing on the motion for a preliminary injunction.

*This *should* seems unlikely to be precatory or directory (nonbinding). The revision has made the payment for part-time faculty mandatory.

2.7 Positives and negatives.

(A) Preference for positives.

If you can state an idea without grammatical negation—especially multiple negation—do so. Instead of *No more than one officer may be present in a polling place at one time*, write *Only one* . . . .

NOT THIS:	BUT THIS:
The board may issue to dentist members of the faculty of a Minnesota school of dentistry, dental hygiene, or dental assisting accredited by the Commission on Dental Accreditation, a license designated as a limited faculty license entitling the holder to practice dentistry within the school and its affiliated teaching facilities, but only for the purposes of teaching or conducting research. The practice of dentistry at a school facility for purposes other than teaching or research is not allowed unless the dentist was a faculty member on August 1, 1993. **Minn. Stat. § 150A.06, subd. 1a(b).**	The board may issue a limited faculty license to a dentist member of the faculty of a Minnesota school of dentistry, dental hygiene, or dental assistance accredited by the Commission on Dental Accreditation. The license entitles the holder to practice dentistry within the school and its affiliated teaching facilities, but only for the purposes of teaching or research. Only a dentist who was a faculty member on August 1, 1993, may practice dentistry at a school facility for a purpose other than teaching or research.
For the purposes of this section, it shall not be deemed cruel or inhumane to transport live poultry in crates so long as not more than 15 pounds of live poultry are allocated to each cubic foot of space in the crate. **18 Pa. Cons. Stat. § 5511(e).**	For the purposes of this section, it is cruel or inhumane to transport live poultry in a crate when more than 15 pounds of live poultry are allocated to each cubic foot of space in the crate.
No licensed lender shall conduct the business of making consumer loans under this Chapter under any name and from or at any place of business within this state, other than that stated in the license. The closing of a consumer loan on immovable property in the office of a notary public shall not violate this Section. Loans made by mail where credit approval is given at the location of the lender and loans made with the use of a lender credit card shall not violate this Section. Loans governed by R.S. 9:3550 that are closed at an insurance agent/broker's location shall not violate this Section provided the loan shall be accepted by a licensed lender. **La. Rev. Stat. § 9:3515(E).**	A licensed lender may conduct the business of making consumer loans under this Chapter only under the name and from or at the place of business in this state named in the license. But a consumer loan on immovable property may be closed in the office of a notary public. A lender may make a loan with the use of a lender credit card. A lender may make a loan by mail if the lender gives credit approval at the lender's location. A loan governed by R.S. 9:3550 may be closed at an insurance agent or broker's location if it is accepted by a licensed lender.

On the desirability of deleting *deem*, see p. 143–44.

NOT THIS:	BUT THIS:
244.370 **Whiskey to be aged—Exception if not labeled as Kentucky whiskey.** No whiskey produced in Kentucky, except whiskey the barrel containing which is branded "Corn Whiskey" under the internal revenue laws, shall be bottled in Kentucky or removed from this state unless such whiskey has been aged in oak barrels for a period of not less than one (1) full year; provided, however, that whiskey aged less than one (1) year may be removed from the state and bottled, or bottled in Kentucky, if the word "Kentucky" or any word or phrase implying Kentucky origin does not appear on the front label or elsewhere on the retail container or package except in the name and address of the distiller as required by federal regulation. For violations of this section, the department shall revoke the permit of the licensee from whose warehouse or premises such whiskey shall have been removed or in which such whiskey shall have been bottled. **Ky. Rev. Stat. § 244.370.**	(A) **Requirements for aging of whiskey.** All Kentucky-produced whiskey must be aged in oak barrels for at least 1 year before bottling or export from the state, unless: (1) the whiskey is in a barrel branded "Corn Whiskey" under the internal-revenue laws; or (2) the whiskey packaging does not use the word "Kentucky" or imply that the whiskey originated in Kentucky, except to provide the distiller's name and address as required by federal regulation. (B) **Loss of permit.** For a violation of (A), the department must revoke the licensee's permit.
§343. Misbranded food. A food shall be deemed to be misbranded— . . . **(l) Pesticide chemicals on raw agricultural commodities** If it is a raw agricultural commodity which is the produce of the soil, bearing or containing a pesticide chemical applied after harvest, unless the shipping container of such commodity bears labeling which declares the presence of such chemical in or on such commodity and the common or usual name and the function of such chemical, except that no such declaration shall be required while such commodity, having been removed from the shipping container, is being held or displayed for sale at retail out of such container in accordance with the custom of the trade. **21 U.S.C. § 343(l).**	**§343. Properly branded food.** . . . (L) **Pesticides.** If a raw agricultural product of the soil bears or contains a pesticide chemical applied after harvest, the product's shipping container must have a label declaring the chemical's presence, its common or usual name, and its function. No label is required after the product has been removed from the shipping container for holding or display for sale at retail, if removal from the container is customary within the trade.

"It is hard to put a price tag on badly constructed legislation. How can we measure the cost of litigating the uncertainties of meaning that are brought about by language that is ambiguous or needlessly vague? And how can we evaluate the cost of finding legislative provisions that have been obscured by inept legislative placement?"

—Leon Jaworski, "The American Bar Association's Concern with Legislative Drafting," in *Professionalizing Legislative Drafting—The Federal Experience* 3, 5 (Reed Dickerson ed., 1973).

(B) Negatives when necessary.

Prohibitions are typically negative by their very nature. Use negatives sensibly when there are no sensible alternatives.

NOT THIS:	BUT THIS:
No member or employee of public employees insurance agency shall gain directly or indirectly from any contract or contracts provided for hereunder; criminal penalties. No elected or appointed official of the state of West Virginia; nor any member, officer, or employees of the Legislature; nor any officer, agent, servant or employee in the executive branch of state government shall have any interest, direct or indirect, in the gain or profits arising from any contract or contracts provided for in this article. Any such person who shall gain, directly or indirectly, from any contract or contracts herein provided for, except as an insured beneficiary thereof, shall be guilty of a misdemeanor, and, upon conviction thereof, shall be punished by a fine not exceeding one thousand dollars, or by imprisonment in the county jail for a period not exceeding one year, or by both, in the discretion of the court: Provided, That nothing in this section shall be construed to prohibit an elected or appointed official of this state, nor an employee of the legislative, judicial or executive branches, from providing health care or entering into contracts provided for in section seventeen of this article. **W. Va. Code § 5-16-21.**	**No profit from contract; criminal penalties.** (A) **Prohibited conduct.** No West Virginia official, elected or appointed, and no West Virginia legislator or executive-branch officer, agent, employee, or servant, may profit directly or indirectly from a contract provided for in this article. (B) **Exceptions.** A person enumerated in (A), or an employee of the judicial branch, may: (1) be an insured beneficiary of such a contract; (2) provide healthcare; and (3) enter into a contract under § 17 of this article. (C) **Criminal penalties.** Violation of (A) is a misdemeanor punishable by a maximum fine of $1,000 or imprisonment up to 1 year in the county jail, or both.

> "The most important thing is knowing what you want to say. The greatest enemy to clear writing is fuzzy thinking. One of the things that you used to hear quite often in the Council of the American Law Institute is something you hear less often today. Back when I was the reporter on the Study of the Division of Jurisdiction in the 1960s, somebody would advance a substantive idea but then say semi-apologetically, 'That might not be draftable. It may just be too complicated.' Something of that sort. Finally I became exasperated, and I said, 'I can draft anything if you will make up your minds what it is you want this statute to say. I can put it down in words, but I have to know what result you want the statute to reach.' That is the overarching problem with legal writing. People aren't really sure what it is they want to say. A hazy mind cannot produce a clear printed page."
>
> —Charles Alan Wright
> Interview with Bryan A. Garner
> Tucson, Arizona, 15 Jan. 1994.

2.8 Gender neutrality.

(A) The goal of invisibility.

Ideally, the question of sexist language or its avoidance will never arise in the reader's mind. True, *he or she* still draws some attention to itself—and if it becomes frequent it is distracting. But sometimes it will be the best you can do: it cannot and should not be viewed as anathema when used sparingly. Contrivances such as *s/he* and *(s)he* are unacceptable to a large proportion of readers, just as the singular *they* is. For now, the best approach is to use any of several devices (see (B)) to achieve invisible gender-neutrality.

NOT THIS:	BUT THIS:
Any person seeking to recover damages pursuant to § 40-28-18 shall file suit no later than one year after the trespass occurred or six months after he knew or should have known of the injury resulting from the trespass. **S.D. Codified Laws § 40-28-20.**	A person seeking to recover damages under § 40-28-18 must file suit within 1 year after the trespass or 6 months after the person knew or should have known about the injury resulting from the trespass.
§ 2502. Vacancies A person appointed to fill a vacancy in the membership of the Commission shall be appointed only for the unexpired term of the member whom he succeeds, and his appointment shall be made in the same manner as the appointment of his predecessor. **44 U.S.C. § 2502.**	**§ 2502. Vacancy.** A person appointed to fill a vacant seat on the Commission may be appointed only for the unexpired term of the predecessor member. The appointment must be made in the same manner as the predecessor's appointment.
§ 3401. Misdemeanors; application of probation laws (a) When specially designated to exercise such jurisdiction by the district court or courts he serves, any United States magistrate judge shall have jurisdiction to try persons accused of, and sentence persons convicted of, misdemeanors committed within that judicial district. **18 U.S.C. § 3401(a).**	**§ 3401. Misdemeanors; application of probation laws.** (A) **Jurisdiction of magistrate judge.** A U.S. magistrate judge of a particular judicial district has jurisdiction to try and sentence a person accused and convicted of a misdemeanor committed within the district if specially designated to exercise this jurisdiction by the district court in charge of the magistrate judge.
222.17 Manifesting and evidencing domicile in Florida. (1) Any person who shall have established a domicile in this state may manifest and evidence the same by filing in the office of the clerk of the circuit court for the county in which the said person shall reside, a sworn statement showing that he or she resides in and maintains a place of abode in that county which he or she recognizes and intends to maintain as his or her permanent home. **Fla. Stat. § 222.17(1).**	**222.17 Proving domicile in Florida.** (A) **Proof.** After establishing a domicile in this state, a person may prove domicile by filing a sworn statement with the clerk's office of the circuit court for the county where the person resides. The statement must show that the person resides in and maintains a place of abode in that county and intends it to be the person's permanent home.

NOT THIS:	BUT THIS:
Whenever the Secretary of the Interior, after reasonable notice and opportunity for hearing, finds that there is a failure to expend funds in accordance with the terms and conditions governing the Federal contribution for such approved projects, he shall notify the Commonwealth that further payments will not be made to the Commonwealth from appropriations under this Chapter until he is satisfied that there will no longer be any such failure. Until he is so satisfied the Secretary of the Interior shall withhold the payment of any financial contributions to the Commonwealth. **30 U.S.C. § 574.**	If, after reasonable notice and opportunity for hearing, the Secretary of the Interior finds that the Commonwealth has failed to expend funds in accordance with the terms and conditions governing the federal contribution for an approved project, the Secretary must notify the Commonwealth that further payments will not be made from appropriations until those responsible for the project provide adequate assurance that no such failure will occur again. Until satisfied, the Secretary may withhold the payment of any financial contribution to the Commonwealth.

(B) Enumeration of nonsexist methods.

With few exceptions, statutes apply to all people without regard to sex. To preserve credibility and fairness, avoid using the pronouns *he* or *she* and the nouns *man* or *woman* whenever possible and practical. Some useful techniques for gender-neutral writing are:

1. Delete personal pronouns whenever possible. Instead of "a conference between a client and his attorney," write "a conference between a client and the client's attorney" or "an attorney–client conference."
2. Use a gender-neutral noun or pronoun such as *anyone*, *client*, *decedent*, *human*, *one*, *person*, or *someone* instead of *man* or *woman*.
3. Repeat the noun, if you can keep repetition to a minimum.
4. Use an article (*a*, *an*, *the*) instead of a possessive pronoun.
5. Use gender-neutral titles (e.g., *police officer*, *firefighter*, *mail carrier*) for gender-specific titles (e.g., *policeman*, *fireman*, *mailman*).
6. Reword the sentence to avoid the need for gender-specific words.
7. Use a plural antecedent (e.g., *contractors* for *contractor*) so you can use a plural pronoun (but see § 2.4, p. 56).
8. Use plural constructions (*they*, *them*, *their*) instead of singular ones (*he*, *she*, *his*, *her*) (but again, see § 2.4, p. 56).
9. Substitute the phrase *he or she* or the phrase *him or her* when you must use gender-specific pronouns.

> "[N]o legal requirement demands retention of the traditional 'male-only' style. It can always be replaced by inclusive language without loss of legal precision or effectiveness."
>
> —Peter Butt & Richard Castle, *Modern Legal Drafting* 158 (2001).

2.9 Handling numbers, percentages, and currency.

(A) Preference for numerals.

Written-out numbers are harder to read than numerals simply because they're undifferentiated from other words. Although in general prose it's customary to spell out one through ten and then to use numerals (apart from currency), in legislation it's desirable to use a numerals-only policy. Some jurisdictions have a policy of italicizing *1* to make it stand out as a numeral when it appears solo; although these *Guidelines* haven't adopted that convention, it's worth considering.

NOT THIS:	BUT THIS:
[A] contract for the sale of goods for the price of five hundred dollars or more is not enforceable by way of action or defense . . . . **Ariz. Rev. Stat. § 47-2201(A).**	A contract for the sale of goods for $500 or more is not enforceable by action or defense . . . .
On any cash advance in an amount in excess of Twenty-nine Dollars and Ninety-nine Cents up to and including the amount of Thirty-five Dollars there shall be allowed an acquisition charge for making the advance not in excess of one-tenth of the amount of the cash advance. In addition thereto, an installment account handling charge shall be allowed not to exceed Three Dollars per month. **Tex. Rev. Civ. Stat. art. 5069-3.16(b) (repealed in 1997).**	On a cash advance of $30 to $35 (inclusive),* a lender may impose an acquisition charge of up to 10% of the amount advanced. The lender may also impose an installment-account handling charge of up to $3 per month.

*Without the word *inclusive*, only amounts of $30.01 to $34.99 might be dealt with in the statute.

(B) No word–numeral doublets.

The age-old convention of doubling up words and numerals—a holdover from scribal days when it was possible for fraudsters to falsify parchments by altering numerals—is no longer justified in printed statutes, or even in contracts for that matter. The doubling encumbers sentences and creates opportunities for discrepancy.

NOT THIS:	BUT THIS:
The State Board of Mental Health is directed to give priority to crisis services and crisis stabilization unit services provided twenty-four (24) hours a day, seven (7) days a week, where trained emergency-crisis response staff triage referrals and respond in a timely and adequate manner to diffuse a current personal crisis situation. **Miss. Code § 41-4-1(2).**	The State Board of Mental Health must give priority to crisis services and crisis-stabilization-unit services that are provided 24 hours a day, 7 days a week, and have trained emergency-crisis-response staff to triage referrals and respond in a timely and adequate manner to defuse people's crises as they occur.

Note the misuse of the word *diffuse* for *defuse*. Literally, to "diffuse" a crisis would be to spread it out so as to make it pervasive—the opposite of what is surely meant here.

The last three words essentially create an actual-case-or-controversy requirement. Mere worries aren't wanted, and the statute gives them no warrant. The word *current* in the original is undesirably vague.

> "Legal writers of old liked to express numbers by both words and figures, as in 'sixty-five (65) years of age.' This is nonsense; once is enough."
> —Lawrence E. Filson, *The Legislative Drafter's Desk Reference* § 27.1, at 311 (1992).

NOT THIS:	BUT THIS:
Where two (2) or more attorneys at law of this state are associated together in practice as attorneys or counselors at law, and one (1) of such attorneys shall be district attorney of his district . . . . Any attorney violating this section shall be deemed guilty of a misdemeanor and, on conviction shall be fined in the sum of not less than Ten Dollars ($10.00) nor more than One Hundred Dollars ($100.00), and shall forfeit his license to practice law in this state. **Miss. Code § 73-3-49.**	If 2 or more attorneys of this state are associated together in practice as attorneys or counselors at law, and 1 attorney is the district attorney of the district . . . . An attorney violating this section is guilty of a misdemeanor and, if convicted, must pay a fine of at least $10 and no more than $100 and forfeit his or her license to practice law in this state.
§ 19-1904. **Additional jurors.** A court may direct that one (1) or more jurors in addition to the regular panel be called and impaneled to sit as alternate jurors. All jurors shall be drawn in the same manner, shall have the same qualifications, shall be subject to the same examination and challenges, shall take the same oath, and shall have the same functions, powers, facilities, and privileges prior to deliberations. At the conclusion of closing arguments, jurors exceeding the number required of a regular panel shall be removed by lot. Those removed by lot may be discharged after the jury retires to consider its verdict. If more than one (1) additional juror is called, each party is entitled to two (2) peremptory challenges in addition to those otherwise allowed by law; provided however, that if only one (1) additional juror is called, each party shall be entitled to one (1) peremptory challenge in addition to those otherwise provided by law. **Idaho Code § 19-1904.**	§ 19-1904. **Additional jurors.** (A) **Impaneling jurors.** A court may direct that 1 or more jurors in addition to the regular panel be called and impaneled to sit as alternate jurors. If 2 or more additional jurors are called, each party is entitled to 2 additional peremptory challenges. If only 1 additional juror is called, each party is entitled to 1 additional peremptory challenge. (B) **Juror selection.** All jurors must: (1) be drawn in the same manner; (2) have the same qualifications; (3) be subject to the same examination and challenges; (4) take the same oath; and (5) have the same functions, powers, facilities, and privileges before deliberations. (C) **Removing excess jurors.** If there are more jurors than required for a regular panel, then at the conclusion of closing arguments, the court must remove the extra jurors by lot. Those removed by lot may be discharged after the jury retires to consider its verdict.

"Opponents of drafting reform argue that we cannot disturb the sanctity of certain wording found in old documents or contracts because that wording has been steeped in time and we change it at our peril. Although no lawyer can ascribe definitive meanings to the wording, we are expected to observe this warning."

—Robert C. Dick, *Legal Drafting* 7 (2d ed. 1985).

NOT THIS:	BUT THIS:
(a)(1) Any member who has acquired five (5) years but less than thirty (30) years of actual service and has attained age sixty-five (65) may retire upon written application filed with the Board of Trustees of the State Police Retirement System. (2) Any member who has acquired five (5) or more years of actual service and has attained age fifty-two (52) may retire upon written application filed with the State Police Retirement System. (3) Any member who acquired thirty (30) or more years of actual service may retire at any age upon written application filed with the board. (4) For those members with less than thirty (30) actual years of service, the age sixty-five (65) requirement shall be reduced by one (1) month for every two (2) months of public safety credit, but in no event to an age younger than fifty-two (52). (b) This application shall set forth at what time, not less than thirty (30) days nor more than ninety (90) days subsequent to the execution and filing thereof, the member desires to be retired. **Ark. Code § 24-6-226(a), (b).**	(A) **Service and age requirements for retiring.** (1) ***Age 65, 5–30 years of service (inclusive).*** A member who has served at least 5 years but less than 30 years and has attained age 65 may retire after filing a written application with the Board of Trustees of the State Police Retirement System. (2) ***Age 52, 5 years of service.*** A member who has served at least 5 years and has attained age 52 may retire after filing a written application with the Board of Trustees. (3) ***Any age, 30 years of service.*** A member who has served at least 30 years may retire at any age after filing a written application with the Board of Trustees. (4) ***Public-safety credit.*** For a member who has served less than 30 years, the age requirement in (A)(1) is reduced by 1 month for every 2 months of public-safety credit, but in no event to an age younger than 52. (B) **Date of retirement.** The application (under A) must state the date when the member plans to retire. The date must be at least 30 days but not more than 90 days after the application is signed and filed.

Must file with the Board.

Must file with the System.

Must file with the Board.

Notice how the revision follows consistent usage in (1)–(3). See § 1.1(D).

(C) Preference for percent sign (%) and section sign (§).

We're after efficient communication and error prevention. *Thirty-three percent* is slower, more cumbersome, and more prone to error than *33%*.

Although some argue that "§" is alien to the general public and therefore confusing, the general public is likewise probably unfamiliar with the pilcrow—the backward P with two downstrokes to mark a paragraph: ¶. Even so, people generally have no difficulty with the pilcrow and focus instead on the number that follows it. They see that they're reading something with numbered paragraphs—a different kind of writing from what they're accustomed to.

The same goes for "§." It's one character, not four (*sec.*) or seven (*section*). The cumulative benefit in streamlining is tremendous—and readers no longer have to focus on a full two words "section 474" when the attention should be on a single unit: § 474.

Further, it takes only a few seconds to become accustomed to this abbreviated form. It's not taxing any readers unduly. In fact, it's doing the opposite: it's sparing them the trouble of reading empty words.

NOT THIS:	BUT THIS:
"Applicable percentage" means 0 percent for the first two credit allowance dates, 12 percent for the next three credit allowance dates and 11 percent for the next two credit allowance dates. **Nev. Rev. Stat. § 231A.040.**	"Applicable percentage" means 0% for the first 2 credit-allowance dates, 12% for the next 3 credit-allowance dates, and 11% for the next 2 credit-allowance dates.
The additional bonds issued shall not exceed twenty-five per centum of the total amount originally issued, and shall bear not more than six per centum interest per annum, and may be made payable in ten annual installments, or lesser number of annual installments as nearly equal as may be, as recommended by the board of viewers having jurisdiction over the same. **Va. Code § 21-411.**	**§ 21-411. Requirements for additional bonds.** The additional bonds issued: (A) must not exceed 25% of the total amount originally issued; (B) must bear no more than 6% annual interest; and (C) may be payable in 10 or fewer annual installments as nearly equal as possible, as recommended by the board of viewers that has jurisdiction over the bonds.
A contract for the rendering of services or the supplying of materials entered into on or after the effective date of this section shall be deemed to include a provision that authorizes the contracting authority, in its sole discretion, to reduce any bond filed by the person contracting to render the services or supply the materials by twenty-five per cent of the total amount of the bond upon demonstration satisfactory to the contracting authority that at least fifty per cent of the services have been rendered or materials have been supplied in accordance with the terms of the contract, and by fifty per cent of the total amount of the bond upon demonstration satisfactory to the contracting authority that at least seventy-five per cent of the services have been rendered or materials have been supplied in accordance with the terms of the contract. **Ohio Rev. Code § 9.313.**	When a contract for rendering services or supplying materials is entered into on or after the effective date of this section, the contracting authority, in its sole discretion, may reduce any bond filed by the person contracting to render the services or supply the materials—in the following amounts: (A) to obtain a 25% bond reduction, the person must demonstrate, to the satisfaction of the contracting authority, that at least 50% of the services have been rendered or materials have been supplied according to the terms of the contract; (B) to obtain a 50% bond reduction, the person must demonstrate, to the satisfaction of the contracting authority, that at least 75% of the services have been rendered or materials have been supplied according to the terms of the contract.

(D) No ".00" for round dollar amounts.

Don't use zeros as part of round dollar amounts. Prefer "$50" over "$50.00." Statutes rarely show cents, which take up extra space and can cause printing errors. Only a statute that needs cents displayed should contain the period and the two extra numerals.

NOT THIS:	BUT THIS:
No person appointed as a member of the Banking Board shall receive any compensation for this service; except, that each appointed member of said Banking Board shall receive $50.00 per day and expenses as paid state employees for each day said Banking Board is in session. **Ala. Code § 5-2A-45.**	A member of the Banking Board will receive $50 per day and expenses (as are paid to state employees) for each day the Banking Board is in session. No other compensation is permitted.
§ 23. Authority is hereby vested in the Illinois Pollution Control Board to conduct hearings on complaints charging that any public water supply owner, owner's manager or agent, official custodian, municipal, state or other official has violated or aided and abetted the violation of Section 1 of this Act, or has refused or neglected to comply with any order issued by the Director, as herein provided for. Based on the determinations of the Illinois Pollution Control Board, the violator shall be penalized by the Illinois Pollution Control Board not less than $100.00 nor more than $1000.00 for each offense. **415 Ill. Comp. Stat. 45/23.**	§ 23. **Compliance hearings.** The Illinois Pollution Control Board may conduct hearings on complaints charging that a public-water-supply owner, an owner's manager or agent, an official custodian, or a municipal, state, or other official has violated or assisted in violating § 1 of this Act, or has refused or neglected to comply with an order issued by the Director as provided for in this statute. Upon determining that a violation has occurred, the Board will fine the violator at least $100 but no more than $1,000 for each offense.

"Columnar tables are actually quite easy to read and follow, if the headings and relationships of the columns are clear and adequately descriptive. And a good table, like a computer spreadsheet, can say with complete precision in half a page what it would take 10 convoluted pages to say in words."

—Lawrence E. Filson, *The Legislative Drafter's Desk Reference* § 9.4, at 93 (1992).

2.10 Calculations, diagrams, charts, and other graphics.

Envision how best to display complex information. Be ingenious. But make sure your graphics are easily understood and can be easily referred to in legal documents. If necessary, retain a compositor competent to lay out your graphics.

Tables can be a moderate challenge in bill-drafting. But if the staff includes someone with minimal proficiency in typesetting, they can be dealt with readily.

NOT THIS:	BUT THIS:
(d) *Annual Benefit Not in Excess of Ten Thousand Dollars ($10,000).* . . . (2) However, if a participant has fewer than 10 years of service with the City of Anniston, then the ten thousand dollar ($10,000) threshold of subsection (d)(1) shall be multiplied by a fraction, a. the numerator of which is the number of years, or part thereof, of service with the City of Anniston and b. the denominator of which is 10. However, in no event shall such fraction be less than 1/10 th. **Ala. Code § 45-8A-22.118(d)(2).**	(D) **Annual benefit not to exceed $10,000.** . . . (2) But if a participant has fewer than 10 years of service with the City of Anniston, the $10,000 threshold of subsection (d)(1) is multiplied by this fraction: $\frac{\text{the number of years (whole or partial) of service}}{10}$ The fraction must be at least 1/10.
"[V]alue of salable copper and other minerals" means: (1) for new copper mineral properties, the sum, for copper and each other mineral produced, of the product of the salable amount of the mineral produced during the interval beginning with the month in which operations on a commercial basis began or recommenced and ending with the last month of production preceding the tax year for which valuation is being determined; multiplied by the normalization factor which is a fraction, the numerator of which is twelve and the denominator of which is the number of months within the interval beginning with the month in which operations on a commercial basis began or recommenced and ending with the last month of production preceding the tax year for which valuation is being determined; further multiplied by the average price for the interval beginning with the month in which operations on a commercial basis began or recommenced and ending with the last month of production preceding the tax year for which valuation is being determined; and (2) for all other copper mineral properties the sum, for copper and each other mineral produced, of the product of the quotient of the salable amount of the mineral produced during the three calendar years immediately preceding the year for which valuation is being determined divided by three; multiplied by the average price for the three-year period. **N.M. Stat. § 7-39-2 (I).**	(3) "Value of salable copper and other minerals" means the result of the applicable calculation below: (1) for new copper-mineral properties, the sum of all the minerals' values—using the months from start or resumption of commercial operations through the last month of production before the tax year for which the valuation will be used—calculated by the formula A×N×P,* using: (a) A = the total salable amount of the mineral produced during those months; (b) N = 12 ÷ the number of those months; and (c) P = the average price of the mineral for those months; and (2) for all other copper-mineral properties, the sum of all the minerals' values, calculated by the formula A×P, using: (a) A = the average annual salable amount of the mineral produced in the 3 calendar years before the tax year for which the valuation will be used; and (b) P = the average price of the mineral for that 3-year period.

*Note the use of a double-dash construction here. See § 4.9(E).

NOT THIS:

Public questions at foot of ballot; instructions to voters

Immediately below the six-point diagram rule to be printed in place of the last two-point hair line rule across the entire ballot, from one four-point rule to the other, shall be printed as near to the center of the ballot as possible the following words: "Public Questions to be voted upon". Below these words and above the first public question, beginning one and one-half inches to the right of the four-point rule at the left of the ballot and extending to not more than one and one-half inches from the four-point rule at the right of the ballot, shall be printed in one line, if possible, the following instructions: "To vote upon the Public Questions printed below, if in favor thereof mark a cross x or plus + in the square at the left of the word 'Yes', and if opposed thereto, mark a cross x or plus + in the square at the left of the word 'No'," underscored with a two-point diagram rule. Below and flush with the left end of said two-point diagram rule shall be printed two separate squares, one under the other, three-eighths of an inch in size formed by two-point diagram rules. Immediately to the right of the upper square shall be printed the word "Yes", and immediately to the right of the lower square shall be printed the word "No". To the right of the words "Yes" and "No" shall be printed a bracket embracing these words and to the right of the bracket shall be printed across the ballot, to not nearer than one and one-half inches from the four-point diagram rule at the right of the ballot, each public question to be voted upon. Below each such public question shall be printed two-point diagram rule beginning one and one-half inches to the right of the four-point rule at the left of the ballot and extending to not nearer than one and one-half inches from the four-point rule at the right of the ballot. In place of the last two-point diagram rule there shall be printed a four-point diagram rule extending across the entire ballot not less than a half inch from the lower edge of the paper and terminating at the lower ends of the four-point diagram rules at either side of the ballot.

N.J. Stat. § 19:14-14.

BUT THIS:

Public questions at foot of ballot; instructions to voters.

(A) **Arrangement of questions and instructions.** Public questions certified for the election must be printed at the bottom of the main ballot, immediately below a six-point rule. This section must have page margins of 1.5 inches on each side and begin with the heading "Public Questions to Be Voted On," followed by these instructions:

> If you're in favor, mark an "x" or "+" in the square to the left of the word "Yes." If you're opposed, mark an "x" or "+" in the square to the left of the word "No."

(B) **Placement of boxes; separation of questions.** The wording of each question must appear in order of ballot number down the right side of the ballot, each accompanied on the left by boxes marked "Yes" and "No," and each question must be separated from the preceding one by a 3-point rule with 1½ inches of space above and below it.

(C) **Illustration.** More printing specifications for the ballot appear in the accompanying illustration.

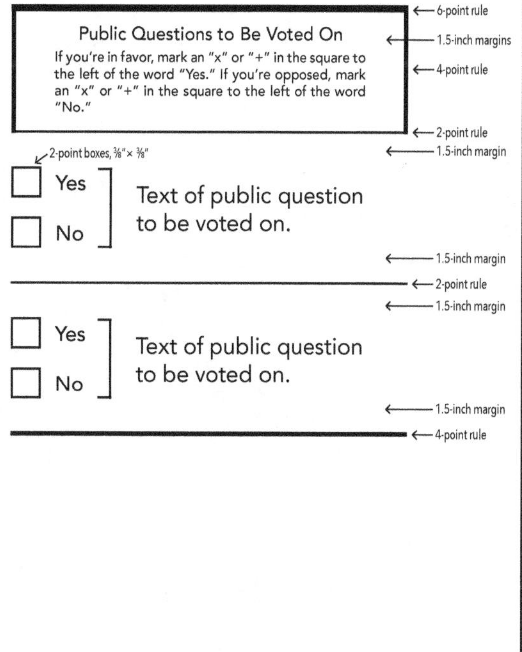

> "[T]here is often a tendency to avoid the use of tables, possibly on the misguided basis that they do not constitute real drafting."
> —Elmer Doonan, *Drafting* § 3.7, at 68 (Julie MacFarland ed., 1995).

3. Structure

3.1 Organization.

(A) Logical arrangement.

Organize rules logically and clearly so that referring to them is relatively easy. Do this by adhering as much as possible to these organizational principles:

- Put rules before exceptions.
- Put more broadly applicable provisions before narrowly applicable ones (except with residual "catchall" provisions).
- Follow the chronological order of contemplated events.
- Couple deadlines with requirements.
- Put penalties after substantive standards and exceptions.

NOT THIS:	BUT THIS:
No money deposited under section 2041 of this title shall be withdrawn except by order of court. In every case in which the right to withdraw money deposited in court under section 2041 has been adjudicated or is not in dispute and such money has remained so deposited for at least five years unclaimed by the person entitled thereto, such court shall cause such money to be deposited in the Treasury in the name and to the credit of the United States. Any claimant entitled to any such money may, on petition to the court and upon notice to the United States attorney and full proof of the right thereto, obtain an order directing payment to him. **28 U.S.C. § 2042.**	(A) **General rule.** Money deposited under § 2041 of this title may be withdrawn only by court order. (B) **Claim for money.** A claimant entitled to withdraw money deposited under § 2041 may petition the court and—upon notice to the United States attorney and full proof of the right to the money—obtain an order directing payment to the claimant. (C) **Unclaimed right to withdraw.** If the right to withdraw the money is adjudicated or undisputed, and the person entitled to claim the deposited money has not claimed it within 5 years, the court must order the money to be deposited in the Treasury in the name and to the credit of the United States.
[Threat of withdrawal.] (A) No funds shall be made available under any applicable program to any educational agency or institution which has a policy of denying, or which effectively prevents, the parents of students who are or have been in attendance at a school of such agency or at such institution, as the case may be, the right to inspect and review the education records of their children. If any material or document in the education record of a student includes information on more than one student, the parents of one of such students shall have the right to inspect and review only such part of such material or document as relates to such student or to be informed of the specific information contained in such part of such material. [The basic requirement, which should come first.] Each educational agency or institution shall establish appropriate procedures for the granting of a request by parents for access to the education records of their children within a reasonable period of time, but in no case more than forty-five days after the request has been made. **20 U.S.C. § 1232g(a)(1)(A).**	(a) ***Parental access to records.*** An educational agency or institution must establish appropriate procedures to grant parents access to their child's educational records within a reasonable time, but in no event more than 45 days after a request has been made. If any material in a student's educational records contains information about another student, a parent may inspect only the material that relates to that parent's child. No funds under any applicable program will be available to an educational agency or institution that has a policy of denying or preventing the parents of students who are attending or have attended the agency's or institution's school the right to inspect and review their child's educational records.

NOT THIS:	BUT THIS:
Submission of copy of accident report to Department of Transportation. Each state and local law enforcement agency shall submit to the Department of Transportation the original document of any accident report prepared by such law enforcement agency or submitted to such agency by a member of the public. If the Department of Driver Services receives a claim requesting determination of security, the Department of Transportation shall provide a copy or an electronic copy of any relevant accident reports to the Department of Driver Services. Any law enforcement agency may transmit the information contained on the accident report form by electronic means, provided that the Department of Transportation has first given approval to the reporting agency for the electronic reporting method utilized. The law enforcement agency shall retain a copy of each accident report. Any law enforcement agency that transmits the data by electronic means must transmit the data using a nonproprietary interchangeable electronic format and reporting method. For purposes of this Code section, the term "nonproprietary" shall include commonly used report formats. All such reports shall be submitted to the Department of Transportation not more than 15 days following the end of the month in which such report was prepared or received by such law enforcement agency. The Department of Transportation is authorized to engage the services of a third party in fulfilling its responsibilities under this Code section. **Ga. Code § 40-9-31.***	**Submitting accident report to Department of Transportation.** (A) **Original required; deadline.** A state or local law-enforcement agency must submit each original accident report to the Department of Transportation—whether the report was prepared by the agency or submitted to the agency by a member of the public. The report must be submitted within 15 days after the end of the month in which the agency prepared or received the report. (B) **Copy of report.** The law-enforcement agency must retain a copy of each accident report. (C) **Requirements for electronic copy.** The information contained in the accident report may be sent electronically if (1) the Department of Transportation has given preapproval, and (2) the report is in an electronic format that is commonly used and readily available. (D) **Request made to Department of Driver Services.** If the Department of Driver Services receives a request for determination of security, the Department of Transportation must provide a physical or electronic copy of any relevant accident report to the Department of Driver Services. (E) **Third-party services.** The Department of Transportation may engage third-party services to fulfill its responsibilities under this section.

The requirement of submitting a report to DOT.

The deadline for submitting a report to DOT is grossly separated from the first sentence. It's buried.

*Note that this example also appears at § 3.5(A).

> "[I]n a code of laws addressed to the people, and to the least intelligent portion of the people, the perfection of science will be attained, when its efforts are not perceived, and its results are characterized by noble simplicity."
>
> —Jeremy Bentham, "A General View of a Complete Code of Laws," in 3 *The Works of Jeremy Bentham* 155, 209 (John Bowring ed., 1843).

NOT THIS:	BUT THIS:
§ 86.3 Waste of gas--Meaning--Prevention--Production of fresh water and oil or gas bearing strata. The term "waste", as applied to gas, in addition to its ordinary meaning, shall include the inefficient or wasteful utilization of gas in the operation of oil wells drilled to and producing from a common source of supply; the inefficient or wasteful utilization of gas from gas wells drilled to and producing from a common source of supply; the production of gas in such quantities or in such manner as unreasonably to reduce reservoir pressure or unreasonably to diminish the quantity of oil or gas that might be recovered from a common source of supply; the escape, directly or indirectly, of gas from oil wells producing from a common source of supply into the open air in excess of the amount necessary in the efficient drilling, completion or operation thereof; waste incident to the production of natural gas in excess of transportation and marketing facilities or reasonable market demand; the escape, blowing or releasing, directly or indirectly, into the open air, of gas from wells productive of gas only, drilled into any common source of supply, save only such as is necessary in the efficient drilling and completion thereof; and the unnecessary depletion or inefficient utilization of gas energy contained in a common source of supply. In order to prevent the waste or to reduce the dissipation of gas energy contained in a common source of supply, in addition to its other powers in respect thereof, the Commission shall have the authority to limit the production of gas from wells producing gas only to a percentage of the capacity of such wells to produce. The production of gas in the State of Oklahoma in such manner and under such conditions as to constitute waste as in this act defined is hereby prohibited, and the Commission shall have authority and is charged with the duty to make rules, regulations, and orders for the prevention of such waste and for the protection of all freshwater strata and oil- or gas-bearing strata encountered in any well drilled for gas. **Okla. Stat. tit. 52, § 86.3.**	**§ 86.3 Waste of gas.** (A) **Waste prohibited.** In Oklahoma, producing gas in a manner constituting waste is prohibited. (B) **Scope of "waste."** In addition to its ordinary meaning, "waste" includes: (1) producing an amount of gas exceeding transportation and marketing facilities or reasonable market demand; (2) producing gas in a way that unreasonably reduces reservoir pressure; (3) producing gas in a way that unreasonably diminishes the recoverable quantity of oil or gas from a common supply source; (4) inefficiently using gas in the operation of an oil or gas well producing from a common supply source; (5) unnecessarily depleting or inefficiently using gas energy contained in a common supply source; and (6) directly or indirectly allowing more gas to escape into the open air from an oil or gas well producing from a common supply source than is necessary to efficiently drill, complete, or operate the well. (C) **Commission's authority.** To prevent waste, the Commission: (1) must make rules, regulations, and orders to prevent waste and protect freshwater strata and oil- or gas-bearing strata encountered in any well drilled for gas; and (2) may limit the amount of gas produced from a gas well to a percentage of its producing capacity.

The prohibition now appears at the fore.

Only at this point in the provision does the reader realize that it's a prohibition.

"Front-load your regulation. . . . [P]ut major matters before minor ones, widely used provisions before rarely used ones, the permanent before the temporary, what to do before penalties for not doing it."

—Thomas A. Murawski, *Writing Readable Regulations* 4 (1999).

(B) Grouping related items together.

Things of like kind need to be kept together, not separated. Otherwise, the drafting seems hodgepodge. An added benefit of headings (see § 1.1(F)) is that they'll help you arrange related ideas sensibly.

NOT THIS:	BUT THIS:
The time, place, and purpose of a special meeting subject to this section shall be publicly announced at least 24 hours before the meeting. Municipal public bodies shall post notices of special meetings in or near the municipal clerk's office and in at least two other designated public places in the municipality, at least 24 hours before the meeting. In addition, notice shall be given, either orally or in writing, to each member of the public body at least 24 hours before the meeting, except that a member may waive notice of a special meeting. **Vt. Stat. tit. 1, § 312(c)(2).**	At least 24 hours before a special meeting subject to this section, a municipal public body must: (A) announce the date, time, place, and purpose of the meeting; (B) post a notice of the meeting in or near the municipal clerk's office and in at least 2 other designated public places in the municipality; and (C) give each member of the public body oral or written notice unless the member waives notice.
§ 123. Animal husbandry. The Maine Agricultural Experiment Station shall conduct scientific investigations in animal husbandry, including experiments and observations on dairy cattle and other domestic animals, and these investigations are under the control of the director of the station with the agreement of the Board of Agriculture. The experiments in animal husbandry may be conducted at any of the farms owned by the State. The board and the director shall seek agreement on all issues. In the event that the agreement can not be reached, final authority rests with the director. **Me. Rev. Stat. tit. 7, § 123.**	**§ 123. Animal husbandry.** (A) **Scientific investigations.** The Maine Agricultural Experiment Station must conduct scientific investigations in animal husbandry, including experiments on and observations of dairy cattle and other domestic animals. The experiments in animal husbandry may be conducted at any State-owned farm. (B) **Director's responsibilities.** The director of the station, with the Board of Agriculture's agreement, controls the investigations described in (A). The board and the director must seek agreement on all issues. If they cannot agree, the director has the final authority.

> "Legal English has long been characterized by another archaic trait: constructions of the type *hereunder*, *therein*, and *wherewith*. These words were common in medieval English. Rather than saying *under it* or *under that*, a speaker of Middle English could say *hereunder* or *thereunder*. And instead of using *with what* or *with which* in questions, Middle English speakers would generally say *wherewith*."
>
> —Peter M. Tiersma, *Legal Language* 93 (1999).

NOT THIS:	BUT THIS:
Definitions and standards for food. When, in the judgment of the commissioner, honest and fair dealing in the interest of consumers will be promoted, the department shall adopt regulations fixing and establishing for food or class of food a reasonable definition and standard of identity, a reasonable standard of quality, and reasonable standards of fill of container. In prescribing a definition and standard of identity for food or class of food in which optional ingredients are permitted, the department shall, for the purpose of promoting honesty and fair dealing in the interest of consumers, designate the optional ingredients which shall be named on the label. The definitions and standards adopted shall conform as far as practicable to the definitions and standards adopted under authority of the federal act. The department shall establish a mobile canned food inspection service available upon request to food packers or processors inside the state. **Alaska Stat. § 17.20.010.**	**Definitions and standards for food.** (A) **Adoption of regulations.** If the commissioner believes that doing so will promote honest and fair dealing in the interest of consumers, the department must adopt regulations establishing definitions and standards for foods or classes of foods that conform as closely as possible to those adopted under 21 U.S.C. § 341. (B) **Standards and definitions.** For standards adopted under (A), the department must establish the following: (1) a reasonable quality standard for any food or class of food; (2) a reasonable container-fill standard for any food or class of food; (3) a reasonable definition and identity standard for any food or class of food. (C) **Labeling.** If a definition or standard for a food or class of foods permits optional ingredients, it must also state which optional ingredients must be named on the label. (D) **Inspections.** The department must establish a mobile canned-food-inspection service and make it available upon request to food packers or processors in the state.

"Judges have suffered much, and continue to suffer much, from bad drafting. In 1857 we find Lord Campbell commenting severely on 'an ill-penned enactment, like too many others, putting Judges in the embarrassing situation of being bound to make sense out of nonsense, and to reconcile what is irreconcilable.'"

—Carleton Kemp Allen, *Law in the Making* 484 (7th ed. 1964) (quoting *Fell v. Burchett*, [1857] 7 E. & B. 537, 539).

3.2 Structural divisions.

(A) The parts.

Use subparts to maximize readability. The parts of a statute are preferably sequenced with a one-level decimal followed by an outline form alternating between letters and numerals. The typical statute, managed properly, won't need more than five levels of breakdown. Subitems should rarely if ever be reached. Throughout this book, the right-column "but this" examples follow our recommended format—without any hand-wringing about the terminology. Every citation is preceded simply by the section symbol (§ 6, or § 6.2, or § 6.2(A)(1)(a)(ii), etc.).

§ 6.2(A)(1)(a)(ii)

---

§ 6. [section: major division heading]
- 6.2 [subsection] [If heading is appropriate—otherwise, straight to (A).]
  - (A) [paragraph]
    - (1) [subparagraph]
      - (a) [item]
        - (ii) [subitem]

NOT THIS:	BUT THIS:
951.01. County prisoners may be put to labor The board of county commissioners of each county may employ all persons in the jail of their respective counties under sentence upon conviction for crime at labor upon the roads, bridges, or other public works of the county where they are so imprisoned, or on other projects for which the governing body of the county could otherwise lawfully expend public funds and which it determines to be necessary for the health, safety, and welfare of the county. **Fla. Stat. § 951.01.**	**§ 951.01. County prisoners at labor.** A board of county commissioners may employ county prisoners to work on: (A) the roads, bridges, or other public works of the county; or (B) any other project for which the county's governing body can lawfully expend public funds to promote the county's health, safety, and welfare.
§ 211. Printing prices on tickets The owner of every place of amusement shall, if a price be charged for admission thereto, cause to be plainly stamped or printed or written on the face of every ticket to be so used, the established price. Such owner shall likewise cause to be plainly stamped, printed or written on the face of each such ticket the maximum premium, which shall not exceed twenty-five percent (25%) of the price of the ticket or the sum of five dollars ($5.00), whichever shall be more, plus lawful taxes, at which such ticket may be resold or offered for resale, other than under section 2(c) or by ticket brokers duly licensed by a city of the first class as of June 1, 2007. **4 Pa. Cons. Stat. § 211.**	**§ 211. Printing prices on tickets.** (A) **Information required.** The owner of a place of amusement that has an admission charge must plainly stamp, print, or write on the face of every ticket: (1) the established admission price; and (2) the maximum resale premium for which the ticket may be resold. (B) **Maximum resale premium.** The maximum resale premium is limited to 25% of the established admission price or $5—whichever is higher—plus lawful taxes. (C) **Exception.** This section does not apply to tickets resold under § 2.3 or by ticket brokers duly licensed by a city of the first class as of June 1, 2007.

The new number (2.3) reflects the hierarchy established above.

(B) Two-part requirement.

At any level, use a subpart only if there is at least one other corresponding subpart. For example, don't use (A) if you don't have a (B), or (1) if you don't have a (2).

This provision does not have a corresponding (b).

NOT THIS:	BUT THIS:
§ 1-21-1201. Definitions. (a) As used in this article: (i) "Owner" means the owner, lessor or sublessor of a residential rental unit and for purposes of notice and other communication required or allowed under this article, "owner" includes a managing agent, leasing agent or resident manager unless the agent or manager specifies otherwise in writing in the rental agreement; (ii) "Rental agreement" means any agreement, written or oral, which establishes or modifies the terms, conditions, rules or any other provisions regarding the use and occupancy of a residential rental unit, . . . **Wyo. Stat. § 1-21-1201.**	**§ 1-21-1201. Definitions.** The following definitions apply in this article. (A) "Owner" means the owner, lessor, or sublessor of a residential rental unit. For purposes of notice and other communication under this article, "owner" includes a managing agent, leasing agent, or resident manager unless the agent or manager specifies otherwise in writing in the rental agreement. (B) "Rental agreement" means an agreement, written or oral, that establishes or modifies the terms, conditions, rules, or other provisions about using and occupying a residential rental unit. . . .

(C) References to structural divisions.

Generally, include an appropriate reference when needed for clarity—particularly if the other provision is on a different level or is not near the reference. Repeating the rule number—*subject to § 4(h)*—is shorter and better than *subject to item (h) of this section*. But omit the full reference to a provision number when not needed for clarity. For example, when referring to a provision on the same level within the same rule, subdivision, or paragraph, you might state:

(a) Except as provided otherwise in (b), a party must . . . .

NOT THIS:	BUT THIS:
The provisions of section seventy-six-a of this article relating to the operation of a farm winery shall also apply to the holder of a license under this section. **N.Y. Alco. Bev. Cont. Law § 76-d(2).**	Section 76-a of this article, relating to the operation of a farm winery, also applies to a license-holder under this section.
Such lien may be discharged . . . by a failure to bring an action to enforce the same within the time prescribed in the preceding section . . . . **N.Y. Lien Law § 142.**	A lien may be discharged . . . if no enforcement lawsuit is filed within the time prescribed in § 141 . . . .
(f) Subsections (a) through (e) are subject to . . . subsection (g) and the other provisions of this part. **U.C.C. § 9-322.**	(f) Paragraphs* (a) through (e) are subject to . . . (g) and the rest of Article 9, part 3.

*The term *paragraph* is used in accordance with § 3.2(A).

NOT THIS:	BUT THIS:
Fees, service and rental charges; fines; sale of surplus or obsolete materials or equipment; deposit and disbursement of receipts. The board of directors of a library established or maintained under this article may fix, establish,* and collect such reasonable fees, service and rental charges as may be appropriate; may assess fines, penalties, damages, or replacement costs for the loss of, injury to, or failure to return any library property or material; and may sell surplus, duplicated, obsolete, or other unwanted materials or equipment belonging to the library. All moneys received from these or other sources in the course of the administration and operation of the library shall be deposited in the library fund and shall be disbursed by the board of directors in the manner prescribed elsewhere in this article. **W. Va. Code § 10-1-9a.**	**Library income.** (A) **Duties of library board.** The board of directors of a library established or maintained under this article may: (1) establish and collect appropriate and reasonable fees, service charges, and rental charges; (2) assess fines, repair costs, or replacement costs for losing, damaging, or failing to return library property; and (3) sell surplus, duplicate, obsolete, or other unwanted library property. (B) **Receipt and disbursement of funds.** All money received in the course of administering and operating the library must be deposited in the library fund, which the board of directors may use as prescribed in § 10-1-6(c).

The substantive changes in (2) probably improve accuracy: repair should be an option.

*What is the difference between *fixing* a fee and *establishing* it? None.

> "A statute should not only be clear and unambiguous, but readable. It ought not to call for the exercise of a cross-word/acrostic mentality which is able to ferret out the meaning from a number of sections, schedules, and regulations."
>
> —*The Preparation of Legislation* ¶ 6.3, at 28 (Lord Renton ed., 1975) (quoting Sir Robert Micklethwait).

3.3 Numbering of subparts.

(A) Default recommendation.

If you have any discretion on the numbering system, you should adopt a method that progresses logically from higher-order to lower-order provisions. The recommended format has major divisions with Arabic numerals; second-level divisions with a single decimal, arranging the numbers that follow the decimal in ascending order from 1 to 999 without regarding them as parts of a mathematical decimal (in sequence: §§ 1.1 . . . 1.99, 1.100, 1.101 . . . 1.199, 1.200, 1.201 . . . 1.299, etc.); third-level divisions signaled by a capital letter in parentheses; fourth-level divisions signaled by an Arabic numeral in parentheses; and fifth-level divisions signaled by lowercase letters in parentheses.

There are many advantages to this numbering system, one being that you'll do better at establishing sets and subsets than you will with other systems. Sections 6.2 and 6.3 must be subsets of 6—whereas if they were merely (b) and (c) you might get sloppy, as experience shows drafters tend to do. Impose this numbering system, and you'll see.

If you have no discretion on the numbering system, do your best to adapt what you can from the scheme recommended here consistently with the system already used in your jurisdiction.

> "*Divide et impera* is the motto of a draftsman as well as of a conqueror."
> —Lord Thring, *Practical Legislation* 47 (2d ed. 1902).

(B) Consistency.

Whatever your numbering system, be rigorously consistent. Avoid the kinds of off-the-wall conventions that can be found in some jurisdictions. In some states, for example, an insertion between 5 and 6 becomes 5c or 5m for reasons that will be inscrutable to all but insiders at the legislative-drafting bureau. If the subparts within 5 are 5.1–5.4, then the new insertion could become 5.5. Or if the insertion needs to be between 5.1 and 5.2, consider 5.1A or (less good) 5.1.5. Or else it could be added to 6—and the main heading for either 5 or 6 could be adjusted to allow for the new matter.

NOT THIS:	BUT THIS:
Sec. 31-1. Resisting or obstructing a peace officer, firefighter, or correctional institution employee. (a) A person who knowingly resists or obstructs the performance by one known to the person to be a peace officer, firefighter, or correctional institution employee of any authorized act within his or her official capacity commits a Class A misdemeanor. (a-5) In addition to any other sentence that may be imposed, a court shall order any person convicted of resisting or obstructing a peace officer, firefighter, or correctional institution employee to be sentenced to a minimum of 48 consecutive hours of imprisonment or ordered to perform community service for not less than 100 hours as may be determined by the court. The person shall not be eligible for probation in order to reduce the sentence of imprisonment or community service. (a-7) A person convicted for a violation of this Section whose violation was the proximate cause of an injury to a peace officer, firefighter, or correctional institution employee is guilty of a Class 4 felony. **720 Ill. Comp. Stat. 5/31-1.**	**§ 31-1. Resisting or obstructing a peace officer, firefighter, or correctional-institution employee.** (A) **Elements of offense.** It is unlawful to knowingly resist or obstruct another person whom one knows is a peace officer, firefighter, or correctional-institution employee performing an authorized act in an official capacity. (B) **Penalty generally.** Violation of (A) is a Class A misdemeanor punishable by imprisonment of at least 48 consecutive hours or at least 100 hours of community service, in addition to any other sentence the court may impose. The offender is not eligible for probation to reduce the sentence of imprisonment or community service. (C) **Penalty with aggravating circumstances.** If a violation of (A) is the proximate cause of an injury to a peace officer, firefighter, or correctional-institution employee, the violation is a Class 4 felony.

This numbering scheme is outré.

"Good text presentation incorporates the latest techniques to help understanding and avoids things that hinder comprehension. The result is a text that is well organized with typestyle, layout, page color, line length, and indentations all designed to communicate the message in the clearest possible way."

—David C. Elliott, *Plain Language: A Global Perspective*, 70 Mich. B.J. 562, 562 (1991).

(C) Avoiding gaps.

Some legislative schemes "reserve" all sorts of subparts for future amendments, so that numbers will run 1-15, 31-38, 51-55, etc., with nothing in the gaps but "Parts 16-31 reserved," or the like. This practice should be discouraged. Instead, all numbers should be accounted for—especially in a codification project in which the statutory framework has had time to mature. If an issue arises in relation to inserting amended matter into an already fully numbered span of provisions, you can always insert an "A" or "B" provision, etc.:

2. [Major division]
   2A. [inserted major division]
   2B. [inserted major division]
3. [Major division]

This approach is preferable to having gaps in the midst of a numerical system.

In some states, section numbers aren't assigned until after the bill has been passed and approved by the governor. For ease of legislators' reading—as well as the governor's reading—we recommend that the numbering system be introduced earlier in the process.

(D) Avoiding romanettes except as a last resort.

The term "romanette" is the drafter's word for the (i), (ii), (iii), etc. that pervade so much traditional-style drafting. They typify drafting that does not feature hanging indents (see § 1.3)—and that therefore consists of margin-to-margin type. If you do try hanging indents with romanettes, their variable width messes up the indents. Hence they're best avoided, or used only as the last (and sixth) level of subenumeration.

NOT THIS:	BUT THIS:
§ 2-2508. Licensure of place of business, fee, exemptions; record retention. . . . (d)(1) A producer of eggs when selling ungraded eggs of the producer's own flock production is exempted from the provisions of this act if: (A) The producer owns 50 or fewer hens; or (B)(i) The producer owns more than 50 hens but fewer than 250 hens; (ii) eggs are washed and clean; (iii) eggs are prepackaged and labeled as ungraded with the name and address of the producer; (iv) cartons are not reused unless all brand markings and other identification is obliterated and the carton is free of foreign material; (v) sales are to consumers only; and (vi) eggs are maintained at a temperature of 45° Fahrenheit or below. (2) If such producer desires to sell graded eggs, the producer shall be permitted to do so if in compliance with this act. **Kan. Stat. § 2-2508(d).**	**§ 2-2508. Licensure of place of business, fee, exemptions; record retention.** . . . (D) **Exemptions for ungraded eggs.** An egg producer that sells ungraded eggs laid by the producer's own flock is exempt from this act if: (1) the producer owns 50 or fewer hens; or (2) the producer owns more than 50 hens but fewer than 250 hens, and: (a) eggs are washed and clean; (b) eggs are maintained at a temperature of 45° Fahrenheit or below; (c) eggs are prepackaged and labeled as ungraded with the name and address of the producer; (d) cartons are not reused unless all brand markings and other identification is obliterated and the carton is free of foreign material; and (e) sales are to consumers only. (E) **Graded eggs.** An egg producer may sell graded eggs laid by the producer's own hens in accordance with this act.

NOT THIS:	BUT THIS:
§ 120.53. Maintenance of orders; indexing; listing; organizational information. (1)(a) Each agency shall maintain 1. All agency final orders. 2. a. A current hierarchical subject-matter index, identifying for the public any rule or order as specified in this subparagraph. b. In lieu of the requirement for making available for public inspection and copying a hierarchical subject-matter index of its orders, an agency may maintain and make available for public use an electronic database of its orders that allows users to research and retrieve the full texts of agency orders by devising an ad hoc indexing system employing any logical search terms in common usage which are composed by the user and which are contained in the orders of the agency or by descriptive information about the order which may not be specifically contained in the order. c. The agency orders that must be indexed, unless excluded under paragraph (c) or paragraph (d), include: (I) Each final agency order resulting from a proceeding under s. 120.57 or s. 120.573. (II) Each final agency order rendered pursuant to s. 120.57(4) which contains a statement of agency policy that may be the basis of future agency decisions or that may otherwise contain a statement of precedential value. (III) Each declaratory statement issued by an agency. (IV) Each final order resulting from a proceeding under s. 120.56 or s. 120.574. **Fla. Stat. § 120.53(1)(a).**	**§ 120.53. Maintenance of orders; indexing; listing; organizational information.** (A) **Order and index maintenance.** Each agency must maintain: (1) all its final orders; and (2) a current hierarchical subject-matter index, identifying for the public any rule or order as specified in this section. (B) **Electronic database.** To satisfy the requirement that a hierarchical subject-matter index of an agency's orders must be made available for public inspection and copying, an agency may maintain and make available for public use an electronic database of its orders that allows users to research and retrieve the full texts of agency orders. The agency must devise an ad hoc indexing system employing any logical search terms in common usage that are composed by the user and are contained in the agency's orders or by descriptive information about the order that may not be specifically contained in the order. (C) **Mandatory indexing.** Unless excluded under paragraph (G) or paragraph (H), the agency orders that must be indexed include: (1) each final agency order resulting from a proceeding under § 120.57 or 120.573; (2) each final order resulting from a proceeding under § 120.56 or 120.574; (3) each final agency order rendered under § 120.57(4) that contains a statement of agency policy that may be the basis of future agency decisions or that may otherwise contain a statement of precedential value; and (4) each declaratory statement issued by the agency.

3.4 Enumerations.

(A) Setting off enumerated items.

Avoid dense blocks of text by laying out numbered or lettered lists whenever possible on separate lines. Structure new paragraphs, subparagraphs, and items in the order in which they naturally occur, assigning each a new number or letter according to its position in the hierarchy.

NOT THIS:	BUT THIS:
(a) **General rule.** -- It is unlawful for any person at any time to hunt, take or trap game or wildlife of any kind or to discharge any firearm or other deadly weapon into or within, or to dress out game or wildlife within, any cemetery or other burial grounds. **34 Pa. Cons. Stat. § 2506(a).**	(A) **Burial ground.** It is unlawful to: (1) hunt, take, trap, or dress game or wildlife of any kind within a cemetery or other burial ground; or (2) discharge any firearm or other deadly weapon within or into a cemetery or other burial ground.
§ 36. Drive-by shooting. . . . (b) **Offense and Penalties.—** (1) A person who, in furtherance or to escape detection of a major drug offense and with the intent to intimidate, harass, injure, or maim, fires a weapon into a group of two or more persons and who, in the course of such conduct, causes grave risk to any human life shall be punished by a term of no more than 25 years, by fine under this title, or both. **18 U.S.C. § 36(b)(1).**	**§ 36. Drive-by shooting.** . . . (B) **Offense.** It is unlawful to fire a weapon into a group of 2 or more persons: (1) to further a major drug offense or to hinder its detection; (2) with intent to intimidate, harass, injure, or maim; and (3) in the course of the conduct, to cause grave risk to a human life. (C) **Penalty.** Violation of (B) is punishable by imprisonment of up to 25 years or a fine under this title, or both.
385:15-1-1. Purpose The rules of this chapter have been promulgated to establish the requirements and procedures whereby an interested party may acquire an oil and gas mining lease from the State of Oklahoma upon school land. Said rules describe the progressive steps that are required in order to lease these properties by the State's sealed bid process. These rules also describe the bond and fee requirements to obtain a lease, the State's consent to assignments, the grounds for lease cancellation, requirements for well and surface maintenance, price guidelines for the computation of the State's royalty, and those reports required to be filed with the State by the Lessee. **Okla. Admin. Code § 385:15-1-1.**	**15-1-1. Purpose.** These rules establish the requirements and procedures for a person to obtain from the State of Oklahoma a lease to mine oil and gas on school land. The rules prescribe: (A) the sealed-bid process; (B) bond and fee requirements; (C) requirements to obtain consent to assign a lease; (D) grounds for lease cancellation; (E) well- and surface-maintenance requirements; (F) guidelines for computing the State's royalties; and (G) reports required to be filed by the Lessee with the State.

NOT THIS:	BUT THIS:
§ 5. Establishment of funds by each entity of government; contributions; withdrawals Sec. 5. Each entity of government may establish such contingency, emergency, unemployment, reserve, retirement, sinking fund, trust, or similar funds as it shall deem reasonable and proper. Contributions to any such fund, to the extent that such contributions are derived from the proceeds of taxes, shall for purposes of this Article constitute appropriations subject to limitation in the year of contribution. Neither withdrawals from any such fund, nor expenditures of (or authorizations to expend) such withdrawals, nor transfers between or among such funds, shall for purposes of this Article constitute appropriations subject to limitation. **Cal. Const. art. 13B, § 5.**	**§ 5. Governmental entity fund establishment, contribution, and withdrawal.** (A) **Allowable funds.** As it considers reasonable and proper, a governmental entity may establish 1 or more of the following funds: (1) contingency; (2) emergency; (3) unemployment; (4) reserve; (5) retirement; (6) sinking; (7) trust; or (8) similar fund. (B) **Contribution from taxes.** If a contribution to a fund is derived from taxes, it is an appropriation and is subject to a contribution-year limit. (C) **Withdrawal or transfer.** A withdrawal from a fund, or an expenditure of (or authorization to expend) a withdrawal from a fund, or a transfer between or among funds is not an appropriation and is not limited.
(a) Service of legal process upon any corporation of this State shall be made by delivering a copy personally to any officer or director of the corporation in this State, or the registered agent of the corporation in this State, or by leaving it at the dwelling house or usual place of abode in this State of any officer, director or registered agent (if the registered agent be an individual), or at the registered office or other place of business of the corporation in this State. If the registered agent be a corporation, service of process upon it as such agent may be made by serving, in this State, a copy thereof on the president, vice-president, secretary, assistant secretary or any director of the corporate registered agent. Service by copy left at the dwelling house or usual place of abode of any officer, director or registered agent, or at the registered office or other place of business of the corporation in this State, to be effective must be delivered thereat at least 6 days before the return date of the process, and in the presence of an adult person, and the officer serving the process shall distinctly state the manner of service in such person's return thereto. Process returnable forthwith must be delivered personally to the officer, director or registered agent. **Del. Code tit. 8, § 321(a).**	(A) **Serving process.** Legal process on a Delaware corporation must be served in Delaware by: (1) delivering a copy personally to: (a) an officer or director of the corporation; (b) the corporation's registered agent; or (c) the president, vice president, secretary, assistant secretary, or any director of the corporation's registered agent, if the agent is itself a corporation; or (2) leaving a copy at: (a) the residence or usual place of abode of an officer or director of the corporation; (b) the residence or usual place of abode of the corporation's registered agent, if the agent is an individual; or (c) the corporation's registered office or other place of business. (B) **Effective service.** If proof of service is due immediately, process must be served personally to be effective—in accordance with (A)(1). Under (A)(2), for process served to a location to be effective, the serving officer must: (1) serve the process in another adult's presence; (2) serve the process at least 6 days before proof of service is due; and (3) clearly state in the proof of service how the officer served the process.

<table>
<tr><th>NOT THIS:</th><th>BUT THIS:</th></tr>
<tr><td>The master of any vessel which, while engaged in laying or repairing submarine cables, shall fail to observe the rules concerning signals that have been or shall be adopted by the parties to the convention described in section 30 of this title with a view to preventing collisions at sea; or the master of any vessel that, perceiving, or being able to perceive the said signals displayed upon a telegraph ship engaged in repairing a cable, shall not withdraw to or keep at distance of at least one nautical mile; or the master of any vessel that seeing or being able to see buoys intended to mark the position of a cable when being laid or when out of order or broken, shall not keep at a distance of at least a quarter of a nautical mile, shall be guilty of a misdemeanor, and on conviction thereof, shall be liable to imprisonment for a term not exceeding one month, or to a fine of not exceeding $500.
47 U.S.C. § 24.</td><td>(A) Master's requirements. The master of a vessel must:
(1) stay at least 1 nautical mile away from a telegraph ship engaged in repairing a cable if the master can perceive the ship's signals;
(2) stay at least a quarter nautical mile away from a buoy that the master can see and that is intended to mark the position of a cable that is broken, out of order, or being laid; and
(3) observe applicable rules concerning signals (as adopted by the parties to the Convention to prevent collisions at sea) while engaged in laying or repairing submarine cables.
(B) Penalty for failure to comply. Violation of (A) is a misdemeanor punishable by imprisonment for up to 1 month or a maximum fine of $500.</td></tr>
<tr><td>It is unlawful, except through regular channels as duly authorized by the sheriff or officer in charge, to introduce into or possess upon the grounds of any county detention facility as defined in s. 951.23 or to give to or receive from any inmate of any such facility wherever said inmate is located at the time or to take or to attempt to take or send therefrom any of the following articles which are hereby declared to be contraband for the purposes of this act, to wit: Any written or recorded communication; any currency or coin; any article of food or clothing; any tobacco products as defined in s. 210.25(11); any cigarette as defined in s. 210.01(1); any cigar; any intoxicating beverage or beverage which causes or may cause an intoxicating effect; any narcotic, hypnotic, or excitative drug or drug of any kind or nature, including nasal inhalators, sleeping pills, barbiturates, and controlled substances as defined in s. 893.02(4); any firearm or any instrumentality customarily used or which is intended to be used as a dangerous weapon; and any instrumentality of any nature that may be or is intended to be used as an aid in effecting or attempting to effect an escape from a county facility.
Fla. Stat. § 951.22(1).</td><td>(A) Prohibited activities. Unless a contraband article as defined in (B) travels through regular channels authorized by the sheriff or officer in charge, it is unlawful to:
(1) introduce contraband into or possess it on the grounds of a county detention facility as defined in § 951.23;
(2) give contraband to or receive it from a current inmate of a county detention facility; or
(3) take contraband from or send contraband to a county detention facility—or to attempt to do so.
(B) Contraband defined. Under this Act, contraband means:
(1) written or recorded communication;
(2) currency or coin;
(3) food;
(4) article of clothing;
(5) tobacco product as defined in § 210.25(11);
(6) cigarette as defined in § 210.01(1);
(7) cigar;
(8) intoxicating or potentially intoxicating beverage;
(9) narcotic, hypnotic, or excitative drug, or other drug of any kind, including nasal inhalators, sleeping pills, barbiturates, and controlled substances as defined in § 893.02(4);
(10) firearm or instrumentality customarily—or intended to be—used as a dangerous weapon; and
(11) instrumentality that can be or is intended to be used as an aid in an escape attempt from a county facility.</td></tr>
</table>

NOT THIS:	BUT THIS:
§ 1341. Frauds and swindles Whoever, having devised or intending to devise any scheme or artifice to defraud, or for obtaining money or property by means of false or fraudulent pretenses, representations, or promises, or to sell, dispose of, loan, exchange, alter, give away, distribute, supply, or furnish or procure for unlawful use any counterfeit or spurious coin, obligation, security, or other article, or anything represented to be or intimated or held out to be such counterfeit or spurious article, for the purpose of executing such scheme or artifice or attempting so to do, places in any post office or authorized depository for mail matter, any matter or thing whatever to be sent or delivered by the Postal Service, or deposits or causes to be deposited any matter or thing whatever to be sent or delivered by any private or commercial interstate carrier, or takes or receives therefrom, any such matter or thing, or knowingly causes to be delivered by mail or such carrier according to the direction thereon, or at the place at which it is directed to be delivered by the person to whom it is addressed, any such matter or thing, shall be fined under this title or imprisoned not more than 20 years, or both. If the violation occurs in relation to, or involving any benefit authorized, transported, transmitted, transferred, disbursed, or paid in connection with, a presidentially declared major disaster or emergency (as those terms are defined in section 102 of the Robert T. Stafford Disaster Relief and Emergency Assistance Act (42 U.S.C. 5122)), or affects a financial institution, such person shall be fined not more than $1,000,000 or imprisoned not more than 30 years, or both. **18 U.S.C. § 1341.**	**§ 1341. Fraud and swindling.** (A) **Fraud through commerce.** It is unlawful to defraud or attempt to defraud anyone by: (1) placing anything in a post office or authorized depository for mail matter to be sent or delivered by the Postal Service; (2) depositing or causing to be deposited anything to be sent or delivered by a private or commercial interstate carrier; (3) taking or receiving anything from the post office or interstate carrier; or (4) knowingly causing anything to be delivered by mail or interstate carrier according to directions on the thing or directions given by the addressee. (B) **"Defraud" defined.** For purposes of (A), "defraud" means to devise or further a scheme or artifice to: (1) obtain money or property by means of false or fraudulent pretenses, representations, or promises; or (2) sell, dispose of, loan, exchange, alter, give away, distribute, supply, or furnish or procure for unlawful use any counterfeit or spurious coin, obligation, security, or other article, or anything represented to be or intimated or held out to be such counterfeit or spurious article. (C) **Penalty.** A violation of (A) is punishable by a fine or imprisonment of up to 20 years, or both. But a violation of (A) is punishable by a fine up to $1 million or imprisonment of up to 30 years, or both, if the violation: (1) occurs in relation to, or involving any benefit authorized, transported, transmitted, transferred, disbursed, or paid in connection with, a presidentially declared major disaster or emergency (as those terms are defined in 42 U.S.C. § 5122); or (2) affects a financial institution.

Subpart (4) is frankly a guess at the meaning. Study the original, and you're likely to be baffled.

> "Clearness is the main object to be aimed at in drawing Acts of Parliament. Clearness depends, first, on the proper selection of words; secondly, on the arrangement and the construction of sentences."
>
> —Lord Thring, *Practical Legislation* 61 (2d ed. 1902).

NOT THIS:	BUT THIS:
(b) (1) Any person may file with the Secretary an application with respect to any drug subject to the provisions of subsection (a) of this section. Such person shall submit to the Secretary as a part of the application (A) full reports of investigations which have been made to show whether or not such drug is safe for use and whether such drug is effective in use; (B) a full list of the articles used as components of such drug; (C) a full statement of the composition of such drug; (D) a full description of the methods used in, and the facilities and controls used for, the manufacture, processing, and packing of such drug; (E) such samples of such drug and of the articles used as components thereof as the Secretary may require; (F) specimens of the labeling proposed to be used for such drug, and (G) any assessments required under section 355c of this title. The applicant shall file with the application the patent number and the expiration date of any patent which claims the drug for which the applicant submitted the application or which claims a method of using such drug and with respect to which a claim of patent infringement could reasonably be asserted if a person not licensed by the owner engaged in the manufacture, use, or sale of the drug. If an application is filed under this subsection for a drug and a patent which claims such drug or a method of using such drug is issued after the filing date but before approval of the application, the applicant shall amend the application to include the information required by the preceding sentence. Upon approval of the application, the Secretary shall publish information submitted under the two preceding sentences. The Secretary shall, in consultation with the Director of the National Institutes of Health and with representatives of the drug manufacturing industry, review and develop guidance, as appropriate, on the inclusion of women and minorities in clinical trials required by clause (A). **21 U.S.C. § 355(b)(1).**	(B) **Application for drug subject to § 355(A).** (1) ***Requirements.*** A person may file with the Secretary an application for approval of a drug subject to § 355(A). The application must include: (a) full investigation reports showing whether the drug is effective and safe for use; (b) a full list of the articles used as components of the drug; (c) a full statement of the drug's composition; (d) a full description of the methods used in, and the facilities and controls used for, manufacturing, processing, and packing the drug; (e) any sample of the drug or articles used as components of the drug that the Secretary may require; (f) specimens of proposed labeling; and (g) any assessments required under § 355(C). (2) ***Patent information required.*** The applicant must also include the patent number and expiration date of any patent claiming the drug or claiming a method of use if the patent's owner could reasonably assert a patent-infringement claim against an unlicensed person engaged in manufacturing, using, or selling the drug. If such a patent is issued after the application filing date but before approval, the applicant must amend the application to include the above information. When the application is approved, the Secretary will publish the submitted patent information. The Secretary must consult with the Director of the National Institutes of Health and drug-manufacturing-industry representatives to develop guidance, as appropriate, on including women and minorities in clinical trials required by § 355(B)(1)(a).

> "Repetition should be studiously excluded. Nothing need be said doubly or trebly. If a thing is said once and then repeated, the courts, which must presume that the Legislature would not do a vain or foolish thing, will endeavor to ascribe some different meaning to the repetitious language."
>
> —Robert K. Cullen, *Mechanics of Statutory Revision*, 24 Or. L. Rev. 1, 14 (1944).

(B) Appositive for foreshadowing.

When introducing an enumeration, consider using an appositive such as *the following* to foreshadow what will follow. Though not required, this language is often helpful.

<table>
<tr><th>NOT THIS:</th><th>BUT THIS:</th></tr>
<tr><td>§ 204. Venue
An action or proceeding over which the district courts have jurisdiction pursuant to section 203 of this title may be brought in any such court in which save for the arbitration agreement an action or proceeding with respect to the controversy between the parties could be brought, or in such court for the district and division which embraces the place designated in the agreement as the place of arbitration if such place is within the United States.
9 U.S.C. § 204.</td><td>§ 204. Venue.
A lawsuit or proceeding for which jurisdiction is proper under § 203 may be brought in either of the following forums:
(A) a district court where venue for the controversy between the parties would otherwise be proper if no arbitration agreement existed; or
(B) a court for the district and division within the United States that embraces the place of arbitration designated by the arbitration agreement.</td></tr>
<tr><td>(a) Communications and information obtained in the course of treatment or evaluation of any client or patient are confidential information. Such confidential information includes the fact that a person is or has been a client or patient, information transmitted by a patient or client or family thereof for purposes relating to diagnosis or treatment, information transmitted by persons participating in the accomplishment of the objectives of diagnosis or treatment, all diagnoses or opinions formed regarding a client's or patient's physical, mental or emotional condition, any advice, instructions or prescriptions issued in the course of diagnosis or treatment, and any record or characterization of the matters hereinbefore described. It does not include information which does not identify a client or patient, information from which a person acquainted with a client or patient would not recognize such client or patient and uncoded information from which there is no possible means to identify a client or patient.
W. Va. Code § 27-3-1(a).</td><td>(A) Confidential information. Communications and information obtained in the course of treating or evaluating a client or patient are confidential information. Confidential information includes the following:
(1) the fact that the person is or has been a client or patient;
(2) information that the patient or client or his or her family provides for diagnostic or treatment purposes;
(3) information provided by those involved in the diagnosis or treatment;
(4) a diagnosis or opinion about the client's or patient's physical, mental, or emotional condition;
(5) advice, instruction, or prescription issued during diagnosis or treatment; and
(6) any record or characterization of the matters covered in (1)–(5).
(B) Exclusion. Confidential information does not include information that provides no means for a person to identify the client or patient.</td></tr>
</table>

(C) Parallel requirements in parallel form.

When stating more than one requirement—and the requirements can be stated in parallel form—put them in a grammatically matching format. Never set forth grammatically mismatched subparts.

NOT THIS:	BUT THIS:
(b) Trial counsel or defense counsel detailed for a general court-martial must be: (1) a member of the State Bar of Texas; and (2) certified as competent to perform those duties by the state judge advocate general. **Tex. Gov't Code § 432.046(b).**	(B) **Qualifications.** Trial counsel or defense counsel detailed for a general court-martial must be: (1) admitted to the State Bar of Texas; and (2) certified as competent to perform those duties by the state judge advocate general.
Discharge of lien Such lien may be discharged by a payment of the amount due thereon, by a failure to bring an action to enforce the same within the time prescribed in the preceding section, by the written consent of the lienor, duly acknowledged and filed with the proper officer to the effect that such lien may be discharged, and by the owner of such sandstone, cement stone, granite, bluestone, limestone or marble filing with such officer an undertaking in an amount equal to twice the sum specified in the notice of lien, executed by one or more sureties who shall justify in such amount and approved by the officer with whom the notice of lien is filed, conditioned for the payment of the sum due such lienor, by reason of such lien, and the cost and expenses of enforcing the same. **N.Y. Lien Law § 142.**	**Discharge of lien.** A lien under § 140 may be discharged if: (A) payment is made in the amount due on the lien; (B) no enforcement lawsuit is brought within the time prescribed under § 141; (C) the lienholder* consents in writing to discharge the lien and that writing is duly acknowledged and filed with the proper officer; or (D) the owner files an undertaking with the proper officer that:† (1) is in an amount equal to 2 times the sum specified in the notice of lien; (2) is executed by 1 or more sureties that have justified the amount; (3) is approved by the officer with whom the notice of lien is filed; and (4) is conditioned on payment of: (a) the amount due under the lien; and (b) the cost and expenses of enforcing the lien.

#1 is a noun phrase.

#2 is a predicate beginning with the completion of a verb phrase.

This listing (A)–(D) is grammatically parallel: each item is an independent clause.

The listing after the word *undertaking* is unparallel.

The listing (1)–(4) is grammatically parallel: each item completes the sentence.

**Lienholder* is superior to *lienor*: see *Garner's Dictionary of Legal Usage* 545 (3d ed. 2011).

†Note that *is* cannot be moved before the colon and deleted in the enumerated items because grammatical parallelism would then be destroyed. That particular edit would make #1 begin with a prepositional phrase functioning adjectivally and #2 through #4 begin with past participles that complete the verb phrase.

> "Consistency between the items in a series . . . requires that the introductory word be appropriate for each item. The reader should be able to read the introductory phrase in conjunction with each item in the series and have it make sense."
>
> —Thomas R. Haggard, *Legal Drafting in a Nutshell* 155 (1996).

(D) Economy of parallelism.

To eliminate repetition and verbiage in enumerations, place terms shared by each of the enumerated items in the lead-in to the list.

NOT THIS:	BUT THIS:
(a) IN GENERAL.—It shall be unlawful for an employing office to intimidate, take reprisal against, or otherwise discriminate against, any covered employee because the covered employee has opposed any practice made unlawful by this chapter, or because the covered employee has initiated proceedings, made a charge, or testified, assisted, or participated in any manner in a hearing or other proceeding under this chapter. **3 U.S.C. § 417(a).**	(A) **Generally.** It is unlawful for an employing office to intimidate, take reprisal against, or otherwise discriminate against any covered employee who has: (1) opposed any practice made unlawful by this chapter; or (2) initiated a proceeding, made a charge, or testified, assisted, or participated in any manner in a hearing or other proceeding under this chapter.
The chain of custody of blood or genetic specimens taken for testing may be established through verified documentation of each change of custody if: (1) the documentation was made at or around the time of the change of custody; (2) the documentation was made in the course of a regularly conducted business activity; and (3) the documentation was made as a regular practice of a business activity. **Ind. Code § 31-14-6-5.**	The chain of custody for blood or genetic specimens taken for testing may be established through verified documentation of each change of custody if the documentation was made: (A) at or around the time of the change of custody; (B) in the course of regularly conducted business activity; and (C) as a regular practice of a business activity.
A prescription drug or medical device is not reasonably safe because of inadequate instructions or warnings when (1) reasonable instructions or warnings regarding foreseeable risks of harm posed by the drug or medical device are not provided to prescribing and other health care providers who are in a position to reduce the risks of harm in accordance with the instructions or warnings; or (2) reasonable instructions or warnings regarding foreseeable risks of harm posed by the drug or medical device are not provided directly to the patient when the manufacturer knew or had reason to know that no health care provider would be in a position to reduce the risks of harm in accordance with the instructions or warnings. **Restatement (Third) of Torts: Products Liability § 8(d) (Tentative Draft No. 2, 1995).**	A prescription drug or medical device is considered not reasonably safe because of inadequate instructions or warnings if reasonable instructions or warnings about foreseeable risks of harm the drug or device poses are not provided to: (A) prescribing and other healthcare providers who are in a position to reduce the risks according to the instructions or warnings; or (B) the patient directly, when the manufacturer knows or has reason to know that no healthcare provider would be in such a position.

The listing (A)–(C) consists of adverbial modifiers.

<table>
<tr><th>NOT THIS:</th><th>BUT THIS:</th></tr>
<tr><td>Work product immunity applies to material or its intangible equivalent if:
(a) The material records or reflects litigation investigation or analysis, but work product does not include facts;
(b) The material was prepared by or for a party or a party's representative, including a party's lawyer, consultant, surety, indemnitor, insurer, or agent; and
(c) The material was prepared in anticipation of litigation, that is, it was prepared for litigation then in progress or its preparation was primarily motivated by the prospect of future litigation.
Restatement of the Law Governing Lawyers § 136(1) (Tentative Draft No. 5, 1992).</td><td>Work-product immunity applies to material or its intangible equivalent if it:
(A) records or reflects litigation investigation or analysis—though work product does not include facts themselves;
(B) was prepared by or for a party or a party's representative, including a party's lawyer, consultant, surety, indemnitor, insurer, or agent; and
(C) was prepared for litigation in progress or anticipated.</td></tr>
<tr><td>[T]he seller shall furnish to the purchaser the following:
(a) Copies of the proposed or existing declaration, the bylaws, and any rules or regulations;
(b) A copy of the proposed or existing articles of incorporation of the association, if it is or is to be incorporated.
(c) A copy of any proposed or existing management contract, employment contract or other contract affecting the use, maintenance or access of all or part of the condominium to which it is anticipated the unit owners or the association will be a party following closing.
(d) A copy of the projected annual operating budget for the condominium including reasonable details concerning the estimated monthly payments by the purchaser for assessments, and monthly charges for the use, rental or lease of any facilities not part of the condominium.
(e) A copy of any lease to which it is anticipated the unit owners or the association will be a party following closing. . . .
Wis. Stat. § 703.33(1).</td><td>(A) Seller's obligations. The seller must give the purchaser a copy of:
(1) the proposed or existing declaration, the bylaws, and any rules or regulations;
(2) the association's proposed or existing articles of incorporation, if it is or will be incorporated;
(3) any proposed or existing management, employment, or other contract affecting the use of, maintenance of, or access to all or part of the condominium to which it is anticipated the unit owners or the association will be a party after closing;
(4) the projected annual operating budget for the condominium, including reasonable details related to the purchaser's estimated monthly payments for assessments, and monthly charges for the use, rental, or lease of any facilities not part of the condominium; and
(5) any lease to which it is anticipated the unit owners or the association will be a party after closing.</td></tr>
</table>

Note that the revision uses a singular noun, whereas the original is inconsistent. See § 2.4.

"It is unfortunate that many lawyers persist in using the word 'ambiguity' to include vagueness. To subsume both concepts under the same name tends to imply that there is no difference between them or that their differences are legally unimportant. Ambiguity is a disease of language, whereas vagueness, which is sometimes a disease, is often a positive benefit. With at least this significant difference between the two concepts, it is helpful to refer to them by different names."

—Reed Dickerson, *The Diseases of Legislative Language*, 1 Harv. J. on Legis. 5, 10 (1964) (footnotes omitted).

NOT THIS:	BUT THIS:
Employment qualifications. No person shall be employed as a Private Security Officer in Guam unless they first meet the following qualifications: (1) He must be at least eighteen (18) years of age; (2) He must be a citizen of the United States or a resident alien; (3) He must not have been convicted in any jurisdiction of any felony for which a full pardon has not been granted; (4) He must not have been declared by any court of competent jurisdiction incompetent by reason of mental disease or defect unless competency has been restored him; (5) He must not suffer from habitual drunkenness or from narcotic addiction or dependence; (6) He must not possess any medical or physical disability which in the judgement of the employer prevents him from performing the duties of a Private Security Officer; and (7) He must not have been discharged from the military service under other than honorable conditions. **10 Guam Code § 71301.**	(A) **Employment qualifications.** To be employed as a private security officer in Guam, a person must: (1) be at least 18 years of age; (2) be a citizen of the United States or a resident alien; (3) not have a felony conviction in any jurisdiction, unless a full pardon was granted; (4) not have been declared incompetent by reason of mental disease or defect by any court of competent jurisdiction, unless competency has been restored; (5) not suffer from habitual drunkenness or narcotic addiction or dependence; (6) not have any medical or physical disability that, in the judgment of the employer, prevents the person from performing the duties of a private security officer; and (7) not have been discharged from the military service other than honorably.

NOT THIS:	BUT THIS:
(b) **Penalties.**— The punishment for a violation of section (a) or an attempt or conspiracy to violate subsection (a) shall be— (1) a fine under this title or imprisonment not more than 1 year, or both, if the offense does not instill in another the reasonable fear of serious bodily injury or death and— (A) the offense results in no economic damage or bodily injury; or (B) the offense results in economic damage that does not exceed $10,000; (2) a fine under this title or imprisonment for not more than 5 years, or both, if no bodily injury occurs and— (A) the offense results in economic damage exceeding $10,000 but not exceeding $100,000; or (B) the offense instills in another the reasonable fear of serious bodily injury or death; (3) a fine under this title or imprisonment for not more than 10 years, or both, if— (A) the offense results in economic damage exceeding $100,000;* or (B) the offense results in substantial bodily injury to another individual; (4) a fine under this title or imprisonment for not more than 20 years, or both, if— (A) the offense results in serious bodily injury to another individual; or (B) the offense results in economic damage exceeding $1,000,000; and (5) imprisonment for life or for any terms of years, a fine under this title, or both, if the offense results in death of another individual. **18 U.S.C. § 43(b).**	(B) **Penalties.** Violation of (A), an attempt to violate (A), or conspiracy to violate (A) is punishable by fine or imprisonment, or both. Length of imprisonment is: (1) up to 1 year if the offense does not cause another person to reasonably fear death or serious bodily injury, and: (a) the offense resulted in no bodily injury; or (b) the economic damage is $10,000 or less; (2) up to 5 years if the offense resulted in no bodily injury, and: (a) the offense caused another person to reasonably fear death or serious bodily injury; or (b) the economic damage is more than $10,000 but no more than $100,000; (3) up to 10 years if: (a) the offense resulted in substantial bodily injury to another person; or (b) the economic damage is more than $100,000 but not more than $1 million; (4) up to 20 years if: (a) the offense resulted in serious bodily injury to another person; or (b) the economic damage exceeds $1 million; or (5) up to and including life if the offense resulted in a person's death.

*Notice the substantive flaw: (3) doesn't specify a range up to $1 million. Under the rule of lenity, (4) should never come into play.

> "There is nothing so discouraging as a long block of solid type. A page of unbroken type is enough to weary and challenge even the most astute minds. Ten to fifteen lines of solid type are usually quite enough; anything from fifteen to twenty-five lines should be re-examined; and anything over twenty-five lines should be broken up."
>
> —Elmer A. Driedger, *The Composition of Legislation* 108 (1957).

(E) Unnumbered "dangling" flush text.

Avoid unnumbered "dangling" sections—that is, flush-left text that, following an enumeration, has no numbered designation. One way to do this is to put enumerations uniformly at the end of a sentence—not at the beginning or in the middle. Each subpart must be assigned a letter or number.

There is a notorious instance of unnumbered dangling flush text—too long to print here—in the Bankruptcy Code. It is contemptuously known in the field as "the hanging paragraph." To avoid its scandal, avert your eyes from 11 U.S.C. § 1325(a)(9).

NOT THIS:	BUT THIS:
(a) **In General.**— Whoever— (1) is required to register under the Sex Offender Registration and Notification Act; (2) (A) is a sex offender as defined for the purposes of the Sex Offender Registration and Notification Act by reason of a conviction under Federal law (including the Uniform Code of Military Justice), the law of the District of Columbia, Indian tribal law, or the law of any territory or possession of the United States; or (B) travels in interstate or foreign commerce, or enters or leaves, or resides in, Indian country; and (3) knowingly fails to register or update a registration as required by the Sex Offender Registration and Notification Act; shall be fined under this title or imprisoned not more than 10 years, or both. (b) **Affirmative Defense.**— In a prosecution for a violation under subsection (a), it is an affirmative defense that— (1) uncontrollable circumstances prevented the individual from complying; (2) the individual did not contribute to the creation of such circumstances in reckless disregard of the requirement to comply; and (3) the individual complied as soon as such circumstances ceased to exist. (c) **Crime of Violence.**— (1) In general.— An individual described in subsection (a) who commits a crime of violence under Federal law (including the Uniform Code of Military Justice), the law of the District of Columbia, Indian tribal law, or the law of any territory or possession of the United States shall be imprisoned for not less than 5 years and not more than 30 years. (2) Additional punishment.— The punishment provided in paragraph (1) shall be in addition and consecutive to the punishment provided for the violation described in subsection (a). **18 U.S.C. § 2250.**	(A) **Requirement to register.** It is unlawful for a person who is required to register under the Sex Offender Registration and Notification Act to knowingly fail to register or update the required registration and: (1) be a sex offender as defined by the Sex Offender Registration and Notification Act because of a conviction under United States law; (2) travel in interstate or foreign commerce; or (3) enter, leave, or reside in Indian country. (B) **Definition.** "United States law" means any federal law—including the Uniform Code of Military Justice—and the laws of the District of Columbia, Indian tribes, and United States territories and possessions. (C) **Uncontrollable-circumstances defense.** It is an affirmative defense to a violation of (A) that an uncontrollable circumstance prevented the person from complying—but the person must have complied with (A) as soon as the circumstance ceased to exist and must not have contributed to creating the circumstance by recklessly disregarding (A). (D) **Penalty.** Violating this Act may result in a fine or imprisonment for up to 10 years, or both. (E) **Enhancement for crimes of violence.** A person who violates (A) and also commits a violent crime under United States law may be imprisoned for 5 to 30 years, to be served consecutively with any penalty imposed under (D).

NOT THIS:	BUT THIS:
SEC. 3. MINIMUM SOUND REQUIREMENT FOR MOTOR VEHICLES. (a) Rulemaking Required.-Not later than 18 months after the date of enactment of this Act [Jan. 4, 2011] the Secretary shall initiate rulemaking, under section 30111 of title 49, United States Code, to promulgate a motor vehicle safety standard- (1) establishing performance requirements for an alert sound that allows blind and other pedestrians to reasonably detect a nearby electric or hybrid vehicle operating below the cross-over speed, if any; and (2) requiring new electric or hybrid vehicles to provide an alert sound conforming to the requirements of the motor vehicle safety standard established under this subsection. The motor vehicle safety standard established under this subsection shall not require either driver or pedestrian activation of the alert sound and shall allow the pedestrian to reasonably detect a nearby electric or hybrid vehicle in critical operating scenarios including, but not limited to, constant speed, accelerating, or decelerating. The Secretary shall allow manufacturers to provide each vehicle with one or more sounds that comply with the motor vehicle safety standard at the time of manufacture. Further, the Secretary shall require manufacturers to provide, within reasonable manufacturing tolerances, the same sound or set of sounds for all vehicles of the same make and model and shall prohibit manufacturers from providing any mechanism for anyone other than the manufacturer or the dealer to disable, alter, replace, or modify the sound or set of sounds, except that the manufacturer or dealer may alter, replace, or modify the sound or set of sounds in order to remedy a defect or non-compliance with the motor vehicle safety standard. The Secretary shall promulgate the required motor vehicle safety standard pursuant to this subsection not later than 36 months after the date of enactment of this Act. **Pedestrian Safety Enhancement Act of 2010, 111 P.L. 373, 124 Stat. 4086.**	**3. Minimum Sound Requirement for Motor Vehicles.** (A) **Regulations required.** By July 4, 2012, the Secretary will start rulemaking under 49 U.S.C. § 30111 to promulgate a motor-vehicle safety standard. This standard must: (1) establish performance requirements for an alert sound that warns blind and other pedestrians of a nearby electric or hybrid vehicle operating below the crossover speed; and (2) require new electric or hybrid vehicles to provide an alert sound conforming to those performance requirements. (B) **Effect on driver or pedestrian.** The standard established under (A): (1) must not require a driver or pedestrian to activate the sound; and (2) must allow a pedestrian to reasonably detect a nearby electric or hybrid vehicle in critical operating scenarios, including constant speed, accelerating, and decelerating. (C) **Manufacturer specifications.** The Secretary must allow manufacturers to provide each vehicle with 1 or more alert sounds complying with the standard. Additionally, the Secretary must: (1) require manufacturers to provide—within reasonable manufacturing tolerance—the same sound or sounds for all vehicles of the same make and model; and (2) prohibit manufacturers from providing any mechanism for anyone to modify the sound or sounds—but the manufacturer or dealer may alter or replace the sound or sounds to remedy a defect or noncompliance with this standard. (D) **Deadline.** The Secretary must promulgate the required standard under (A) no later than 36 months after this Act's enactment date.

Unnumbered dangling flush text.

"One of the hardest things for a lawyer to do is to write short sentences."
—Alfred F. Conard, *New Ways to Write Laws*, 56 Yale L.J. 458, 474 (1947).

(F) Bullets.

Use bullets to ease the reading of a list only if no citation to any individual item is likely. As in the first example, "dangling" text is unobjectionable after a list of bulleted items because the numbering sequence hasn't been broken. Use bullets sparingly in legislation.

<table>
<tr><th>NOT THIS:</th><th>BUT THIS:</th></tr>
<tr><td>As between client and lawyer, decisions such as the following are allocated to the client within the meaning of § 32(3) and may not be irrevocably delegated to the lawyer: whether and on what terms to settle a claim; how to plead in a criminal prosecution; whether to choose to waive jury trial in a criminal prosecution; whether to testify in a criminal prosecution; and whether to appeal in a civil proceeding or criminal prosecution. A client may from time to time authorize a lawyer to make those decisions for the client, except to the extent that other law (such as criminal procedure rules governing pleas, jury trial waiver, and defendant testimony) requires the client's personal participation or approval.
Restatement (Third) of the Law Governing Lawyers § 33 (Tentative Draft No. 5, 1992).</td><td>Between client and lawyer, certain decisions are allocated to the client under § 32(3) and cannot be irrevocably delegated to the lawyer. These decisions include:
• whether and on what terms to settle a claim;
• how to plead in a criminal prosecution;
• whether to waive jury trial in a criminal prosecution;
• whether to testify in a criminal prosecution; and
• whether to appeal in a civil or criminal case.
A client may on occasion authorize a lawyer to make those decisions, unless other law (such as criminal-procedure rules governing pleas, jury-trial waiver, and defendant testimony) requires the client's personal participation or approval.</td></tr>
<tr><td>The flag should be displayed on all days, especially on New Year's Day, January 1; Inauguration Day, January 20; Martin Luther King Jr.'s birthday, third Monday in January; Lincoln's Birthday, February 12; Washington's Birthday, third Monday in February; Easter Sunday (variable); Mother's Day, second Sunday in May; Armed Forces Day, third Saturday in May; Memorial Day (half-staff until noon), the last Monday in May; Flag Day, June 14; Father's Day, third Sunday in June; Independence Day, July 4; National Korean War Veterans Armistice Day, July 27; Labor Day, first Monday in September; Constitution Day, September 17; Columbus Day, second Monday in October; Navy Day, October 27; Veterans Day, November 11; Thanksgiving Day, fourth Thursday in November; Christmas Day, December 25; and such other days as may be proclaimed by the President of the United States; the birthdays of States (date of admission); and on State holidays.
4 U.S.C. § 6(d).</td><td>The flag should be displayed on all days, especially the following:
• January: New Year's Day, January 1; Inauguration Day, January 20; Martin Luther King Jr.'s birthday, third Monday in January;
• February: Lincoln's Birthday, February 12; Washington's Birthday, third Monday in February;
• March/April: Easter Sunday (variable);
• May: Mother's Day, second Sunday in May; Armed Forces Day, third Saturday in May; Memorial Day (half-staff until noon), last Monday in May;
• June: Flag Day, June 14; Father's Day, third Sunday in June;
• July: Independence Day, July 4; National Korean War Veterans Armistice Day, July 27;
• September: Labor Day, first Monday in September; Constitution Day, September 17;
• October: Columbus Day, second Monday in October; Navy Day, October 27;
• November: Veterans Day, November 11; Thanksgiving Day, fourth Thursday in November;
• December: Christmas Day, December 25; and
• Additional: other days proclaimed by the President of the United States; the dates of admission of States; and State holidays.</td></tr>
</table>

Flush text is acceptable after bullets. See § 3.4(F).

(G) Capitalization.

As long as the syntax of a sentence flows from one subpart into the next, without a sentence-ending period, begin each enumerated item with a lowercase character—not uppercase. Only stand-alone provisions should begin with a capital letter.

NOT THIS:	BUT THIS:
Unclaimed animals. A political subdivision or a person contracting under s. 173.15 (1) that has custody of an animal considered unclaimed under sub. (5)(c) or (6) or s. 173.13 (3)(c) or 173.19 or an unwanted animal may do any of the following: (a) Release the animal to any person other than the owner if all of the following apply: 1. The person provides his or her name and address. 2. If licensure is required by statute or ordinance, the animal is licensed or assurance of licensure is given by evidence of prepayment. 3. If vaccination is required by statute or ordinance, the animal is vaccinated or assurance of vaccination is given by evidence of prepayment. 4. Any charges imposed by the political subdivision or person contracting under s. 173.15 (1) for custody, care, vaccination and treatment are paid or waived. (b) If the animal is not a dog or cat, sell the animal at public auction, including sale at a licensed animal market. (c) Euthanize the animal. (d) If the animal is a stray or abandoned dog, release the dog under s. 174.13. **Wis. Stat. § 173.23(1m).**	(A) **Unclaimed animals.** A political subdivision or a person that contracts under § 173.15(1) and that has custody of an unwanted animal or an animal considered unclaimed under § 173.15(5)(c), 173.15(6), 173.13(3)(c), or 173.19 may do any of the following: (1) release the animal to a person other than the owner if: (a) the recipient provides his or her name and address; (b) the animal is licensed (if required by statute or ordinance), or assurance of licensure is given by evidence of prepayment; (c) the animal is vaccinated (if required by statute or ordinance), or assurance of vaccination is given by evidence of prepayment; and (d) any charges imposed by the political subdivision or contracting person for custody, care, vaccination, and treatment are paid or waived; (2) release the animal if it is a stray or abandoned dog under § 174.13; (3) sell the animal at public auction if it is not a dog or cat, including sale at a licensed animal market; or (4) euthanize the animal.

"As are the words, such is the law. Laws can only be made with words. Life, liberty, property, honour—everything which is dear to us—depends upon the choice of words."

—Jeremy Bentham, "A General View of a Complete Code of Laws," in 3 *The Works of Jeremy Bentham* 155, 207–08 (John Bowring ed., 1843).

Note the unidiomatic pairing of *require* with *from*, as opposed to *to*: the revision uses *to* with both *require* and (in compliance with traditional legal usage) *prohibit*. See *Garner's Dictionary of Legal Usage* 717 (3d ed. 2011).

NOT THIS:	BUT THIS:
§ 19-0919. General powers 1. Nothing in this title shall be construed to require or prohibit the department from: a. extending compliance schedules, issuing variances or relaxing performance standards at any specific facility or stationary source, so long as such extension, issuance or relaxation does not result in: (i) violation of any primary federal ambient air quality standard or any state ambient air quality standard; or (ii) failure to make reasonable further progress in a non-attainment area pursuant to the federal clean air act; or (iii) failure to attain the interim control target pursuant to section 19-0909 of this title; or (iv) failure to attain the final control target pursuant to section 19-0911 of this title; or (v) violation of the nitrogen control program pursuant to section 19-0913 of this title; or (vi) creation of a public or private nuisance. b. Continuing any special limitations until January first, nineteen hundred ninety-six or reauthorize any special limitation which has expired after the effective date of this title and prior to January first, nineteen hundred eighty-six. c. Allowing any conversion or modification of a facility or stationary source to burn coal as a boiler fuel. 2. Nothing in this title shall be construed to establish a statewide cap or limitation on acid deposition precursors such that new sources would be excluded for the state. **N.Y. Envtl. Conserv. Law § 19-0919.**	**§ 19-0919. General powers.** (A) **Discretionary authority.** This title does not require or prohibit the department to: (1) extend compliance schedules, issue variances, or relax performance standards at a facility or stationary source, as long as the extension, issuance, or relaxation does not result in the: (a) violation of a primary federal or state ambient-air-quality standard; (b) failure to make reasonable further progress in a nonattainment area under the federal Clean Air Act; (c) failure to attain the interim control target under § 19-0909; (d) failure to attain the final control target under § 19-0911; (e) violation of the nitrogen-control program under § 19-0913; or (f) creation of a public or private nuisance; (2) continue a special limit until January 1, 1996, or reauthorize a special limit expiring after this title's effective date and before January 1, 1986; and (3) allow any facility or stationary source to be converted or modified to burn coal as a boiler fuel. (B) **No cap on acid-deposition precursors.** This title does not establish a statewide cap or limit on acid-deposition precursors that would exclude new sources for the state.

"Overdefining bedevils modern legal documents. . . . Drafters feel compelled to define every term, even terms that are used once only or in one clause only. The result is page after page of definitions."
—Peter Butt & Richard Castle, *Modern Legal Drafting* 119 (2001).

NOT THIS:	BUT THIS:
§ 316. Prescription monitoring program. (a) The Department must provide for a prescription monitoring program for Schedule II, III, IV, and V controlled substances that includes the following components and requirements: (1) The dispenser must transmit to the central repository, in a form and manner specified by the Department, the following information: (A) The recipient's name. (B) The recipient's address. (C) The national drug code number of the controlled substance dispensed. (D) The date the controlled substance is dispensed. (E) The quantity of the controlled substance dispensed. (F) The dispenser's United States Drug Enforcement Administration registration number. (G) The prescriber's United States Drug Enforcement Administration registration number. (H) The dates the controlled substance prescription is filled. (I) The payment type used to purchase the controlled substance (i.e.* Medicaid, cash, third party insurance). (J) The patient location code (i.e. home, nursing home, outpatient, etc.) for the controlled substances other than those filled at a retail pharmacy. (K) Any additional information that may be required by the department by administrative rule, including but not limited to information required for compliance with the criteria for electronic reporting of the American Society for Automation and Pharmacy or its successor. **720 Ill. Comp. Stat. 570/316(a)(1).**	**§ 316. Prescription-monitoring program.** (A) The Department must provide a prescription-monitoring program for Schedule II, III, IV, and V controlled substances. The program must include the following components and requirements: (1) in the form and manner specified by the Department, the dispenser must forward the following information to a central repository: (a) recipient's name; (b) recipient's address; (c) national drug-code number of the controlled substance dispensed; (d) date the controlled substance was dispensed; (e) quantity of the controlled substance dispensed; (f) dispenser's United States Drug Enforcement Administration registration number; (g) prescriber's United States Drug Enforcement Administration registration number; (h) date the controlled-substance prescription was filled; (i) payment type used to purchase the controlled substance—Medicaid, cash, third-party insurance, etc.; (j) patient-location code—home, nursing home, outpatient, etc.—for a controlled substance not filled at a retail pharmacy; and (k) any additional information that the department requires by administrative rule, including information required for compliance with the criteria for electronic reporting of the American Society for Automation and Pharmacy or its successor.

*The statute appears to misuse *i.e.* for *e.g.* See *Garner's Modern English Usage* 480 (4th ed. 2016).

> "Definition can be taken only so far. Using different words by way of description or explanation or paraphrase can in itself change the meaning or alter the emphasis. The definition can itself be subjected to relentless and subtle interpretation, distracting attention from the word itself. At the end of the day it may simply be undesirable, unnecessary, even impossible, to take the matter any further. A dog is a dog is a dog."
>
> —Alec Samuels, *Stalking Defined*, 18 Statute L. Rev. 244, 245–46 (1997).

(H) Avoiding unhelpful enumeration, or "splintering."

NOT THIS:	BUT THIS:
§ 27-75-3. Enactment of compact. (8) To adopt uniform mandatory rules with respect to regulatory compliance requirements for: (i) Foreign insurer eligibility requirements; (ii) Surplus lines policyholder notices; . . . . **R.I. Gen. Laws § 27-75-3, art. I (8).**	**§ 27-75-3. Enactment of compact.** (8) **Uniform rules.** To adopt uniform, mandatory rules governing regulatory compliance for foreign-insurer-eligibility requirements and surplus-lines-policyholder notices; . . . .
§ 371a. Exemptions from registration. (a) Notwithstanding any other provisions of law relating to registration fees for trailers the following shall be exempt from registration: (1) wood splitters; and (2) pole dinkeys. (b) When any such trailer is used upon a public highway it shall have attached a red reflector which shall be so displayed as to be clearly visible from the rear, under normal atmospheric conditions, or a reflectorized slow moving vehicle symbol of a standard type approved by the Commissioner. (c) A person in violation of this section shall be fined not more than $25.00 for each offense. **Vt. Stat. tit. 23, § 371a.**	**§ 371a. Exemption from registration.** (A) **Exempt trailers.** Despite any other provisions of law relating to registration fees for trailers, wood splitters and pole dinkeys are exempt from registration. (B) **Mandatory reflectors.** When a wood splitter or pole dinkey is used on a public highway it must have attached: (1) a red reflector clearly visible from the rear under normal atmospheric conditions; or (2) a reflectorized slow-moving-vehicle symbol of a standard type approved by the Commissioner. (C) **Penalty.** Violation of (B) is punishable by a fine of up to $25 for each offense.

"Special definitions should be sparingly used, and only for the purpose of avoiding tedious repetitions, or of explaining terms which would be ambiguous without them."

—Sir Courtenay Ilbert, *Legislative Methods and Forms* 281 (1901).

3.5 Key Terms and Their Definitions.

(A) Sparing use of definitions.

Minimize defined terms by (1) resorting to them only when no other device works well; and (2) trying instead to explain your meaning in the immediate context.

NOT THIS:	BUT THIS:
Submission of copy of accident report to Department of Transportation. Each state and local law enforcement agency shall submit to the Department of Transportation the original document of any accident report prepared by such law enforcement agency or submitted to such agency by a member of the public. If the Department of Driver Services receives a claim requesting determination of security, the Department of Transportation shall provide a copy or an electronic copy of any relevant accident reports to the Department of Driver Services. Any law enforcement agency may transmit the information contained on the accident report form by electronic means, provided that the Department of Transportation has first given approval to the reporting agency for the electronic reporting method utilized. The law enforcement agency shall retain a copy of each accident report. Any law enforcement agency that transmits the data by electronic means must transmit the data using a nonproprietary interchangeable electronic format and reporting method. For purposes of this Code section, the term "nonproprietary" shall include commonly used report formats. All such reports shall be submitted to the Department of Transportation not more than 15 days following the end of the month in which such report was prepared or received by such law enforcement agency. The Department of Transportation is authorized to engage the services of a third party in fulfilling its responsibilities under this Code section. **Ga. Code § 40-9-31.***	**Submitting accident report to Department of Transportation.** (A) **Original required; deadline.** A state or local law-enforcement agency must submit each original accident report to the Department of Transportation—whether the report was prepared by the agency or submitted to the agency by a member of the public. The report must be submitted no later than 15 days after the end of the month in which the agency prepared or received the report. (B) **Copy of report.** The law-enforcement agency must retain a copy of each accident report. (C) **Requirements for electronic copy.** The information contained in the accident report may be sent electronically if (1) the Department of Transportation has given preapproval, and (2) the report is in an electronic format that is commonly used and readily available. (D) **Request made to Department of Driver Services.** If the Department of Driver Services receives a request for determination of security, the Department of Transportation must provide a physical or electronic copy of any relevant accident report to the Department of Driver Services. (E) **Third-party services.** The Department of Transportation may engage third-party services to fulfill its responsibilities under this section.

Strange and unnecessary definition of *nonproprietary.*

*Note that this example also appears at § 3.1(A).

(B) Placement.

With a provision-specific defined term, generally use it first and then promptly define it—as opposed to defining it before using it.

NOT THIS:	BUT THIS:
§ 874 Kickbacks from public works employees. Whoever, by force, intimidation, or threat of procuring dismissal from employment, or by any other manner whatsoever induces any person employed in the construction, prosecution, completion or repair of any public building, public work, or building or work financed in whole or in part by loans or grants from the United States, to give up any part of the compensation to which he is entitled under his contract of employment, shall be fined under this title or imprisoned not more than five years, or both. **18 U.S.C. § 874.**	**§ 874 Kickback from public-works employee.** (A) **Offense.** It is unlawful to use force, intimidation, threat of procuring dismissal from employment, or other method to induce a person employed in the construction, prosecution, completion, or repair of a public building, to give up any compensation owed to that person under an employment contract. (B) **Definition of public building.** "Public building" in (A) includes a public work and a building or work financed in whole or in part by a loan or grant from the United States. (C) **Penalty.** Violation of (A) is punishable by imprisonment of up to 5 years or a fine, or both.
Every common carrier by railroad while engaging in commerce between any of the several States or Territories, or between any of the States and Territories, or between the District of Columbia and any of the States or Territories, or between the District of Columbia or any of the States or Territories and any foreign nation or nations, shall be liable in damages to any person suffering injury while he is employed by such carrier in such commerce, or, in case of the death of such employee, to his or her personal representative, for the benefit of the surviving widow or husband and children of such employee; and, if none, then of such employee's parents; and, if none, then of the next of kin dependent upon such employee, for such injury or death resulting in whole or in part from the negligence of any of the officers, agents, or employees of such carrier, or by reason of any defect or insufficiency, due to its negligence, in its cars, engines, appliances, machinery, track, roadbed, works, boats, wharves, or other equipment. Any employee of a carrier, any part of whose duties as such employee shall be the furtherance of interstate or foreign commerce; or shall, in any way directly or closely and substantially, affect such commerce as above set forth shall, for the purposes of this chapter, be considered as being employed by such carrier in such commerce and shall be considered as entitled to the benefits of this chapter. **45 U.S.C. § 51.**	(A) **Railroad liability.** A railroad carrier is liable for an employee's injury or death resulting in whole or in part from: (1) the negligence of an officer, agency, or employee of the carrier; or (2) a negligent defect or insufficiency in the carrier's property such as a car, engine, appliance, track, work, boat, roadbed, or wharf. (B) **Key terms.** (1) "Employee" means a person employed by a railroad carrier whose duties either further or directly or closely and substantially affect interstate or foreign commerce. (2) "Railroad carrier" includes only those carriers engaging in commerce between: (a) the States or Territories; (b) the States and Territories; (c) the States or Territories and the District of Columbia; or (d) a State or Territory or the District of Columbia and any foreign nation or nations. (C) **Damages.** A railroad carrier found liable must pay damages: (1) to the employee suffering the injury; or (2) if the employee has died, to the employee's personal representative for the benefit of the employee's surviving spouse and children; or, if none, then of the employee's parents; or, if none, then of the next-of-kin dependent on the employee.

NOT THIS:	BUT THIS:
4931.10 Transmitting advertising by facsimile device. (A) As used in this section: (1) "Advertisement" means a message or material intended to cause the sale of realty, goods, or services. (2) "Facsimile device"* means a device that electronically or telephonically receives and copies onto paper reasonable reproductions or facsimiles of documents and photographs through connection with a telephone network. (3) "Pre-existing business relationship" does not include transmitting an advertisement to the owner's or lessee's facsimile device. (B)(1) No person shall transmit an advertisement to a facsimile device unless the person has received prior permission from the owner or, if the device is leased, from the lessee of the device to which the message is to be sent to transmit the advertisement; or the person has a pre-existing business relationship with such owner or lessee. Division (B)(1) of this section does not apply to a person who transmits an advertisement to a facsimile device located on residential premises. (2) No person shall transmit an advertisement to a facsimile device located on residential premises unless the person has received prior written permission from the owner or, if the device is leased, from the lessee of the device to which the message is to be sent to transmit the advertisement. In addition to any other penalties or remedies, a recipient of an advertisement transmitted in violation of division (B)(2) of this section may bring a civil action against the person who transmitted that advertisement or caused it to be transmitted. In that action, the recipient may recover one thousand dollars for each violation. (C) When requested by the owner or lessee, the transmission shall occur between seven p.m. and five a.m. This section applies to all such advertisements intended to be so transmitted within this state. **Ohio Rev. Code § 4931.10.**	**4931.10 Sending advertisements to fax machines.** (A) **General prohibition.** No person may fax an advertisement before getting permission from the receiving device's owner or lessee unless the person has a preexisting business relationship with the owner or lessee. (B) **Key terms.** (1) "Advertisement" means any message or material intended to help sell realty, goods, or services. (2) "Preexisting business relationship" does not include sending an advertisement to the owner's or lessee's facsimile device. (C) **Residences.** (1) ***Written consent.*** If the fax machine is located at a residence, the sender must have prior written permission from the receiving machine's owner or lessee before sending an advertisement. (2) ***Civil penalty.*** In addition to any other penalties or remedies, a recipient of an advertisement violating (C)(1) may bring a civil lawsuit against the person who sent or caused the advertisement to be sent. A recipient may be awarded $1,000 for each violation. (D) **Timing.** If the owner or lessee so requests, an advertisement may be sent by fax only between 7:00 p.m. and 5:00 a.m.

Unnumbered dangling flush text: see § 3.4(E).

*Some lawyers insist on printing "facsimile transmission" on their business cards—even though ordinary people haven't used this terminology since the mid-1980s. People know what a "fax" is and what "to fax" means. No definition is necessary or even desirable. And note that the statute made itself almost instantly defunct by defining *facsimile device*: many if not most faxes today have nothing to do with a "telephone network." See § 3.5(A).

"Definition sections should, as a rule, be placed towards the end of a Bill."
—Sir Courtenay Ilbert, *Legislative Methods and Forms* 281 (1901).

(C) Glossary.

If defined terms appear pervasively within a statute, collect them in an alphabetically arranged glossary (definition or key-terms section) either at the outset or at the end. If the glossary is extensive, it may serve as an index. That is, provision-specific definitions won't be moved to the glossary. Instead the glossary will list the key term, in alphabetical order, with a brief note stating that the term is defined in § XX (whatever it might be).

(D) Precise terminology.

Use precise definitional terms: *means*, *includes*, and *does not include*. Avoid especially *shall mean*.

NOT THIS:	BUT THIS:
For the purposes of this section, the word "obligations" shall mean fines and penalty assessments, court-ordered restitution or reimbursement to any person injured as a result of the offense, successful completion of all treatment and rehabilitation programs the person is required to take, full payment of all fees for such programs, and any other costs which may be ordered by the court. **N.H. Rev. Stat. § 265-A:22.**	In this section, the term "obligation" means a fine or penalty; court-ordered restitution or reimbursement to any person injured as a result of an offense; successful completion of all required treatment and rehabilitation programs; full payment of all fees for such programs; and any other cost that the court may order.

(E) No counterintuitive definitions.

Ensure that your definitions seem intuitively right—that is, make sure that the term defined reasonably fits the stipulated definition.

NOT THIS:	BUT THIS:
The term "merchandise" includes any objects, wares, goods, commodities, intangibles, securities, bonds, debentures, stocks, real estate or services. **Iowa Code § 714.16(1)(i).**	(1) The term "investments" includes commodities, intangibles, securities, bonds, debentures, and stocks. (2) The term "merchandise" includes any objects, wares, and goods. (3) The term "services" does not include unpaid services. (4) The term "real estate" includes land, any structures on the land, anything attached to the land, and any crops growing on the land.

It's very strange to think of services, real estate, or stocks and bonds as "merchandise." Either develop four genera (as at right) or come up with a distinctive new genus such as "sellables."

4. Syntax

Use a syntactic arrangement that enhances clarity, logic, and readability.

4.1 Kernel sentence parts together.

Subject and verb shouldn't be widely separated. They should be kept together, preferably toward the beginning of the sentence. Don't try to stuff all qualifications into one sentence. See also § 4.6 (Interruptive phrases).

Noun clause as subject . . .

. . . and complete predicate 47 words later.

Even this slight subject-verb separation requires improvement.

NOT THIS:	BUT THIS:
§ 474A. Deterrents to counterfeiting of obligations and securities (a) Whoever has in his control or possession, after a distinctive paper has been adopted by the Secretary of the Treasury for the obligations and other securities of the United States, any similar paper adapted to the making of any such obligation or other security, except under the authority of the Secretary of the Treasury, is guilty of a class B felony. **18 U.S.C. § 474A.**	**§ 474A. Counterfeiting U.S. obligations and securities prohibited; class B felony.** (A) **Elements of offense.** It is unlawful to control or possess a paper adapted to making counterfeits of any paper or security of the United States. A "paper or security of the United States" means any distinctive paper adopted by the Secretary of the Treasury for obligations and securities of the United States. This provision does not apply to those acting under the authority of the Secretary of the Treasury. Violation of this provision is a class B felony.
(1) **Information sharing.** The Secretary, in consultation with the Secretary of Transportation, shall establish a program to provide appropriate information that the Department has gathered or developed on the performance, use, and testing of technologies that may be used to enhance railroad, public transportation, and surface transportation security to surface transportation entities, including railroad carriers, over-the-road bus operators and terminal owners and operators, motor carriers, public transportation agencies, owners or operators of highways, pipeline operators, and State, local, and tribal governments that provide security assistance to such entities. **6 U.S.C. § 1114(a)(1).**	(1) ***Information sharing.*** In consultation with the Secretary of Transportation, the Secretary will establish a program to provide appropriate information that the Department has gathered or developed on the performance, use, and testing of technologies that may be used to enhance railroad, public-transportation, and surface-transportation security. This information must be provided to: (a) surface-transportation entities, including railroad carriers, over-the-road bus operators, terminal owners and operators, motor carriers, public-transportation agencies, owners or operators of highways, and pipeline operators; and (b) state, local, and tribal governments that provide security assistance to such entities.

> "The art of legislative drafting is the ability to visualize the many different grammatical forms and methods that can be used to convey ideas, to select those that best express them and then, by a process of conversion of modifiers from one form to another and from one position to another, to arrange the elements of the sentence so as to communicate the legal ingredients clearly and precisely."
> —Elmer A. Driedger, *The Composition of Legislation* xxvi (1957).

The subject-verb separation here results from misplaced conditions. See § 4.1.

NOT THIS:	BUT THIS:
(a) Application; contents (1) Any alien lawfully admitted for permanent residence, or (2) any alien lawfully admitted to the United States pursuant to clause 6 of section 3 of the Immigration Act of 1924, between July 1, 1924, and July 5, 1932, both dates inclusive, who intends to depart temporarily from the United States may make application to the Attorney General for a permit to reenter the United States, stating the length of his intended absence or absences, and the reasons therefor. Such applications shall be made under oath, and shall be in such form, contain such information, and be accompanied by such photographs of the applicant as may be by regulations prescribed. **8 U.S.C. § 1203.**	(A) **Application; contents.** (1) ***Prior permission to reenter.*** An alien intending to leave the United States temporarily may apply to the Attorney General for a permit to reenter if the alien: (a) is lawfully admitted to the United States for permanent residence; or (b) was admitted under the Immigration Act of 1924, § 3, clause 6, between July 1, 1924, and July 5, 1932. (2) ***Prerequisites.*** The alien must apply under oath and state the reasons for and length of the intended absence. The alien's application must conform to any requirements as to its form, information, and photographs.
The directors designated in the articles of incorporation shall, until their successors take office, direct the exercise of all powers of a China Trade Act corporation except such as are conferred upon the stockholders by law or by the articles of incorporation or bylaws of the corporation. Thereafter the directors elected in accordance with the bylaws of the corporation shall direct the exercise of all powers of the corporation except such as are so conferred upon the stockholders. In the exercise of such powers the directors may appoint and remove and fix the compensation of such officers and employees of the corporation as they deem advisable. **15 U.S.C. § 151.**	Until their successors take office, directors designated in the articles of incorporation will exercise all powers of a China Trade Act corporation except those conferred on the stockholders by law, the articles of incorporation, or the bylaws of the corporation. Then the directors elected in accordance with the corporation's bylaws will exercise all corporate powers except those conferred on the stockholders. In exercising their powers, the directors may appoint and remove corporate officers and employees, and fix their compensation, as they consider advisable.
(b) **Communication with third parties.** Except as provided in section 1692b of this title, without the prior consent of the consumer given directly to the debt collector, or the express permission of a court of competent jurisdiction, or as reasonably necessary to effectuate a postjudgment judicial remedy, a debt collector may not communicate, in connection with the collection of any debt, with any person other than the consumer, his attorney, a consumer reporting agency if otherwise permitted by law, the creditor, the attorney of the creditor, or the attorney of the debt collector. **15 U.S.C. § 1692c(b).**	(B) **Communication with third parties.** Except as provided in § 1692b, in connection with collecting a debt a debt collector must not communicate with any person other than the consumer, the consumer's attorney, a consumer-reporting agency (if otherwise permitted by law), the creditor, the creditor's attorney, or the debt collector's own attorney, unless: (1) the consumer has consented directly to the debt collector; (2) a court of competent jurisdiction has authorized it; or (3) it is reasonably necessary to carry out a postjudgment judicial remedy.

4.2 Principle of end weight.

End sentences emphatically—with a word or phrase that can receive stress. Remember that in good English, the last position in the sentence, not the first, is the most important.

NOT THIS:	BUT THIS:
The company may specify on a certificate the expiration date of the policy. **Me. Rev. Stat. tit. 29-A, § 1606(5).**	On a certificate, the company may specify the policy's expiration date.
Not later than five (5) days following the convening of each regular legislative session, the governor shall transmit to the legislature a budget document setting forth his financial plan for the next fiscal year, and having the character and scope set forth. **Idaho Code § 67-3506.**	No later than 5 days after convening a regular legislative session, the governor must send to the legislature a budget specifically setting forth a financial plan for the coming fiscal year.
Any new member serving only a portion of a seven-year term in office may continue to serve until a successor is appointed and has qualified, except that such member may not continue to serve for more than one year after the date on which the term of the member would otherwise expire, unless reappointed. **5 U.S.C. § 1202(b).**	A new member serving only part of a 7-year term in office may continue to serve until a successor is appointed and has qualified. But unless reappointed, the new member cannot serve for more than 1 year after the date on which the term would otherwise expire.

"It is beyond a doubt that many of the more positive errors and gross defects of legislation are to be prevented by observing a very few intelligible and simple rules, which any person capable of dividing grammatically a sentence of his native language would be competent to apply. Through neglect of such rules a law, good in its substance, is rendered confused in its form, proportionally difficult to be understood and applied, and sometimes is even made inoperative, or, what is worse, a delusion and a snare."

—George Coode, *On Legislative Expression; or the Language of the Written Law* 5 (2d ed. 1852).

4.3 Conditions—in general.

Place conditions where they can be read most easily, preferably using the word *if.* Use *when* (not *where*) if the sentence needs an *if* to introduce another unrelated clause or if the condition is something that may occur with regularity.

(A) Short condition.

If a condition is relatively short and seeing it first would help the reader avoid a miscue, put it at the beginning of the sentence.

NOT THIS:	BUT THIS:
§ 13-3-2. Assent as essential to contract. Withdrawal of proposition. The consent of the parties being essential to a contract, until each has assented to all the terms, there is no binding contract; until assented to, each party may withdraw his bid or proposition. **Ga. Code. § 13-3-2.**	**§ 13-3-2. No contract without consent.** The parties' consent is essential to a contract. Until each consents to all the terms: (A) there is no binding contract; and (B) each party may withdraw its offer.

(B) Long condition and short main clause.

If a condition is long and the main clause is short, put the main clause first and move directly into the condition.

NOT THIS:	BUT THIS:
§ 15-5-4. Collusion of parties. Whenever it appears that the absence, adultery, cruelty, desertion, or other cause of complaint was committed or occasioned by the collusion of the parties, and done or contrived with an intention to procure a divorce, no divorce shall be decreed. **R.I. Gen. Laws § 15-5-4.**	**§ 15-5-4. Collusion of parties.** A divorce must not be decreed if it appears that the parties, intending to procure a divorce, have colluded to commit or occasion the absence, adultery, cruelty, desertion, or other cause of complaint.
Packages of cigarettes manufactured, imported, or packaged (1) for export from the United States or (2) for delivery to a vessel or aircraft, as supplies, for consumption beyond the jurisdiction of the internal revenue laws of the United States shall be exempt from the requirements of this chapter, but such exemptions shall not apply to cigarettes manufactured, imported, or packaged for sale or distribution to members or units of the Armed Forces of the United States located outside of the United States. **15 U.S.C. § 1340.**	Cigarettes are exempt from the requirements of this chapter if they are manufactured, imported, or packaged either for export from the United States or for delivery as supplies to a vessel or aircraft for consumption beyond the jurisdiction of federal tax laws. But this exemption does not apply to cigarettes manufactured, imported, or packaged for sale or distribution to members or units of the Armed Forces of the United States located outside the United States.

Note that this provision also falls into the category of subject-verb separation. See § 4.1

NOT THIS:	BUT THIS:
Where the value of the marital-property portion of a spouse's entitlement to future payments can be determined at dissolution, the court may include it in reckoning the worth of the marital property assigned to each spouse. Where the value of the future payments is not known at the time of dissolution, where their receipt is contingent on future events or not reasonably assured, or where for other reasons it is not equitable under the circumstances to include their value in the property assigned at the time of dissolution, the court may decline to do so. **Principles of the Law of Family Dissolution: Analysis and Recommendations § 4.08(3) (Tentative Draft No. 1, 1995).**	If the value of the marital-property portion of a spouse's entitlement to future payments can be determined at dissolution, the court may include it in determining the worth of each spouse's marital-property portion. But the court may decline to do so if: (A) the future payments' value is not known at dissolution; (B) the future payments' receipt is contingent on future events or not reasonably assured; or (C) it is otherwise not equitable under the circumstances to include the future payments' value in the property assigned at dissolution.
§ 45-9-60. Indemnification of public officers and officials who are required to be bonded In the event that a public officer or official has a money judgment returned against him in an action or is otherwise subjected to monetary liability by an aggrieved party, by his bond carrier, or both as a result of an act of omission or commission of a subordinate employee of the public officer or official and in the event that said public officer or official shall, as a result of such action, be required to expend his personal moneys, said officer or official shall be indemnified out of funds otherwise available to the public official's or officer's department or office, provided that authorization for such indemnification payment by the department or office shall be contingent on issuance of an official opinion of the Attorney General declaring that the judgment against or liability of the public officer or official was not due to an act of omission or commission of the public officer or official which constituted a breach of a duty imposed by law on the officer or official. In the event that the Attorney General is the public official seeking indemnification under this article, the Governor shall make the determination as to whether or not the liability of the Attorney General was due to an act of omission or commission of the Attorney General which constituted a breach of a duty imposed by law. **Ga. Code § 45-9-60.**	**§ 45-9-60. Indemnification of a bonded public officer or official.** (A) **Requirements for indemnification.** A public officer or official must be indemnified out of his or her department's or office's public funds if the officer or official: (1) receives an adverse money judgment or is otherwise subjected to monetary liability by an aggrieved party, the aggrieved party's bond carrier, or both; (2) supervises a subordinate employee whose act of omission or commission caused the adverse money judgment or other monetary liability; and (3) is required to expend personal money. (B) **Attorney General's opinion required.** Before a department or office may authorize an indemnity payment, the Attorney General must issue an official opinion declaring that the public officer's or official's judgment or liability under (A) was not caused by the public officer's or official's omission or act that constituted the breach of a legal duty. (C) **Governor's determination.** If the Attorney General seeks indemnity under this article, the Governor must determine whether the liability resulted from the Attorney General's omission or act that constituted the breach of a legal duty.

(C) Long condition and long main clause.

If both the condition and the main clause are long, foreshadow the condition and put it at the end of the sentence. If there are several conditions, a phrase such as *under the following circumstances* will foreshadow the conditions at the end.

NOT THIS:	BUT THIS:
An emergency medical services provider or licensed child placement agency shall take possession of a child who appears to be sixty days of age or younger if the child is voluntarily delivered to the provider or agency by the child's parent and the parent does not express an intent to return for the child. Any provider or agency who takes possession of a child pursuant to this section shall perform any act necessary to protect the physical health and safety of the child. **S.D. Codified Laws § 25-5A-27.**	An emergency-medical-services provider or licensed child-placement agency must take possession of a child and perform any action necessary to protect the child's physical health and safety if: (A) the child appears to be no more than 60 days old; and (B) the child's parent: (1) voluntarily delivers the child to the provider or agency; and (2) does not express an intent to return for the child.
84.11 Local bridge construction and reconstruction. (6a) COUNTY BOARD ACTION. If any city, village or town which is required by the order of the department to pay a portion of the cost of a bridge project under sub. (1m) fails to comply with sub. (6) and provide the portion of the cost which it is required to pay, or if the city, village or town does not hold a regular or special meeting within 30 days after the date of the department's finding, determination and order, the county board of the county in which the city, village or town is located may take action to provide such portion, and to assess all or part thereof against the city, village or town as a special tax, in one or more installments as the county board determines. **Wis. Stat. § 84.11(6a).**	**§ 84.11 Local bridge construction and reconstruction.** 6.1 **County board action.** In either of the following circumstances, the county board where a city, town, or village is located may take action—including assessing a special tax in one or more installments against the city, town, or village—to help pay the part of the cost of a bridge that the city, town, or village has been ordered to pay by the department under (§ 1.13): (A) if the city, town, or village has failed to comply with (6) and pay its proportional share; or (B) if the city, town, or village did not hold a regular or special meeting within 30 days after the department's finding, determination, and order.

The odd numbering of the original is provisionally adjusted here to accord with § 3.3(A). In practice, it might need to be fixed a little differently.

> "Where exceptions are numerous they should (as in the instances of numerous cases and numerous conditions) be placed in separate members of the section or even in a separate section. Where the enumeration of the exception is short, compared with the enumeration of the particulars not excepted, it is often convenient to state the exceptions first."
>
> —Lord Thring, *Practical Legislation* 77 (2d ed. 1902).

(D) Hidden conditions.

Unearth hidden conditions to make them explicit, using the word *if.* This little word is among the most important ones in the drafter's vocabulary.

NOT THIS:	BUT THIS:
An order of revival issued upon a judgment or decree during the period of twelve years from the rendition or from the date of an order reviving the judgment or decree, extends the effect and operation of the judgment or decree with the lien thereby created and all the remedies for its enforcement for the period of twelve years from the date of the order. **D.C. Code § 15-103.**	If a revival order is issued on a judgment or decree within 12 years after it was rendered or revived, the order extends the effect of the judgment or decree—with the lien it created and all its enforcement remedies—for 12 years from the order's date.
556G.1 Unclaimed personal property held by a dry cleaning establishment. All property deposited with a dry cleaning establishment which remains unclaimed for a period of four months after the establishment has attempted to contact the owner of the property by ordinary mail one time at the property owner's last known mailing address, may be presumed abandoned and disposed of by delivering the property to a local nonprofit charitable organization. **Iowa Code § 556G.1.**	**556G.1 Unclaimed property held by dry-cleaner.** If property deposited with a dry-cleaner remains unclaimed for 4 months after the dry-cleaner has tried to contact the property's owner by ordinary mail at the last known mailing address, it may be presumed abandoned. To dispose of the property, the dry-cleaner may deliver it to a local nonprofit charitable organization.
(b) **Information regarding certain goods.** The Secretary may also cause to be disseminated information regarding food, drugs, devices, tobacco products, or cosmetics in situations involving, in the opinion of the Secretary, imminent danger to health or gross deception of the consumer. Nothing in this section shall be construed to prohibit the Secretary from collecting, reporting, and illustrating the results of the investigations of the Department. **21 U.S.C. § 375(b).**	(B) **Information regarding certain goods.** If, in the opinion of the Secretary, a situation involves gross deception of a consumer or imminent danger to a consumer's health, the Secretary may also disseminate information about food, drugs, devices, tobacco products, or cosmetics. Nothing in this section prohibits the Secretary from collecting, reporting, and illustrating the results of the Department's investigations.

> "A proviso usually designates an exception or a qualification and almost invariably its subject matter is better dealt with in a new sentence or even a new clause."
>
> —Edward Kerr, *Plain Language: Is It Legal?*, 52 Law Soc'y J. 52, 58 (1991).

Does this really mean to say that partnerships and corporations are precluded? The contractors must be individuals? It seems like an error deriving from some people's euphemistic use of *individual* instead of *person*.†

NOT THIS:	BUT THIS:
(1) The Parks and Wildlife Department, the successor to the Game, Fish and Oyster Commission* is authorized to take rough fish and turtles from any of the public fresh waters of this State by means of crews operated by the Commission or contracts entered into with individuals, through the use of seines or nets or other devices and under such rules and regulations and contracts as it shall prescribe, when said Commission shall find that rough fish or turtles exist in any such waters in numbers detrimental to the propagation and preservation of game fish. **Tex. Rev. Civ. Stat. § 4050c(1) (repealed in 1975).**	(1) ***Reducing rough fish or turtles.*** If the Parks and Wildlife Department finds that rough fish or turtles exist in the State's public freshwaters in numbers detrimental to the propagation and preservation of game fish, the Department may take them through contractors or Department crews by seine, net, or other device. The crews and contractors must comply with any regulations the Department prescribes.
§ 18-8406. Notification of duty to register — prior to release. With respect to a juvenile sex offender sentenced to a period of detention the county shall provide, prior to release, written notification of the duty to register. With respect to a juvenile sex offender committed to the custody of the department of juvenile corrections, the department shall provide, prior to release, written notification of the duty to register. The written notification shall be a form provided by the Idaho state police and shall be signed by the juvenile and the parents or guardian of the juvenile. One (1) copy shall be retained by the department of juvenile corrections, one (1) copy shall be provided to the offender, and one (1) copy shall be submitted within three (3) working days to the central registry. **Idaho Code § 18-8406.**	**§ 18-8406. Notification of duty to register—before release.** (A) **Informing juvenile of duty.** If a juvenile sex offender has been sentenced to a period of detention with the county or committed to the custody of the department of juvenile corrections, the county or department—whichever has custody—must provide the juvenile with written notification of his or her duty to register upon release. (B) **Notification form.** The written notification under (A) must be a form provided by the Idaho state police. The juvenile and his or her parents or guardian must sign the form. The department of juvenile corrections must retain 1 copy; 1 copy must be provided to the offender; and 1 copy must be submitted within 3 working days to the central registry.

*Note the missing comma at the end of this appositive phrase.

†On the avoidance of *individual* except when contrasted with a group, see *Garner's Modern English Usage* 507–08 (4th ed. 2016); R.W. Burchfield, *The New Fowler's Modern English Usage* 391–92 (3d rev. ed., 2004); *Merriam-Webster's Concise Dictionary of English Usage* 418–19 (2002); and Eric Partridge, *Usage and Abusage: A Guide to Good English* 153 (Janet Whitcut ed., 1994).

4.4 Exceptions.

Place exceptions where they can be read most easily in the legislative sentence.

(A) When to state first.

If an exception is short, state it briefly at the beginning. This arrangement within the sentence promotes the principle of end weight. See § 4.2.

NOT THIS:	BUT THIS:
No money deposited under section 2041 of this title shall be withdrawn except by order of court. **28 U.S.C. § 2042.**	Unless the court orders otherwise, money deposited under § 2041 must not be withdrawn.

(B) When to state last.

If an exception cannot be stated briefly, put it at the end of the sentence or provision.

NOT THIS:	BUT THIS:
Except as provided by section 1303(b) (relating to waiting period after application), the license shall not be issued prior to the third day following the date of the most recent of the two applications therefor. **23 Pa. Cons. Stat. § 1307.**	The license may be issued no sooner than 3 days after the most recent of the 2 applications, unless § 1303(b)—relating to the waiting period after application—provides otherwise.

"The price of clarity, of course, is that the clearer the document the more obvious its substantive deficiencies. For the lazy or dull, this price may be too high."

—Reed Dickerson, *Clear Legal Drafting: What's Holding Us Back?*, 11 ALI-ABA CLE Rev. 3 (1980).

4.5 Provisos.

(A) *Provided that.*

Eliminate this phrase and all variations on it. Provisos can mean *if*, *except*, or *also*—and their uncertain syntactic reach is a recurrent cause of ambiguity.

NOT THIS:	BUT THIS:
No prisoner shall be compelled to labor more than 10 hours per day nor be subject to punishment for any refusal to labor beyond such limit; provided, that the 10 hours shall be the time embraced from the leaving to the return of the prisoner to his or her place of detention. **Fla. Stat. § 951.08.**	A prisoner must not be required to work more than 10 hours per day and must not be punished for refusing to work longer. The 10 hours begin when the prisoner leaves the place of detention and end when the prisoner returns.
In the case of a minor spouse, the right of election may be exercised in whole or in part only by the spouse's guardian; in the case of an incapacitated spouse, the right of election may be exercised in whole or in part only by the spouse's guardian or by his agent in accordance with section 5603(d) if the power of attorney qualifies as a durable power of attorney under section 5604 (relating to durable powers of attorney); provided, that, in each case, the election shall be exercised only upon order of the court having jurisdiction of the minor's or the incapacitated person's estate, after finding that exercise of the right is advisable. **20 Pa. Cons. Stat. § 2206.**	If the spouse is incapacitated or is a minor, the spouse's guardian may fully or partly exercise the right of election. If the spouse is incapacitated, an agent may make the election under § 5603(d) if the power of attorney qualifies as durable under § 5604. The election of a minor's or incapacitated person's estate must be by court order if the court finds the election appropriate.

This provision seems anomalous. Marriage normally removes the disabilities of minority.

"Little can be done to improve the quality of legislation unless those concerned in the process are willing to modify some of their most cherished habits."

—*The Preparation of Legislation* ¶ 1.10, at 3 (Lord Renton ed., 1975).

NOT THIS:	BUT THIS:
Prior to publishing a notice of a foreclosure sale, as required by section 14, the creditor, or if the creditor is not a natural person, an officer or duly authorized agent of the creditor, shall certify compliance with this subsection in an affidavit based upon a review of the creditor's business records. The creditor, or an officer or duly authorized agent of the creditor, shall record this affidavit with the registry of deeds for the county or district where the land lies. The affidavit certifying compliance with this subsection shall be conclusive evidence in favor of an arm's-length third party purchaser for value, at or subsequent to the resulting foreclosure sale, that the creditor has fully complied with this section and the mortgagee is entitled to proceed with foreclosure of the subject mortgage under the power of sale contained in the mortgage and any 1 or more of the foreclosure procedures authorized in this chapter; provided that, the arm's-length third party purchaser for value relying on such affidavit shall not be liable for any failure of the foreclosing party to comply and title to the real property thereby acquired shall not be set aside on account of such failure. The filing of such affidavit shall not relieve the affiant, or other person on whose behalf the affidavit is executed, from liability for failure to comply with this section, including by reason of any statement in the affidavit. **Mass. Gen. Laws ch. 244, § 35C(b).**	Before publishing a foreclosure notice to comply with § 14, the creditor or its agent must complete an affidavit certifying, based on business records, that the creditor is in compliance with this provision. The creditor or its agent must record this affidavit with the deeds registry for the county or district where the land is. The affidavit will be conclusive evidence of an arm's-length third-party purchase for value. The affidavit permits the mortgagee to proceed with foreclosure under the power of sale and any of the foreclosure procedures authorized in this Act. An arm's-length third-party purchaser for value relying on the affidavit is not liable for the foreclosing party's noncompliance. The title to the property cannot be set aside because of such noncompliance. Filing the affidavit does not relieve the affiant, or anyone else on whose behalf the affiant has filed, from liability for noncompliance with this section.

This provision is called a "subsection" in one place and a "section" later. Confusing. See §§ 1.1(D), 3.2(A).

(B) *Provided, however, that.*

Often thought to create exceptions only, this wording can also create conditions and mere additions. Reword.

NOT THIS:	BUT THIS:
The board shall have a corporate seal and perpetual existence: Provided, That the board may be dissolved by the affirmative vote of at least sixty percent of the persons elected to the governing body or bodies and: Provided, however, That a governing body may withdraw from any board created by agreement of two or more governing bodies upon the affirmative vote of at least sixty percent of the persons elected to such governing body. **W. Va. Code § 10-2-4a.**	The board must have a corporate seal. Unless the board's governing body dissolves the board with an affirmative vote of at least 60% of the body's elected members, the board will have perpetual existence. A governing body may withdraw from any board created by agreement with 1 or more other governing bodies upon the affirmative vote of at least 60% of the withdrawing body's elected members.

The original is quite unclear, especially with its strange combination of ideas in the first sentence. The revision is an educated guess about its meaning.

4.6 Interruptive phrases.

(A) Avoiding subject-verb and verb-object separation.

Try moving an interruptive phrase from midsentence to the beginning or end. Unless there is some special reason for separating the kernel parts of the sentence—subject, verb, and object—don't do it. See also § 4.1 (Kernel sentence parts together).

NOT THIS:	BUT THIS:
All special elections which are authorized or required by law, unless the applicable law otherwise requires, shall be held on Tuesday. **Iowa Code § 39.2(1)(a).**	All special elections authorized or required by law must be held on Tuesday unless the applicable law requires otherwise.
The director may execute, subject to the provisions of subsections (b), (c) and (d) of this section and as permitted by applicable federal law, prescription drug purchasing agreements with . . . all departments [etc.]. **W. Va. Code § 5-16C-4(a).**	Subject to (b), (c), and (d) and as permitted by applicable federal law, the director may execute prescription-drug purchasing agreements with . . . all departments [etc.].
§ 873. Blackmail. Whoever, under a threat of informing, or as a consideration for not informing, against any violation of any law of the United States, demands or receives any money or other valuable thing, shall be fined under this title or imprisoned not more than one year, or both. **18 U.S.C. § 873.**	**§ 873. Blackmail prohibited.** (A) **Offense.** It is unlawful to demand or receive money or anything of value by threatening to inform others, or by not informing others, about a violation of federal law. (B) **Penalty.** Violation of this provision is punishable by imprisonment up to 1 year or a fine, or both.
(b) **Initiation by Secretary; grant applications and budgets** The Secretary, within thirty days after a request by any Indian tribe, shall initiate a[n] eligibility study to determine whether there is justification to encourage and maintain a tribally controlled college or university, and, upon a positive determination, shall aid in the preparation of grant applications and related budgets which will insure successful operation of such an institution. **25 U.S.C. § 1806.**	(B) **Secretary's initiation; grant applications and budgets.** Within 30 days after a request by an Indian tribe, the Secretary must initiate an eligibility study to determine whether there is justification to encourage and maintain a tribally controlled college or university. Upon a positive determination, the Secretary must help prepare grant applications and related budgets to ensure the institution's successful operation.
A court, at the request of a mortgagee, should appoint a receiver if the mortgage is in default and the mortgage or other agreement contains either a mortgage on the rents or a provision authorizing appointment of a receiver to take possession and collect rents upon mortgagor default. **Restatement (Third) of Property: Security (Mortgages) § 4.3(b) (Tentative Draft No. 3, 1994).**	At the mortgagee's request, a court should appoint a receiver if the mortgage is in default and the mortgage or other agreement contains either a mortgage on the rents or a provision authorizing the appointment of a receiver to take possession and collect rents upon the mortgagor's default.

NOT THIS:	BUT THIS:
A patent for a claimed invention may not be obtained, notwithstanding that the claimed invention is not identically disclosed as set forth in section 102, if the differences between the claimed invention and the prior art are such that the claimed invention as a whole would have been obvious before the effective filing date of the claimed invention to a person having ordinary skill in the art to which the claimed invention pertains. **35 U.S.C. § 103.**	Even if a claimed invention is not identically disclosed as set forth in § 102, a patent cannot be obtained for it if the differences between the prior art and the claimed invention are such that before its effective filing date, the claimed invention as a whole would have been obvious to a person with ordinary skill in the pertinent art.

(B) Adverbial interruptive phrases.

Put an adverbial interruptive phrase after the first auxiliary verb in a verb phrase, not before it. In other words, split verb phrases.*

NOT THIS:	BUT THIS:
Emergency limitations. The Commissioner of Banks, with the approval of the Governor, may impose a limitation upon the amounts withdrawable or payable from withdrawable accounts of State associations during any specifically defined period when such limitation is in the public interest and welfare. **N.C. Gen. Stat. § 54B-125.**	**Right to impose limit when necessary.** The Commissioner of Banks may, with the Governor's approval, impose a limit on the amounts withdrawable or payable from withdrawable accounts of State associations during any specifically defined period when a limit is in the public interest and welfare.
The Attorney General or the county attorney of the county in which a postsecondary institution is located, at the request of the commission or on his or her own accord, may bring any appropriate action or proceeding in any court of competent jurisdiction to enforce the Postsecondary Institution Act. **Neb. Rev. Stat. § 85-2420.**	To enforce the Postsecondary Institution Act, the Attorney General or the county attorney of the postsecondary institution's county may—on his or her own initiative or at the Commission's request—bring an appropriate lawsuit in a court of competent jurisdiction.
Each life insurance policy issued between the effective date of this code and the operative date of s. 627.476 shall provide: (1) That, in the event of default in any premium, the insurer will grant, upon proper request not later than 60 days after the due date of the premium in default, a paid-up nonforfeiture benefit on a plan stipulated in the policy . . . . **Fla. Stat. § 627.475(1).**	Each life-insurance policy issued between this code's effective date and the operative date of § 627.476 must provide: (A) that if a premium is in default, the insurer will, upon proper request within 60 days after the due date of the premium in default, grant a paid-up nonforfeiture benefit on a plan stipulated in the policy . . . .

*This is an age-old principle that only true grammarians seem to know. Don't mistakenly associate split verbs with split infinitives. *See Garner's Modern English Usage* 25 (4th ed. 2016) (s.v. "Adverbs (A)").

NOT THIS:	BUT THIS:
§ 9606 Abatement actions. **(a) Maintenance, jurisdiction, etc.** In addition to any other action taken by a State or local government, when the President determines that there may be an imminent and substantial endangerment to the public health or welfare or the environment because of an actual or threatened release of a hazardous substance from a facility, he may require the Attorney General of the United States to secure such relief as may be necessary to abate such danger or threat, and the district court of the United States in the district in which the threat occurs shall have jurisdiction to grant such relief as the public interest and the equities of the case may require. The President may also, after notice to the affected State, take other action under this section including, but not limited to, issuing such orders as may be necessary to protect public health and welfare and the environment. **42 U.S.C. § 9606(a).**	**§ 9606 Abatement actions.** (A) **Government's right to protect public; jurisdiction.** Upon determining that a hazardous substance's potential or actual release might imminently and substantially endanger the public welfare or environment, the President may—along with other state or local government action—require the U.S. Attorney General to secure the relief necessary to stop this danger. The U.S. district court in the district where the threat occurs has jurisdiction to grant whatever relief the public interest and the equities of the case may require. The President may also, after giving notice to the affected state, take other necessary action to protect the public welfare and environment, including issuing executive orders.

(C) Other interruptive phrases.

For an interruptive phrase that must appear midsentence—because of what it modifies—use a double-dash construction instead of commas.

NOT THIS:	BUT THIS:
When a person discusses with a lawyer the possibility of their forming a client-lawyer relationship and even if no such relationship arises, the lawyer must: (1) Protect the person's confidential information as stated in Chapter 5 and the person's property as stated in § 56-58 and avoid conflicts of interest as stated in § 213; and (2) Use reasonable care to the extent the lawyer advises or provides other legal services for the person. **Restatement (Third) of the Law Governing Lawyers § 27 (Tentative Draft No. 5, 1992).**	When a person and a lawyer discuss the possibility of their forming a client-lawyer relationship—even if no such relationship arises—the lawyer must: (A) protect the person's confidential information, as stated in Chapter 5, and the person's property, as stated in §§ 56–58; (B) avoid conflicts of interest, as stated in § 213; and (C) use reasonable care in providing advice or other legal services to the person.

> "If it could be made to be generally recognised that essentials of every law are simple, and that their direct expression is the perfection of law writing, the greatest defects of our statute law would cease."
>
> —George Coode, *On Legislative Expression; or the Language of the Written Law* 68 (2d ed. 1852).

4.7 Modifiers.

(A) Putting related words together.

To avoid ambiguity, place a modifier right beside the word or phrase it modifies.

NOT THIS:	BUT THIS:
The members of the governing board shall be entitled to one vote each on such board. . . . **R.I. Gen. Laws § 2-16.1-2, art. IV(b).**	Each member of the governing board has 1 vote. . . .

(B) When to rephrase.

If moving a misplaced modifier will not cure the ambiguity, rephrase the sentence.

NOT THIS:	BUT THIS:
A person who, knowing that another person is intoxicated, sells, barters, delivers, or gives away an alcoholic beverage to the intoxicated person commits a Class B misdemeanor. **Ind. Code § 7.1-5-10-15(a).**	It is unlawful to sell, barter, deliver, or give an alcoholic beverage to someone that one knows to be intoxicated. Violation of this provision is a Class B misdemeanor.
§ 35. Client under a disability. . . . (3) If a client described in Subsection (1) has a guardian or other person legally entitled to act for the client, the client's lawyer must treat the guardian or other person as the person entitled to act with respect to the client's interests in the matter, unless: (a) The lawyer represents the client in a matter against the interests of such person; or (b) The person instructs the lawyer to act in a manner that the lawyer knows will violate the person's legal duties toward the client. **Restatement (Third) of the Law Governing Lawyers § 35(3) (Tentative Draft No. 5, 1992).**	**§ 35 Client with disability.** . . . (C) **Guardian stands in client's shoes; exceptions.** If a client described in Subsection (A) has a guardian or other person legally entitled to act for the client, the client's lawyer must treat that guardian or other person as the person entitled to act in the client's interests in the matter, unless: (1) the lawyer represents the client in a matter against that person's interests; or (2) the client instructs the lawyer to act in a manner that the lawyer knows will violate the person's legal duties toward the client.

Note the miscue: is the person to act respectfully?

> "Although formulae are now commonly used in legislation, I have been surprised at the number of people who have a 'math attack' at the very mention of the word 'formula'."
>
> —David C. Elliott, *Tools for Simplifying Complex Legislation*, 3 N.Z.J. Tax'n L. & Pol'y 153, 156 (1997).

Simply moving *caused by the defect* wouldn't cure the miscue here: "harm caused by the defect to persons or property" leaves one to wonder whether it's the product or the people and property that are defective.

NOT THIS:	BUT THIS:
Liability of commercial seller or distributor of defective used products. One engaged in the business of selling or otherwise distributing used products who sells or distributes a defective used product is subject to liability for harm to persons or property caused by the defect if the defect: (a) results from the seller's* failure to exercise reasonable care; or (b) is a manufacturing defect under § 2(a) or a defect that may be inferred under § 3 and the seller's marketing of the product would cause a reasonable person in the position of the buyer to expect the used product to present no greater risk of defect than if the product were new; or (c) is a defect under § 2 or § 3 in a used product remanufactured by the seller or a predecessor in the commercial chain of distribution of the used product. **Restatement (Third) of Torts: Products Liability § 8 (Proposed Final Draft 1997).**	**Liability for selling or distributing used defective products.** If a person engaged in the business of selling or otherwise distributing used products sells or distributes a defective used product, that person is liable for harm the defect causes to persons or property if the defect: (A) results from the seller or distributor's failure to exercise reasonable care; (B) is a manufacturing defect under § 2(a)—or a defect that may be inferred under § 3—and the seller or distributor's marketing of the product would cause a reasonable buyer or distributee to expect the used product to present no greater defect risk than if it were new; or (C) is a defect under § 2 or 3 in a used product remanufactured by the seller or distributor—or a predecessor in the product's commercial distribution chain.

*Note the shift in terminology by which *or distributor* has been dropped after *seller*—which could be read in (a)–(c) as not applying to *distributors*.

> "If a document looks terrifying it does not matter how easy the words are: they will never be read."
>
> —Alan Siegel, "Language Follows Logic: Practical Lessons in Legal Drafting" (remarks at Conference of Experts in Clear Legal Drafting, Nat'l Ctr. for Admin. Justice, 2 June 1978), in Reed Dickerson, *Materials on Legal Drafting* 295 (1981).

4.8 Prepositional phrases.

(A) Minimizing *of*-phrases.

Of-phrases tend to encumber a sentence. Do what you can to minimize them while keeping your language normal and idiomatic. Although all prepositional phrases require some caution, *of* requires it to a greater degree. Use a possessive as opposed to an *of*-phrase when you can do so unambiguously.

Many legislative drafters have been taught a retrograde dogma: that *of*-genitives should always be preferred to normal possessives—the *convenience of the debtor* as opposed to *the debtor's convenience.* The syntactic consequences of this dogma are cumulatively debilitating to the prose, which becomes ever more ponderous and clumsy. The counteracting preference against *of*-phrases is among the most significant reforms contained in these *Guidelines*.

NOT THIS:	BUT THIS:
§ 20. Resignation or refusal of office The only evidence of a refusal to accept, or of a resignation of the office of President or Vice President, shall be an instrument in writing, declaring the same, and subscribed by the person refusing to accept or resigning, as the case may be, and delivered into the office of the Secretary of State. **3 U.S.C. § 20.**	**§ 20. Resigning or refusing office.** The only effective evidence of a person's resignation or refusal to accept the office of President or Vice President is a signed, written instrument delivered to the Secretary of State's office.
The marriage license shall be issued if it appears from properly completed applications on behalf of each of the parties to the proposed marriage that there is no legal objection to the marriage. **23 Pa. Cons. Stat. § 1307.**	A marriage license must be issued if it appears from both parties' properly completed applications for the proposed marriage that there is no legal objection to the marriage.
Newly constructed rental housing financed in whole or in part with the funds set aside pursuant to this subdivision shall remain affordable to, and occupied by, very low income households, persons of low income, and persons and families of moderate income for not less than 55 years. **Cal. Gov't Code § 8191(3).**	For at least 55 years, newly constructed rental housing financed in whole or in part with the funds set aside under this subdivision must remain affordable to and occupied by very-low-income households, low-income persons, and moderate-income persons and families.

> "The word 'such' is not infrequently used in Acts when the word 'the' or 'that' would be more correct. In the first place, 'the' or 'that' is better English; and in the next place, the general use of the word 'such' may cause confusion to arise when it is desired to use the word 'such' in its correct meaning."
> —Sir Alison Russell, *Legislative Drafting and Forms* 87 (4th ed. 1938).

NOT THIS:	BUT THIS:
Unless the Mayor considers it to be in the best interest of the District to do otherwise, all securities abandoned under § 41-109 must be held for at least 3 years before the Mayor may sell them. If the Mayor sells any securities delivered pursuant to § 41-109 before the expiration of the 3-year period, any person making a claim pursuant to this chapter before the end of 3 years is entitled to either the proceeds of the sale of the securities or the market value of the securities at the time the claim is made, whichever is greater, less any deduction for fees pursuant to § 41-123(c). A person making a claim under this chapter after the expiration of this period is entitled to receive either the securities delivered to the Mayor by the holder, if they still remain in the hands of the Mayor, or the proceeds received from the sale, less any amounts deducted pursuant to § 41-123(c); but no person has any claim under this chapter against the District, the holder, any transfer agent, registrar, or other person acting for or on behalf of a holder for any appreciation in the value of the property occurring after delivery by the holder to the Mayor. **D.C. Code § 41-122(d).**	All securities abandoned under § 41-109 must be held for at least 3 years before sale, unless the Mayor considers it to be in the District's best interest to do otherwise. If the Mayor sells any securities delivered under § 41-109 before the 3-year period expires, any claimant under this Act within that period is entitled to the proceeds from the securities' sale or the securities' market value when the claim is made (whichever is greater), less any deductions under § 41-123(c). After this period expires, the claimant is entitled to receive either the securities that the holder delivered to the Mayor, if they still remain in the Mayor's hands, or the sale's proceeds, less any deductions under § 41-123(c). But no person has a claim under this Act against the District, the holder, or a transfer agent, registrar, or other person acting for a holder, for appreciation in the property's value occurring after the holder has delivered the property to the Mayor.

(B) Changing to adjective.

When feasible, change prepositional phrases to adjectives—including phrasal adjectives (see § 4.9(G)).

NOT THIS:	BUT THIS:
[N]othing contained herein may be construed as limiting any other powers of a housing authority. **N.D. Cent. Code § 23-11-36.**	[N]othing in this Act limits any other housing-authority powers.
Whoever violates subsection (1) shall be guilty of a felony of the third degree, punishable as provided in s. 775.082, s. 775.083, or s. 775.084. **Fla. Stat. § 951.22(2).**	Violation of (1) is a third-degree felony punishable under § 775.082, 775.083, or 775.084.

> "Legal writing is notorious for using language that no one else uses. Words such as *hereby*, *hereinbefore*, and *thereto* do not add precision to a statute. They just give the statute a legal smell."
>
> —Susan Krongold, *Writing Laws: Making Them Easier to Understand*, 24 Ottawa L. Rev. 495, 526 (1992).

(C) Changing to possessive.

When feasible, change prepositional phrases to possessives. Avoid the *of*-genitive if a possessive is idiomatically available.

NOT THIS:	BUT THIS:
[T]he proposed or existing articles of incorporation of the association, if it is or is to be incorporated . . . . **Wis. Stat. § 703.33.**	The association's proposed or existing articles of incorporation, if it is or will be incorporated . . . .
Right of entry. A cable operator, upon receiving a request for service by a tenant or landlord, has the right to enter property of the landlord for the purpose of making surveys or other investigations preparatory to the installation. Before such entry, the cable operator shall serve notice upon the landlord and tenant, which notice shall contain the date of the entry, the name and address of the cable operator, the name and address of the landlord, from whom the request for service was received, and a citation to this act. The cable operator is liable to the landlord for any damages caused by such entry but such damages shall not duplicate damages paid by the cable operator pursuant to section eight of this article. **W. Va. Code § 24D-2-6.**	**Entering the property.** Upon receiving a tenant's or landlord's request for service, a cable operator may enter the property before the installation to make a survey or other preparatory investigation. Before entering, the cable operator must give the landlord and tenant notice, specifying the entry date, the cable operator's name and address, the requesting landlord's name and address, and a citation to this Act. The cable operator is liable to the landlord for any damage that the entry causes as long as this liability does not duplicate damages that the cable operator has paid under § 24D-2-8.

"The lawyer, like the theologian, is faced with a number of texts that he regards as authoritative, and that are supposed to settle any question that can conceivably arise. Each text was at one time drawn up by someone who presumably meant something by it; but once the document has left its author's hands it is the document that matters, not any unexpressed meaning that still remains in the author's mind. For the lawyer the words of the document are authoritative as words, and there is generally no possibility of obtaining further information from the author, either because the author is dead, or because of rules of evidence precluding reference to him."

—Glanville Williams, *Language and the Law* (pt. 2), 61 L.Q. Rev. 179, 191 (1945).

4.9 Punctuation.

Use standard punctuation in accordance with *The Redbook: A Manual on Legal Style* (3d ed. 2013) and *The Chicago Manual of Style* (16th ed. 2010). Only a few common pitfalls are illustrated here.

(A) Colon before indented enumerations.

Use a colon—not a dash or other punctuation mark—as a lead-in to subparts.

NOT THIS:	BUT THIS:
§ 6504. National standards for organic production. To be sold or labeled as an organically produced agricultural product under this title, an agricultural product shall— (1) have been produced and handled without the use of synthetic chemicals, except as otherwise provided in this title; (2) except as otherwise provided in this title and excluding livestock, not be produced on land to which any prohibited substances, including synthetic chemicals, have been applied during the 3 years immediately preceding the harvest of the agricultural products; and (3) be produced and handled in compliance with an organic plan agreed to by the producer and handler of such product and the certifying agent. **7 U.S.C. § 6504.**	**§ 6504. Requirements for organic products.** To be sold or labeled as organically produced under this title, an agricultural product must be: (A) produced and handled without using synthetic chemicals, unless this title provides otherwise; (B) produced on land that has not had prohibited substances—e.g., synthetic chemicals—applied during the 3 years before the harvest of the agricultural products, except for livestock and as otherwise provided in this title; and (C) produced and handled in compliance with an organic plan that is agreed to both by the product's producer and handler and by the certifying agent.

(B) Semicolon at end of nonterminal parts.

Put a semicolon at the end of each subpart. End each subpart except the last with a semicolon (with the next to last followed by a conjunction—*and* or *or*).

NOT THIS:	BUT THIS:
(b) A statement is not hearsay if the declarant testifies at the trial or hearing and is subject to cross-examination concerning the statement and the statement is (1) inconsistent with the declarant's testimony, and was given under oath subject to the penalty of perjury at a trial, hearing, or other proceeding, or in a deposition, or (2) consistent with the declarant's testimony and is offered to rebut an express or implied charge against the witness of recent fabrication or improper influence or motive, or (3) an identification of a person made after perceiving the person. Such prior statements are substantive evidence. **D.C. Code § 14-102(b).**	(B) **Not hearsay.** A statement is substantive evidence, not hearsay, if: (1) the declarant testifies at the trial or hearing and is subject to cross-examination about the statement; and (2) the statement is: (i) inconsistent with the declarant's testimony and was given under oath subject to the penalties of perjury at a trial, hearing, or other proceeding, or deposition; (ii) consistent with the declarant's testimony and is offered to rebut an express or implied charge against the witness of recent fabrication or improper influence or motive; or (iii) indicative of a person's identity after the declarant perceived the person.

(C) Comma after introductory phrase.

Place a comma after an introductory phrase or subordinate clause.

NOT THIS:	BUT THIS:
At the expiration of sixty days from the date of written notice to the commission the employer no longer is liable under the terms of this title . . . . **S.C. Code § 42-1-390.**	At the end of 60 days after the date of written notice to the Commission, the employer is no longer liable under this title . . . .

(D) Serial comma and semicolon.

Use the serial comma or the serial semicolon before *and* or *or* in a series. It prevents more ambiguities than people suspect, and it never creates an ambiguity in competent writing.

NOT THIS:	BUT THIS:
The seller shall furnish to the purchaser the following: . . . (c) A copy of any proposed or existing management contract, employment contract or other contract affecting the use, maintenance or access of all or part of the condominium to which it is anticipated the unit owners or the association will be a party following closing. **Wis. Stat. § 703.33.**	The seller must give the purchaser the following: . . . (C) A copy of any proposed or existing management contract, employment contract, or other contract affecting the use, maintenance, or access of all or part of the condominium if the unit owners or the association may be a party to the contract after closing.

(E) Double-dash construction for important interpolations.

Prefer dashes to parentheses or commas for interpolated ideas that need emphasis. This represents a huge shift for many legislative drafters who have been taught to avoid all dashes at all costs. The reason is obscure and ill-founded. Far from creating ambiguities, dashes disambiguate many constructions and make the sense much plainer to readers of legislative texts. For more examples, consult any of the four major sets of federal court rules (Civil, Criminal, Appellate, Evidence). The bias against dashes is wayward and backward. Used in moderation, they are an important part of any good writer's arsenal. Without them, commas are required to take on too many duties. The commas proliferate, and the writing becomes a slog.

NOT THIS:	BUT THIS:
To the extent that the authority to decide is not allocated to the client by § 33, other provisions of this Restatement, or a valid agreement or instruction, a lawyer may take any lawful measure reasonably calculated to advance a client's objectives as defined by the client in a matter in which the lawyer represents the client, consulting with the client as required by § 31. **Restatement (Third) of the Law Governing Lawyers § 32(3) (Tentative Draft No. 5, 1992).**	When the client is not allocated decision-making authority by § 33, by this Restatement's other provisions, or by a valid agreement or instruction, a lawyer may take any lawful measure reasonably calculated to advance a client's objectives—as the client defines them—in a matter in which the lawyer represents the client, consulting with the client as § 31 requires.

NOT THIS:	BUT THIS:
§ 27-12A-40. Creation of Insurance Fraud Unit. (d) Investigators of the unit shall have all the powers vested in law enforcement officers of the State of Alabama, including, but not limited to, the powers of arrest and the power to serve process, but only as necessary to enforce this chapter, and shall perform the duties, responsibilities, and functions as may be required for the unit to carry out its duties and responsibilities pursuant to this chapter. No person shall serve as investigator of the unit who has not met the minimum standards established for law enforcement officers by the Alabama Peace Officers' Standards and Training Commission, or other standards as may be provided hereafter by law. **Ala. Code § 27-12A-40(d).**	**§ 27-12A-40. Insurance-Fraud Unit.** (D) **Investigators' powers & qualifications.** The unit's investigators have all the powers vested in law-enforcement officers of the State of Alabama, including the powers of arresting and serving process—but only as necessary to enforce this Act. An investigator must perform the duties, responsibilities, and functions required for the unit to carry out its duties and responsibilities. An investigator must meet the minimum standards established for law-enforcement officers by the Alabama Peace Officers' Standards and Training Commission, or other standards provided by law.

(F) No hyphen for most prefixed terms.

Eliminate hyphens from prefixed words: *nonparty* and *pretrial*, not *non-party* and *pre-trial*. Exceptions include *cross-claim* and words using the prefix *self-* or *quasi-*. Also, use a hyphen if:

(1) the solid form might lead the reader to mistake the syllables (*anti-inflammatory*, *co-occurrence*, *non-insider*);

(2) the main word is a proper name (*non-United States citizen*, *pre-Memorial Day*);

(3) the prefix is part of a noun phrase (*non-high-school athletics*); or

(4) there might be any confusion in meaning (*pre-judicial career* vs. *prejudicial testimony*; *re-sent* vs. *resent*; *re-sign* vs. *resign*).

NOT THIS:	BUT THIS:
The petition in a cross-claim shall be served on the co-party in the manner prescribed by Article 1314. Citation of the co-party shall not be necessary. . . . **La. Stat. Code Civ. Proc. art. 1072.**	The petition in a cross-claim must be served on the coparty in the manner prescribed by Article 1314. Citation of the coparty is not necessary. . . .
(b) Under a cooperative work-education program established under subsection (a), a director . . . may, without regard to any applicable non-statutory limitation on the number of authorized personnel or on the aggregate amount of any personnel cost . . . (1) make an offer [etc.]. **10 U.S.C. § 2195(b).**	Under a cooperative work-education program established under (a), a director . . . may—without regard to an applicable nonstatutory limit on the number of authorized personnel or on the aggregate amount of any personnel cost . . . (1) make an offer [etc.].
The Commissioner is authorized to require an ante mortem and post-mortem inspection of all livestock slaughtered by licensees . . . . **Ga. Code § 26-2-205.**	The Commissioner is authorized to require antemortem and postmortem inspections of all livestock slaughtered by licensees . . . .

(G) Hyphenating phrasal adjectives.

For clarity and polish, hyphenate phrasal adjectives. That is, if two or more consecutive words make sense only when understood together as an adjective modifying a noun that follows, those words (excluding the noun) should be hyphenated. Three exceptions: (1) when a two-word phrase contains an adverb ending in *-ly* followed by an adjective <closely held corporation> <federally recognized tribe>; (2) when the phrase consists of a proper noun <several United States citizens>; and (3) when the phrase has been naturalized from a foreign language <ex officio member> <prima facie case>.

NOT THIS:	BUT THIS:
The sexual assault program fund is a special account in the general revenue fund. **Tex. Gov't Code § 420.008(a).**	The sexual-assault-program fund is a special account in the general-revenue fund.
Criminal history record information requested under this section . . . may not be released or disclosed by a domestic relations office . . . . **Tex. Gov't Code § 411.1285(c).**	Criminal-history-record information requested under this section . . . must not be released or disclosed by a domestic-relations office . . . .
[T]he Secretary may authorize a ski area permittee to provide such other seasonal or year-round natural resource-based recreational activities . . . . **16 U.S.C. § 497b(c)(1).**	[T]he Secretary may authorize a ski-area permittee to provide other seasonal or year-round natural-resource-based recreational activities . . . .

> "More words should not be used than are necessary to make the meaning clear. Every superfluous word may raise a debate in Parliament, and a discussion in court."
>
> —Sir Courtenay Ilbert, *Legislative Methods and Forms* 247 (1901).

5. Words and Phrases

5.1 Pronouns and their antecedents.

(A) Preference for pronouns when unambiguous.

Some lawyers misguidedly avoid all pronouns. Yes, they can sometimes be ambiguous—be careful. But they are also necessary to a readable style.

NOT THIS:	BUT THIS:
(1) The cost of acquisition of ballot boxes and voting booths, voting machines or electronic voting systems and regular maintenance thereof shall be borne by the municipalities in which the boxes, booths, machines, or systems are used. **Wis. Stat. § 5.68(1).**	(A) **Equipment costs.** The cost of acquiring and maintaining ballot boxes, voting booths, voting machines, and voting systems must be borne by the municipality in which they are used.

Note also how the zombie nouns have been eliminated (see § 1.2(E)).

(B) Necessity of an antecedent.

Ensure that every pronoun is preceded by a proper referent (noun). An adjective or a possessive cannot function as a pronoun's antecedent.

The first *their* has no antecedent: *spousal,* an adjective, doesn't suffice.

NOT THIS:	BUT THIS:
The objective of this Chapter is to allocate property by principles . . . that respect both spousal ownership rights in their property and the equitable claims that each spouse has on the property in consequence of their marital relationship . . . . **Principles of the Law of Family Dissolution: Analysis and Recommendations § 4.02 (Tentative Draft No. 1, 1995).**	This Chapter's objective is to allocate property by principles that . . . respect both spouses' ownership rights in their property and the equitable claims each spouse has on the property because of the marital relationship . . . .

(C) Avoiding cataphora.

Ensure that a referent precedes a pronoun, not vice-versa. That is, avoid what rhetoricians call "cataphora" or "anticipatory reference." Use a noun twice rather than having a pronoun precede its referent.

NOT THIS:	BUT THIS:
Following its approval of the report of the jury of view, the commissioners court may order . . . . **Tex. Transp. Code § 254.018.**	After approving the jury-of-view report, the commissioners court may order . . . .

(D) Agreement in number.

Ensure that a pronoun agrees in number with its antecedent.

NOT THIS:	BUT THIS:
Unless the context otherwise requires, this chapter applies to transactions in goods; they do not apply to any transaction . . . . **Or. Rev. Stat. § 72.1020.**	Unless the context requires otherwise, this Act applies to transactions in goods. It does not apply to any transaction . . . .
Whoever, owing allegiance to the United States, levies war against them or adheres to their enemies . . . . **18 U.S.C. § 2381.**	It is unlawful for a person owing allegiance to the United States to levy war against it or to adhere to its enemies . . . .

Once treated as a plural proper noun, *United States* has been predominantly singular in American English since the late 1800s. See *Garner's Dictionary of Legal Usage* 914 (3d ed. 2011).

> "Lawyers particularly like describing the obvious: 'The sum of one hundred pounds (£100)'; 'The 29th day of September.' What else is £100 if not a sum, and what is the 29th September if not a day?"
>
> —Mark Adler, *Clarity for Lawyers: The Use of Plain English in Legal Writing* 54 (1990).

5.2 Relative pronouns.

(A) *That* vs. *which.*

Use *that*, not *which*, as a restrictive relative pronoun. This injunction is generally (and usefully) followed in American English: it lends grammatical rigor to avoid the word *which* unless it follows a comma, dash, parenthesis, or preposition. True, this convention isn't followed in British English. But it is highly recommended in all English-language contexts.*

What am I talking about? A restrictive *that*-clause is necessary to the essential meaning of a sentence; a nonrestrictive *which*-clause (which might, for example, appear within parentheses) could be dropped from the sentence with no loss of essential meaning—as with the parenthetical *which*-clause earlier in this sentence:

Ex.: Briefing that is helpful should be encouraged in all cases. (*Unhelpful briefing shouldn't be encouraged.*)

Ex.: Briefing, which is helpful, should be encouraged in all cases. (*All briefing should be encouraged.*)

Understand how word choice is reinforced by punctuation. A commaless *which* is ambiguous.

NOT THIS:	BUT THIS:
In prescribing a definition . . . , the department shall . . . designate the optional ingredients which shall be named on the label. **Alaska Stat. § 17.20.010.**	In prescribing a definition . . . , the department must . . . designate the optional ingredients that must be named on the label.
[A]ny intoxicating beverage or beverage which causes or may cause an intoxicating effect . . . . **Fla. Stat. § 951.22.**	[A]ny beverage that can cause intoxication . . . .
He must not possess any medical or physical disability which in the judgement of the employer prevents him from performing the duties of a Private Security Officer . . . . **10 Guam Code Ann. § 71301(7).**	A person must not possess any medical or physical disability that—in the judgment of the employer—prevents that person from performing a Private Security Officer's duties . . . .

*For more on this subject, see *Garner's Modern English Usage* 900–02 (4th ed. 2016); *The Chicago Manual of Style* § 5.220, at 298; § 6.22, at 314 (16th ed. 2010).

(B) Nonrestrictive *which*.

Unless it is preceded by a preposition, use *which* only as a nonrestrictive relative pronoun, and set it off with a comma.

NOT THIS:	BUT THIS:
§ 35. Imparting or conveying false information. (a) Whoever imparts or conveys or causes to be imparted or conveyed false information, knowing the information to be false, concerning an attempt or alleged attempt being made or to be made, to do any act which would be a crime prohibited by this chapter or chapter 97 or chapter 111 of this title shall be subject to a civil penalty of not more than $1,000 which shall be recoverable in a civil action brought in the name of the United States. **18 U.S.C. § 35(a).**	**§ 35. Imparting or conveying false information.** (A) **The Crime.** It is unlawful to knowingly impart or convey, or cause to be imparted or conveyed, false information about any current or future act or attempted act that would be a crime prohibited by this chapter, chapter 97, or chapter 111 of this title. Violation of this provision is punishable by a civil penalty of up to $1,000, which is recoverable in a civil lawsuit brought in the name of the United States.
Any person who willfully threatens to commit a crime which will result in death or great bodily injury to another person, with the specific intent that the statement, made verbally,* in writing, or by means of an electronic communication device, is to be taken as a threat, even if there is no intent of actually carrying out, which, on its face and under the circumstances in which it is made, is so unequivocal, unconditional, immediate, and specific as to convey to the person threatened, a gravity of purpose and an immediate prospect of execution of the threat, and thereby causes that person reasonably to be in sustained fear for his or her own safety or for his or her immediate family's safety, shall be punished by imprisonment in the county jail not to exceed one year, or by imprisonment in the state prison. **Cal. Penal Code § 422(a).**	(A) **Prohibited threats.** It is unlawful to make an oral, written, or electronic communication constituting a criminal threat. A statement is a criminal threat if: (1) the statement: (a) threatens a crime that would result in a person's death or serious physical injury; (b) is unequivocal, unconditional, immediate, and specific; and (c) is intended to be taken as a threat, regardless of intent to carry it out; and (2) the threatened person reasonably: (a) believes that the threatened activity could be carried out; and (b) fears for the person's own safety or that of his or her immediate family. (B) **Penalty.** Violation of (A) is punishable by imprisonment of up to 1 year in state prison or county jail.

The *whiches* in this provision are sloppy—especially the second one.

*This statute appears to misuse *verbally* (in words) for *orally* (in speech). See *Garner's Modern English Usage* 941–42 (4th ed. 2016).

(C) Remote relatives.

Avoid so-called "remote relatives"—the relative pronoun *that* or *which* (or sometimes even *who*) separated from the noun to which it refers. Place the relative pronoun directly after the word it modifies.†

NOT THIS:	BUT THIS:
The State Board of Education shall annually submit a budget recommendation to the Governor and General Assembly that contains recommendations for funding for pre-school through grade 12. **105 Ill. Comp. Stat. 5/2-3.47.**	The State Board of Education must annually submit to the Governor and General Assembly a budget recommendation that contains funding for preschool through grade 12.

†For more on remote relatives, see *Garner's Modern English Usage* 784–86 (4th ed. 2016) (s.v. "Remote Relatives").

NOT THIS:	BUT THIS:
§ 34. Penalty when death results Whoever is convicted of any crime prohibited by this chapter, which has resulted in the death of any person, shall be subject also to the death penalty or to imprisonment for life. **18 U.S.C. § 34.**	**§ 34. Penalty when death results.** A person convicted of a crime that is prohibited by this Act and that has resulted in the death of a person is subject to the death penalty or life imprisonment.
Where one spouse has made a gift of marital property to a third party which is substantial relative to the total value of the marital property, and in which the other spouse did not concur, the court should augment the other spouse's share of the remaining marital property by one-half of the value of such a gift. **Principles of the Law of Family Dissolution: Analysis and Recommendations § 4.16 (Tentative Draft No. 1, 1995).**	If 1 spouse has given a third party marital property that constitutes a substantial part of the total marital estate and the other spouse did not concur in the gift, the court should augment the other spouse's share of the remaining marital property by half the gift's value.
Chapter 11. Legislative organization, procedures and staffing. **§ 11.242. Powers, duties, and functions as to statutory revision** The powers, duties, and functions of the Office of Legislative Services in the operation and maintenance of a statutory revision program shall be as follows: (1) To conduct a systematic and continuing study of the statutes and laws of this state for the purpose of reducing their number and bulk, removing inconsistencies, redundancies, and unnecessary repetitions and otherwise improving their clarity and facilitating their correct and proper interpretation; and for the same purpose, to prepare and submit to the Legislature reviser's bills and bills for the amendment, consolidation, revision, repeal, or other alterations or changes in any general statute or laws or parts thereof of a general nature and application of the preceding session or sessions which may appear to be subject to revision. Any revision, either complete, partial, or topical, prepared for submission to the Legislature shall be accompanied by revision and history notes relating to the same, showing the changes made therein and the reason for such recommended change. **Fla. Stat. § 11.242.**	**§ 11.242. Powers, duties, and functions to revise statutes.** In operating and maintaining a statutory-revision program, the Office of Legislative Services has the following powers, duties, and functions: (A) to conduct a systematic and continuing study of Florida's laws to reduce their number and bulk; (B) to remove inconsistencies, redundancies, and unnecessary repetition; (C) to improve clarity and facilitate proper interpretation; and (D) to submit to the Legislature reviser's bills and bills for any change in an earlier general statute that may appear to need revision, along with revision and history notes showing each recommended change and the reason for it.

> "A good law gathers strength from direct statement; a bad one may hide under confused language."
> —Chester Lloyd Jones, *Statute Law Making in the United States* 93 (1912).

5.3 Conjunctions.

(A) Conjunctive and disjunctive subparts.

When clauses or phrases are joined conjunctively (*and*) or disjunctively (*or*), put the conjunction at the end of the next-to-last item only—not after each item. In legal drafting, polysyndeton (the use of *and* or *or* at the end of each item) has no place.

NOT THIS:	BUT THIS:
§ 1-1. Common law of the State; exceptions. The common law of England, as ascertained by English and American decisions, is declared to be the common law of the State of Hawaii in all cases, except as otherwise expressly provided by the Constitution or laws of the United States, or by the laws of the State, or fixed by Hawaiian judicial precedent, or established by Hawaiian usage; provided that no person shall be subject to criminal proceedings except as provided by the written laws of the United States or of the State. **Haw. Rev. Stat. § 1-1.**	**§ 1-1. Common law of the State; exceptions.** (A) **Common law.** The common law of the State of Hawaii is the common law of England, as ascertained by English and American decisions. (B) **Exceptions.** The common law is superseded by: (1) the U.S. Constitution or federal or state statutes; (2) Hawaiian judicial precedent; and (3) established Hawaiian usages. (C) **Criminal proceedings.** Only the written laws of Hawaii or the United States apply in criminal matters.
§ 27-75-3. **Enactment of compact.** (2) To protect the premium tax revenues of the compacting states through facilitating the payment and collection of premium tax on non-admitted insurance; and to protect the interests of the compacting states by supporting the continued availability of such insurance to consumers; and to provide for allocation of premium tax for non-admitted insurance of multi-state risks among the states in accordance with uniform allocation formulas to be developed, adopted, and implemented by the commission. **R.I. Gen. Laws § 27-75-3, art. I (2).**	**§ 27-75-3. Enactment of compact.** (2) **Tax revenues and nonadmitted insurance.** The compact will: (a) protect the premium-tax revenues of the compacting states by supporting the payment and collection of premium tax on nonadmitted insurance; (b) protect the interests of the compacting states by supporting the continued availability of nonadmitted insurance to consumers; and (c) allocate premium tax for nonadmitted insurance of multi-state risks among the states according to uniform-allocation formulas developed, adopted, and implemented by the commission.

(B) *But* vs. *and.*

Use *but* instead of *and* to introduce a contrasting idea.

NOT THIS:	BUT THIS:
All appointments are subject to confirmation by the General Assembly if in session when such appointments are made, and if not in session, then at its next succeeding session. **Va. Code § 23-49.14(d).**	An appointment is subject to confirmation by the General Assembly if in session when the appointment is made, but if not in session, then at the Assembly's next succeeding session.

"Anything *and/or* can do, ordinary English can do better."
—David Mellinkoff, *Legal Writing: Sense and Nonsense* 56 (1982).

(C) Preference for *But* over *However* as a sentence-starter.

Use *But* to start a sentence in preference to *However* or other even more cumbersome contrasting words.* Don't place a comma after an initial *But*.

NOT THIS:	BUT THIS:
However, the association may not exercise an election . . . if the receiver, rehabilitator, or liquidator . . . disaffirmed the reinsurance agreement. **Wash. Rev. Code § 48.32A.075(14)(a).**	But the association cannot exercise an election . . . if the receiver, rehabilitator, or liquidator . . . has disaffirmed the reinsurance agreement.
The reporting requirement . . . does not apply to the discovery of abuse or neglect that occurred during childhood if it is discovered after the child has become an adult. However, if there is reasonable cause to believe other children are or may be at risk of abuse or neglect by the accused, the reporting requirement . . . does apply. **Wash. Rev. Code § 26.44.030(2).**	If abuse or neglect that occurred during childhood is discovered after the child has become an adult, the reporting requirement . . . does not apply. But if there is reasonable cause to believe that other children are or may be at risk of abuse or neglect by the accused, the reporting requirement . . . does apply.

(D) Avoiding comma splices with *however*.

Avoid the grammatical blunder of splicing together two independent clauses with the conjunctive adverb *however*. The mistake is called a "comma splice," also known as a run-on sentence.

NOT THIS:	BUT THIS:
Notwithstanding s. 160.19 (1) and (2), the department is not required to promulgate or amend rules that define design or management criteria for aquifer storage and recovery systems to minimize the amount of a specified substance in groundwater or to maintain compliance with the preventive action limit for a specified substance, however, the department shall promulgate rules that define design or management criteria for aquifer storage and recovery systems to maintain compliance with drinking water standards promulgated under ss. 280.11 and 281.17 (8). **Wis. Stat. § 160.257(2).**	Despite §§ 160.19(1) and 160.19(2), the department need not promulgate or amend rules defining design or management criteria for aquifer storage-and-recovery systems either to minimize the amount of a specified substance in groundwater or to comply with the preventive-action limit for a specified substance. But the department must promulgate such rules† to comply with drinking-water standards under §§ 280.11 and 281.17(8).

*For a collection of myriad authorities defending this age-old practice, see *Garner's Modern English Usage* 133–34, 878 (4th ed. 2016).

†The phrase *such rules* here means "rules of this kind"—that is, rules that define design or management criteria for aquifer storage-and-maintenance systems.

> "I am well aware of the prejudice which exists against all attempts to state the law simply."
>
> —James Fitzjames Stephen, *A Digest of the Law of Evidence* xix (4th ed. 1893).

5.4 Specific words and forms to avoid.

action (in the sense of "lawsuit"). Prefer *lawsuit*—if for no reason other than avoiding the miscue that ordinary readers will have in thinking that *action* might refer merely to an act.

NOT THIS:	BUT THIS:
§ 3504. Investigations; civil actions. (a) The Attorney General shall investigate diligently violations under section 3503 involving Government funds. If the Attorney General finds that a person has violated or is violating section 3503, the Attorney General may bring a civil action under this section against that person. (b) (1) A person may bring a civil action for a violation of this chapter for the person and for the Government in the name of the Government if any Government funds are involved. The person bringing the action is referred to as the qui tam plaintiff. **33 V.I. Code § 3504(a), (b)(1).**	**§ 3504. Investigations; civil lawsuits.** (A) **Duty to investigate.** The Attorney General must diligently investigate violations under § 3503 involving Government funds, and may bring a civil lawsuit against a violator. (B) **Qui tam lawsuit.** (1) If this Act is violated and Government funds are involved, a person (the "qui tam plaintiff") may bring a civil lawsuit for the person and for the Government in the name of the Government.
§ 37-2-9. Publication of notice where representatives of defendant nonresidents, etc.; when action revived. When the plaintiff shall make an affidavit that the representatives of the defendant, or any of them, in whose name the action may be ordered to be revived, are nonresidents of the state, or have left the same to avoid the service of the order, or so concealed themselves that the order cannot be served upon them or that the names and residence of the heirs or devisees of the person against whom the action may be ordered to be revived, or some of them are unknown to the affiant, a notice may be published as provided in Chapter XCIV, notifying them to appear on a day therein named and show cause why the action should not be revived against them, and if sufficient cause be not shown to the contrary, the action shall stand revived. **N.M. Stat. § 37-2-9.**	**§ 37-2-9. Publication of notice for unavailable representatives of defendants; when lawsuit revived.** (A) **Publication of notice.** Notice may be published, as provided in Chapter 94, if the plaintiff states in an affidavit that: (1) any representative of the defendant: (a) is a nonresident of the state; (b) has left the state to avoid service of the order; or (c) has hidden to avoid service of the order; or (2) the plaintiff does not know the name and residence of an heir or devisee of the person against whom the lawsuit may be revived. (B) **Contents of notice.** The notice must notify the defendant's representative that: (1) the lawsuit may be revived in the defendant's name; (2) the representative must appear on a specified date and show cause why the lawsuit should not be revived; and (3) if sufficient cause is not shown, the lawsuit will be revived.

> "[T]he symbol 'and/or,' though increasingly popular in legal documents, should under no circumstances be allowed to corrupt the statute book."
> —Sir Alison Russell, *Legislative Drafting and Forms* 101 (4th ed. 1938).

aforesaid. See *said* (p. 157).

all of. Delete *of* when possible.

NOT THIS:	BUT THIS:
Any person whose employment is permanent under this section on December 21, 1995, shall retain all of the rights and privileges of such permanent employment after that date. **Wis. Stat. § 119.42(3).**	A person whose employment is permanent under this section on December 21, 1995, retains all the rights and privileges of this permanent employment after that date.

and/or. Use *or* or *and*, or *or . . . both*. If *and/or* joins the last two items of a list consisting of three or more items, try *any or all of the following* as the lead-in to the list. But remember: if *and* is the right word, use *and*.

NOT THIS:	BUT THIS:
For the purposes of this article, the term "itinerant vendor" shall mean a merchant, other than a merchant with an established retail store, who transports to a building, vacant lot, or other location, including a location where a fee is charged for the privilege of offering or displaying goods for sale and/or where a fee is charged to prospective buyers for admission to the area where goods are offered or displayed for sale . . . . **N.Y. Gen. Bus. Law § 37(1).**	"Itinerant vendor" means a merchant who transports goods to a building, vacant lot, or other location to offer or display them for sale—not including a merchant with an established retail store. This definition includes a location where a fee is charged to prospective buyers or sellers for admission.
If an insurance company licensed to do business in this state offers or purports to offer to renew any commercial liability and/or property insurance policy at less favorable terms as to the dollar amount of coverage or deductibles, higher rates, and/or higher rating plan, the new terms, the new rates and/or rating plan may take effect on the renewal date of the policy if the insurer has sent to the policyholder notice of the new terms, new rates and/or rating plan at least 30 days prior to the expiration date. . . . **Minn. Stat. § 60A.351.**	If an insurance company licensed to do business in this state offers or purports to offer to renew any commercial-liability or property-insurance policy at a higher rate or a higher rating plan, or with less favorable terms for the dollar amount of coverage or deductible, the insurer must send the policyholder notice of the new rating plan and the new terms at least 30 days before the policy expires. Otherwise, the changes will not take effect on the policy's renewal date. . . .

"[C]onfused language often evidences confused thought; pretentious words may be used to conceal poverty of concept; loose phraseology may have its roots in sloppy analysis. Technical, 'insider' language can also evidence a conscious or unconscious slant with that language. There is simply less incentive to try to see things in the ways of ordinary people if ordinary people are outside the circle of those with whom one is trying to communicate."

—John A. Bell, *Prose of Law: Congress as a Stylist of Statutory English* 39–40 (1981).

NOT THIS:	BUT THIS:
§ 58-65-120. Medical, dental and hospital service associations and agent to transact business through licensed agents only No medical and/or dental or hospital service association; nor any agent of any association shall on behalf of such association or agent, knowingly permit any person not licensed as an agent as provided by law, to solicit, negotiate for, collect or transmit a premium for a new contract of medical and/or dental or hospital service certificate or to act in any way in the negotiation for any contract or policy; provided, no license shall be required of the following: (1) Persons designated by the association or subscriber to collect or deduct or transmit premiums or other charges for medical and/or dental care or hospital contracts, or to perform such acts as may be required for providing coverage for additional persons who are eligible under a master contract. (2) An agency office employee acting in the confines of the agent's office, under the direction and supervision of the duly licensed agent and within the scope of such agent's license, in the acceptance of request for insurance and payment of premiums, and the performance of clerical, stenographic, and similar office duties. N.C. Gen. Stat. § 58-65-120.	**§ 58-65-120. Medical-, dental-, and hospital-service associations must transact business through licensed agents.** (A) **General rule.** A medical-, dental-, or hospital-service association, or an agent of that association, must not knowingly permit an unlicensed agent to solicit, negotiate for, collect, or send a premium for a new medical, dental, or hospital contract or policy or to participate in any negotiation. (B) **Exceptions.** The following are not required to be a licensed agent: (1) a person designated by the association or subscriber to: (a) collect, deduct, or send premiums or other charges for medical or dental care or hospital contracts; or (b) arrange for coverage of additional persons eligible under a master contract; (2) an agency-office employee acting in the confines of the agent's office, under the direction and supervision of the duly licensed agent, and within the scope of that agent's license: (a) in the acceptance of requests for insurance and payment of premiums; or (b) in the performance of clerical, stenographic, and similar office duties.

> "[T]here is no need to refer to 'the said article' or 'the article hereinbefore mentioned'; anything conveyed by the extra words is already covered by 'the' alone."
>
> —Mark Adler, *Clarity for Lawyers: The Use of Plain English in Legal Writing* 60 (1990).

any. Try *a*, *an*, or *other* instead. But *any* is preferable to *if any* (see p. 148). And see *such as* (p. 161).

NOT THIS:	BUT THIS:
§ 875. Interstate communications. (a) Whoever transmits in interstate or foreign commerce any communication containing any demand or request for a ransom or reward for the release of any kidnapped person, shall be fined under this title or imprisoned not more than twenty years, or both. **18 U.S.C. § 875(a).**	**§ 875. Interstate communications.** (A) **Prohibition and penalty.** It is unlawful to transmit in interstate or foreign commerce a communication containing a demand or request for a ransom or reward for the release of a kidnapped person. Violation of this title is punishable by imprisonment of up to 20 years or a fine, or both.
State, county and municipal officers, departments, boards and commissions, and all school districts in this State, shall require applications in writing for employment by them, upon such application forms as they may severally prescribe, which shall include information as to active or honorary membership in or affiliation with all membership associations and organizations. The provisions of this section shall not apply to any office or position which by law is filled by the vote of the qualified electors in any general or special election. **S.C. Code § 1-1-540.**	(A) **Written applications.** The following must require a written employment application for a prospective employee that they may hire: (1) state, county, and municipal offices; (2) departments, boards, and commissions; and (3) school districts. (B) **Requirements.** In addition to any other information that an employer mentioned in (A) may require, the application must include information about active or honorary membership in or affiliation with all membership associations and organizations. (C) **Exemption for elective office.** This section does not apply to a position filled by the vote of qualified electors in a general or special election.
§ 1.14 Tribal ordinances or customs enforced. Any tribal ordinance or custom heretofore or hereafter adopted by the governing council of the Sac and Fox Indian settlement in Tama county in the exercise of any authority which it may possess shall, if not inconsistent with any applicable civil law of the state, be given full force and effect in the determination of civil causes of action pursuant to sections 1.12 to 1.15. **Iowa Code § 1.14.**	**§ 1.14 Effect of tribal ordinance or custom.** When the governing council of the Sac and Fox Indian settlement in Tama County exercises its authority to adopt a tribal ordinance or custom before or after this section's effective date, that ordinance or custom has full effect in lawsuits under §§ 1.12 to 1.15, as long as it is not inconsistent with other applicable state law.

> "A judge puts before himself the printed page of the statute book; it is mirrored on the retina of his eye and from this impression he has to reproduce the thought of the law-giving body."
> —John Chipman Gray, *The Nature and Sources of the Law* 171 (2d ed. 1921).

commence & expire. Instead of these hyperformal words, try *begin* and *end.*

NOT THIS:	BUT THIS:
The sentence of community parole supervision for life shall commence immediately upon the expiration of the term of imprisonment imposed upon such person by the court or upon such person's release from probation or parole supervision or upon the expiration of a continuance without a finding or upon discharge from commitment to the treatment center pursuant to section 9 of chapter 123A, whichever first occurs. . . . **Mass. Gen. Laws ch. 6, § 178H(2).**	The sentence of community-parole supervision for life begins immediately upon the earliest of the following: (A) when the person's term of imprisonment ends; (B) when the person is released from probation or parole supervision; (C) when a continuance without a finding ends; or (D) when the person is discharged from commitment to a treatment center under § 123A(9).
Fire protection districts subject to the conditions hereinafter set forth may, pursuant to the discretion of the fire protection board, contract with individual property owners whose property is situated outside of the external boundaries of the fire protection district within the state of Idaho or within any neighboring state to provide for the same measure of fire protection to such contracting property owner as is provided to property owners within the boundaries of such contracting fire protection districts. All such contracts shall be for a term of one (1) year and shall commence at 12:01 a.m. on January 1 of such year and expire at 12 midnight on December 31 of such year. . . . **Idaho Code § 31-1431.**	At the discretion of the fire-protection board, a fire-protection district may contract with a property owner whose property is situated within Idaho and outside the district's external boundaries or within any neighboring state to provide the property owner with the same fire protection as is provided to property owners within the fire-protection district's boundaries. Any such contract must be for a term of 1 calendar year, beginning at 12:01 a.m. each January 1 . . . .

commencing _____ and until and including _____. Instead, write *begin(ning)* _____ *through* _____.

NOT THIS:	BUT THIS:
Regular terms of the Supreme Court shall commence on the first Monday of October in each year and continue until and including the last day of June of the ensuing year, but the court may, in its discretion, adjourn from time to time. **Ala. Code § 12-2-8.**	Regular terms of the Supreme Court begin on the first Monday of October in each year and continue through June 30 of the next year. But the court may, in its discretion, adjourn from time to time.

> "There ought to be a certain simplicity and candor in the laws; made to punish the iniquity of men, they themselves should be clad with the robes of innocence."
>
> —Charles de Secondat Baron de Montesquieu, 2 *The Spirit of Laws* 169 (1748; Thomas Nugent trans., 1900).

NOT THIS:	BUT THIS:
If such bonds or notes are payable in installments, the installments remaining unpaid may be called for redemption only (i) in the inverse order of their maturity or, (ii) in equal proportionate amounts; provided, however, that for bonds issued during the one-year period commencing July first, nineteen hundred eighty-eight, and for bonds issued during the one-year period commencing July first, nineteen hundred eighty-nine, and for bonds issued during the one-year period commencing July first, nineteen hundred ninety, and for bonds issued during the three-year period commencing July first, nineteen hundred ninety-one, and for bonds issued during the period from July first, nineteen hundred ninety-four up until and including July fifteenth, nineteen hundred ninety-seven and for bonds issued during the period from July fifteenth, nineteen hundred ninety-seven up until and including July fifteenth, two thousand, and for bonds issued during the period from July fifteenth, two thousand up until and including July fifteenth, two thousand three, and for bonds issued during the period from July fifteenth, two thousand three up until and including July fifteenth, two thousand six, and for bonds issued during the period from July fifteenth, two thousand six up until and including July fifteenth, two thousand nine, and for bonds issued during the period from July fifteenth, two thousand six up until and including July fifteenth, two thousand twelve, and for bonds issued during the period from July fifteenth, two thousand nine up until and including July fifteenth, two thousand fifteen, installments remaining unpaid on such bonds may be called for redemption prior to their date of maturity in such amounts, at such times in such manner and pursuant to such terms as may be determined by the finance board of a municipality, school district or district corporation at the time of the issuance thereof. **N.Y. Local Fin. Law § 53.00(b).**	(A) **Installment payments.** If the bonds or notes are payable in installments, the unpaid installments may be called for redemption only in the inverse order of their maturity or in equal proportionate amounts. (B) **Redemption of unpaid installments.** Installments unpaid on a bond issued during the following periods may be called for redemption before their maturity date in the amounts, at the times, in the manner, and under the terms determined by the finance board of a municipality, school district, or district corporation: • each 1-year period from July 1, 1988, from July 1, 1989, and from July 1, 1990; • the 3-year periods from July 1, 1991 through July 1, 1994, from July 1, 1994 through July 15, 1997, from July 15, 1997 through July 15, 2000, from July 15, 2000 through July 15, 2003, from July 15, 2003 through July 15, 2006, from July 15, 2006 through July 15, 2009; and • the 6-year periods from July 15, 2006 through July 15, 2012, and from July 15, 2009 through July 15, 2015.

deem. Use *treated as* or *considered* or a present-tense verb such as *is* or *does*.

NOT THIS:	BUT THIS:
A seller shall be deemed to do business in this state if the seller . . . . **Cal. Bus. & Prof. Code § 17511.3.**	A seller does business in this state if the seller . . . .
Any person violating the provisions of this section shall be deemed guilty of a misdemeanor . . . . **Wis. Stat. § 175.10(2).**	A person who violates this section is guilty of a misdemeanor . . . .

NOT THIS:	BUT THIS:
A person not a partner is deemed to know of a limitation on the authority of a partner to transfer real property held in the name of the partnership if a certified copy of the filed statement containing the limitation on authority is of record in the office for recording transfers of that real property. **N.D. Cent. Code § 45-15-03(4).**	A person who is not a partner is considered to know the limit on the partner's authority to transfer real property held in the partnership's name if a certified copy of the filed statement containing the limit on authority is on record in the office for recording transfers of that property.

every. Prefer *a* or *an*.

NOT THIS:	BUT THIS:
Every person liable for any tax imposed by this title, or for the collection thereof, shall keep such records, render such statements, make such returns, and comply with such rules and regulations as the Secretary may from time to time prescribe. **26 U.S.C. § 6001.**	A person liable for a tax or the collection of a tax that this title imposes must keep records, render statements, make returns, and comply with the regulations that the Secretary may occasionally prescribe.

except as. Use *unless* when you can—especially when referring to some future action by the court or by the parties. Sometimes you'll need *except as* in reference to another legislative provision {*except as permitted in § 101, no creditor may* . . .} in the sense "except to the extent that."

Miscue: This sounds as if the list of persons is provided by local rule.

The rewrite reflects the numbering system recommended in § 3.3(A).

NOT THIS:	BUT THIS:
Except as the parties may stipulate under the provisions of subdivision (a) of this rule, the arbitrator shall be appointed by the Court Administrator or Superior Court Clerk from a list of persons, as provided by local rule . . . . **Ariz. Rev. Stat. § 16- 73(b).**	Unless the parties stipulate otherwise under (A), the Court Administrator or Superior Court Clerk will appoint the arbitrator from a list of persons in accordance with local rule . . . .
§ 61-7. **Board; composition; compensation; duties.** . . . (b) Except as otherwise provided by resolution of the board or this act, all ordinances, resolutions, and other legislative acts of the district shall be adopted by the board and certified to, recorded and published, in the same manner as are ordinances, resolutions, or other legislative acts of the county of Napa. (c) Except as otherwise provided by resolution of the board, the budget for the district shall be prepared, presented, and approved by the board in accordance with those procedures applicable to the budget for the County of Napa, except that at least 14 votes are required to approve or modify the budget. **Cal. Water Code § 61-7(b)–(c).**	§ 61-7. **Board; composition; compensation; duties.** . . . (B) **Board authority.** Unless a board resolution or this Act provides otherwise, the board must adopt, certify to, record, and publish any district ordinance, resolution, and other legislative act in the same manner as a Napa County ordinance, resolution, or other legislative act. (C) **Budget duties.** Unless a board resolution provides otherwise, the board must prepare, present, and approve the district's budget in accordance with Napa County's budget procedures. But at least 14 votes are required to approve or modify the budget.

NOT THIS:	BUT THIS:
Except as provided otherwise by written agreement between the director or officer and the credit union, a director or officer who is a party to a proceeding may apply for indemnification to the court conducting the proceeding or to another court of competent jurisdiction. **Wis. Stat. § 186.088(1).**	Unless a written agreement between the director or officer and the credit union provides otherwise, a director or officer who is a party to a proceeding may apply for indemnity to the court conducting the proceeding or to another court of competent jurisdiction.
Subject to his duty to liquidate the estate for prompt distribution and to the provisions of the will, if any, the personal representative may invest the funds of the estate but shall have no duty to do so. Any such investment, except as the court or the will may otherwise authorize or direct, shall be restricted to: . . . **20 Pa. Cons. Stat. § 3316.**	Subject to the personal representative's duty to liquidate the estate for prompt distribution and to any provisions of the will, the representative may invest the estate's funds—but has no duty to do so. Unless the court or the will otherwise directs or authorizes, any investments are restricted to: . . .

except that. Prefer *but*, especially by beginning a new sentence. See § 5.3(C).

NOT THIS:	BUT THIS:
Circulation records maintained by the public library in the District of Columbia which can be used to identify a library patron who has requested, used, or borrowed identified library materials from the public library and the specific material that patron has requested, used, or borrowed from the public library, shall be kept confidential, except that the records may be disclosed to officers, employees, and agents of the public library to the extent necessary for the proper operation of the public library. **D.C. Code § 39-108(a).**	The District of Columbia public library must keep confidential all its maintained circulation records that could identify a library patron and the specific material that the patron has requested, used, or borrowed from the library. But the library may disclose those records to its officers, employees, and agents as necessary for its proper operation.

except when. Use *unless.*

NOT THIS:	BUT THIS:
Except when he is accompanied by his counsel, the judge must inform the defendant of his right to remain silent and that anything he says may be used against him. **N.C. Gen. Stat. § 15A-602.**	Unless the defendant is accompanied by counsel, the judge must inform the defendant of: (A) the right to remain silent; and (B) the fact that anything the defendant says may be used against him or her.
The tax for supporting ambulance and rescue squads serving the borough shall not exceed the rate specified in subsection (a)(9) except when the question is submitted to the voters of the borough in the form of a referendum which will appear on the ballot in accordance with the election laws of the Commonwealth, in which case the rate shall not exceed two mills. **8 Pa. Cons. Stat. § 1302(e).**	The tax for supporting ambulance and rescue squads serving the borough must not exceed the rate specified in (a)(9) unless the question is submitted to the borough voters in the form of a referendum appearing on the ballot in accordance with the Commonwealth's election laws, in which case the rate must not exceed 2 mills.

NOT THIS:	BUT THIS:
Stations or levels shall have a passageway around the working shaft so that crossing over the hoisting compartments may be avoided. Sumps shall be securely covered. At shaft stations a gate or guard rail shall be provided and kept in place across the shaft, except when a cage, skip or bucket is being loaded, but may be temporarily removed for repairs or other operations if proper precaution is taken to prevent danger to persons. . . . **Ariz. Rev. Stat. § 27-348.**	A station or level must have a passageway around the working shaft so that crossing over the hoisting compartment may be avoided. A sump must be securely covered. A shaft station must have a gate or guardrail and must be kept in place across the shaft unless a cage, skip, or bucket is being loaded. The gate or guardrail may be temporarily removed for repairs or other operations if proper precaution is taken to prevent danger to persons. . . .

except with [+ *noun*]. Use *unless* [+ *verb*].

The failure to require consent in writing appears to be a substantive flaw.

NOT THIS:	BUT THIS:
Any health care provider may designate one or more individuals to be contacted by the private review agent for information or data. In the event of any such designation, the private review agent shall not contact other employees or personnel of the health care provider except with prior consent to the health care provider. **Ga. Code § 33-46-4(9).**	A healthcare* provider may designate 1 or more persons whom the private-review agent may contact for information or data. If the provider does so, the agent must not contact the provider's other employees or personnel unless the provider first consents in writing.

following. If you mean "after," write *after.*

NOT THIS:	BUT THIS:
When senatorial districts are realigned following a decennial census, members of the state executive committee previously elected or appointed shall continue in office until the expiration of their terms. . . . At the first election of executive committee members following the realignment of senatorial districts, members shall be elected from the newly established districts. **W. Va. Code § 3-1-9.**	When senatorial districts are realigned after a decennial census, previously elected or appointed members of the state executive committee continue in office until their terms expire. . . . At the first election of executive-committee members after the realignment of senatorial districts, members are elected from the newly established districts.

*On the preferred one-word spelling of *healthcare*, see n.* at p. 11.

> "Errors are harder to find in dense and convoluted prose. Removing legalese helps lay bare any oversights in the original. This can benefit not only the client for whom the document is drawn, but also the drafter, for it forces the drafter to reappraise the text and consider what the client really intended."
> —Peter Butt & Richard Castle, *Modern Legal Drafting* 89 (2001).

forthwith. Use *promptly* (with very little delay) or *immediately* (with no delay) instead. Better yet, state a specific period or deadline.

NOT THIS:	BUT THIS:
When it appears to the Attorney General that any person has formed or published a lottery, or taken any measures for that purpose, or is engaged in selling or otherwise distributing tickets, certificates, shares or interests therein, whether such lottery originated in this State or not, he shall immediately make complaint in the name of the State to the Superior Court for an injunction to restrain such person from further proceedings therein. If satisfied that there is sufficient ground therefor, such court shall forthwith issue such injunction and thereupon it shall order notice to be served on the adverse party to appear and answer to said complaint. . . . **Me. Rev. Stat. tit. 17-A, § 958(1).**	If it appears to the Attorney General that a person has formed or published a lottery; has taken any measures to that end; or is engaged in selling or otherwise distributing tickets, certificates, or shares or interests in them, regardless of whether the lottery originated in this State, the Attorney General must promptly complain on behalf of the State to the Superior Court and seek an injunction to restrain the person from continuing the lottery activities. If the court is satisfied that there is sufficient ground for an injunction, the court must issue it promptly and order notice to be served on the adverse party to appear and answer the complaint. . . .

hereof, herein, hereby, hereto, hereunder, therein, thereof, thereto, and the like. Use everyday words instead, especially demonstrative pronouns such as *that*, *this*, *these*, and *those*.

NOT THIS:	BUT THIS:
Whoever shall put any dead animal, carcass or part thereof, or other filthy substance, into any well . . . . **Neb. Rev. Stat. § 28-1304.**	A person who puts a dead animal, its carcass, its parts, or any other filthy substance* into a well . . . .
Poultry and poultry products are an important source of the Nation's total supply of food. They are consumed throughout the Nation and the major portion thereof moves in interstate or foreign commerce. **21 U.S.C. § 451.**	Poultry products are important to the Nation's food supply. Most of them move through interstate or foreign commerce.
(c) The Secretary, in his discretion, may waive the limitation provisions of subchapter I of chapter 81 of title 5 with respect to notice of injury and filing of claims under this subchapter, whenever the Secretary shall find that, because of circumstances beyond the control of an injured person or his beneficiary, compliance with such provisions could not have been accomplished within the time therein specified. **42 U.S.C. § 1706(c).**	(C) **Waiving notice of injury and filing of claims.** The Secretary may waive the limitation provisions of 5 U.S.C. §§ 8101–8152 for notice of injury and filing of claims upon finding that—because of circumstances beyond his or her control—the injured person or beneficiary could not have complied with the limitation provisions within the specified time.

*Note that this phrase (*filthy substance*) is vague—perhaps unconstitutionally so. It may be redeemed by the *ejusdem generis* canon of construction. *See* Antonin Scalia & Bryan A. Garner, *Reading Law: The Interpretation of Legal Texts* § 32, at 199–213 (2012). What is intended to be covered? Animal spoor? Human remains? Bodily fluids? Used chewing tobacco? Bleach? Chemicals? The wording is predictably problematic.

NOT THIS:	BUT THIS:
Unless the motion and the files and records of the case conclusively show that the prisoner is entitled to no relief, the court shall cause notice thereof to be served upon the United States attorney, grant a prompt hearing thereon, determine the issues and make findings of fact and conclusions of law with respect thereto. **28 U.S.C. § 2255(b).**	Unless the prisoner's motion or the challenged case's records conclusively show that the prisoner should not receive relief, the court must notify the United States Attorney, grant a proper hearing, determine the issues, and make findings of fact and conclusions of law about the sentence's challenge.
[N]o State or any political subdivision thereof may adopt, enforce, or continue in effect any provision of any law or regulation (including any remedy or penalty applicable to any violation thereof) with respect to termination (or the furnishing of notification with respect thereto) of any such franchise or to the nonrenewal (or the furnishing of notification with respect thereto) of any such franchise relationship unless . . . . **15 U.S.C. § 2806(a)(1).**	No State or any of its political subdivisions may adopt, enforce, or perpetuate a legal or regulatory provision or associated remedy or penalty regarding a petroleum franchise's termination, nonrenewal, or notice of termination or nonrenewal, unless . . . .

if any. Try placing *any* before the noun.

NOT THIS:	BUT THIS:
§ 1588. Articles of association; minimum requirements Articles of association of cooperative housing corporations shall contain the following provisions in addition to those required by chapter 17 of this title: (1) a statement that the cooperative housing corporation shall have only one class of stock; (2) a statement of restrictions, if any, upon transfer of shares; (3) the rate of dividend, if any, allocable to membership shares which shall not exceed six percent per annum on invested capital; (4) reservation of the right of the cooperative housing corporation to acquire membership shares; (5) basis of distribution of assets in event of dissolution; (6) the method of allocation of ownership and voting interests in the cooperative housing corporation; and (7) the conditions, if any, under which the cooperative housing corporation shall have a right of first refusal upon proposed transfer of cooperative interests. **Vt. Stat. tit. 11, § 1588.**	**§ 1588. Articles of association; minimum requirements.** A cooperative-housing corporation's articles of association must contain the following provisions in addition to those required by chapter 17 of this title: (A) a statement that the corporation has only 1 class of stock; (B) a statement of any restrictions on transferring shares; (C) the rate of any dividend allocable to membership shares—limited to no more than 6% per year on invested capital; (D) reservation of the corporation's right to acquire membership shares; (E) the basis for distributing assets if the corporation dissolves; (F) the method of allocating ownership and voting interests in the corporation; and (G) any conditions under which the corporation has a right of first refusal on a proposed transfer of cooperative interests.

including but not limited to; including without limitation; including without limiting the generality of the foregoing; etc. The recommended course is to put the following definition in an interpretation act: "'Including' means 'including but not limited to.'"

NOT THIS:	BUT THIS:
The provisions of this title shall not apply to the following powers of attorney: 1. a power of attorney given primarily for a business or commercial purpose, including without limitation: (a) a power to the extent it is coupled with an interest in the subject of the power; (b) a power given to or for the benefit of a creditor in connection with a loan or other credit transaction; (c) a power given to facilitate transfer or disposition of one or more specific stocks, bonds or other assets, whether real, personal, tangible or intangible . . . . **N.Y. Gen. Oblig. Law § 5-1501C.**	This title does not apply to the following powers of attorney: (A) one given primarily for a business or commercial purpose, including a power: (1) coupled with an interest in the subject of the power; (2) given to or for the creditor's benefit in connection with a loan or other credit transaction; or (3) given to facilitate the transfer or disposition of 1 or more specific stocks, bonds, or other assets, whether real, personal, tangible, or intangible. . . .

Note that the revision also demonstrates economy of parallelism (see § 3.4(D)).

in the event of + [*zombie noun*]. Try to change to *if.*

NOT THIS:	BUT THIS:
Not later than 18 months after the date of enactment of the Rail Safety Improvement Act of 2008, the Secretary of Transportation shall prescribe regulations that require railroad carriers— (1) to provide emergency escape breathing apparatus suitable to provide head and neck coverage with respiratory protection for all crewmembers in locomotive cabs on freight trains carrying hazardous materials that would pose an inhalation hazard in the event of release; . . . **49 U.S.C. § 20166.**	No later than 18 months after the Rail Safety Improvement Act of 2008 is enacted, the Secretary of Transportation must prescribe regulations that require railroad carriers: (1) to provide emergency-escape breathing apparatuses with suitable head and neck coverage for respiratory protection for all crew members in locomotive cabs on freight trains carrying hazardous materials that would pose an inhalation hazard if released; . . .
In carrying out these responsibilities, the Secretary shall . . . develop a mechanism whereby United States citizens can voluntarily request to be placed on a list in order to be contacted in the event of an evacuation, or which, in the event of an evacuation, can maintain information on the location of United States citizens in high risk areas submitted by their relatives; . . . . **22 U.S.C. § 4802(b)(2).**	In carrying out these responsibilities, the Secretary must . . . develop a way for citizens to join a list to be contacted if an evacuation is called and for relatives of U.S. citizens in high-risk areas to maintain information on their location.

in the event that. Use *if.*

NOT THIS:	BUT THIS:
(f) **Disposition of controlled substances or list I chemicals** In the event the Attorney General suspends or revokes a registration granted under section 823 of this title, all controlled substances or list I chemicals owned or possessed by the registrant pursuant to such registration at the time of suspension or the effective date of the revocation order, as the case may be, may, in the discretion of the Attorney General, be placed under seal. **21 U.S.C. § 824(f).**	(f) **Disposition of controlled substances or list-I chemicals.** If the Attorney General suspends or revokes a registration granted under § 823, all controlled substances or list-I chemicals the registrant owns or possesses at revocation may, with the Attorney General's approval, be sealed.
§ 27300. Results of election; limitation upon subsequent proceedings In the event that a majority of the votes cast at the election are in favor of the exclusion, the board, upon completion of the canvass, shall make an order excluding the area from the district. In the event that a majority of the votes cast at the election are opposed to the exclusion, the measure fails and no proceedings for exclusion of the area may be subsequently initiated within one year. **Cal. Pub. Util. Code § 27300.**	**§ 27300. Results of election; limit on later proceedings.** (A) **If the proposition carries.** If a majority of the votes favor exclusion, the board must, on completion of the canvass, order the area to be excluded from the district. (B) **If the proposition fails.** If a majority of the votes oppose exclusion, the measure fails. No proceedings for area exclusion may be initiated within the next year.

limitation. Unless referring to a statute of limitations, use *limit.*

NOT THIS:	BUT THIS:
[L]oans or extensions of credit secured by a segregated deposit account in the lending state bank are not subject to a limitation based on unimpaired capital and unimpaired surplus . . . . **Alaska § 06.05.205(C)(6).**	A loan or extension of credit secured by a segregated deposit account in the lending state bank is not subject to a limit based on unimpaired capital and unimpaired surplus . . . .
Section 76113. Sections 76107 to 76110 shall not be considered to impose the following limitations . . . [a] limitation on the right of a person to engage in diving for recreational purposes in and upon the Great Lakes or the bottomlands of the Great Lakes. **Mich. Comp. Laws § 324.76113(a).**	**§ 76113. No Limitation on Certain Rights to Dive.** Sections 76107 to 76110 do not limit . . . a person's right to dive in and on the Great Lakes or the bottomlands of the Great Lakes for recreational purposes.

"[T]he moment has come when the reflex use of 'shall' should be abandoned in favour of 'must.'"

—Martin Cutts, *Unspeakable Acts?: Clarifying the Language and Typography of an Act of Parliament* § 9.13, at 11 (1993).

not later than. Use *no later than* or *within.* "*Within* 10 days after entry of judgment" is usually better than "*no later than* 10 days after entry of judgment." But the latter may be needed if you want to allow the act to be done before the entry of judgment as well as in the following 10 days.

NOT THIS:	BUT THIS:
Not later than January 1 of each odd-numbered year the commission shall submit to the lieutenant governor, speaker of the house of representatives, and each other member of the legislature a report documenting the committee's recommendations and comments . . . . **Tex. Gov't Code § 411.0197(f).**	No later than January 1 of each odd-numbered year, the commission must submit to the lieutenant governor and each member of the legislature a report documenting the committee's recommendations and comments . . . .
The findings of the Board of County Commissioners of Clatsop County with respect to an application shall be set out concisely in writing, and a copy served on the applicant not later than the 10th day after they are rendered. Not later than the 30th day after receipt of a copy of such findings or within such further time as the county board authorizes on a showing of good cause, an applicant may request a rehearing . . . . **Or. Rev. Stat. § 273.875.**	When the Clatsop County Board of Commissioners makes findings regarding an application, it must set out the findings concisely in writing and serve a copy on the applicant within 10 days after the findings are rendered. Within 30 days after receiving a copy of the findings, or within the further time authorized by the Board upon a showing of good cause, an applicant may request a rehearing . . . .

not less than. Try *at least.*

NOT THIS:	BUT THIS:
Not less than 5 days' written notice of the hearing under par. (b) shall be sent to the pupil and, if the pupil is a minor, to the pupil's parent or guardian. **Wis. Stat. § 119.25(2)(c).**	At least 5 days before the hearing, written notice of the hearing under (b) must be sent to the pupil and, if the pupil is a minor, to the pupil's parent or guardian.
Sec. 2201. Performance standards (a) In general The Secretary shall, in coordination with the Secretary of Agriculture, not less frequently than every 2 years, review and evaluate relevant health data and other relevant information, including from toxicological and epidemiological studies and analyses, current Good Manufacturing Practices issued by the Secretary relating to food, and relevant recommendations of relevant advisory committees, including the Food Advisory Committee, to determine the most significant foodborne contaminants. **21 U.S.C. § 2201(a).**	**§ 2201. Performance standards.** (A) **Generally.** At least every 2 years, in coordination with the Secretary of Agriculture, the Secretary must determine the most significant foodborne contaminants. They must review and evaluate relevant health data and other relevant information, including toxicological and epidemiological studies and analyses, current Good Manufacturing Practices issued by the Secretary relating to food, and relevant recommendations of relevant advisory committees, such as the Food Advisory Committee.

not more than. Try *up to.*

NOT THIS:	BUT THIS:
2073. Penalties. Any person who willfully performs any act prohibited, or willfully fails to perform any act required, by the provisions of this title [50 U.S.C. Appx. §§ 2071 et seq.] or any rule, regulation, or order thereunder, shall, upon conviction, be fined not more than $10,000 or imprisoned for not more than one year, or both. **50 U.S.C. App. § 2073.**	**§ 2073. Prohibition and penalty.** It is unlawful to willfully perform any act prohibited, or to fail to perform any act required, by this Act [50 U.S.C. Appx. §§ 2071 et seq.] or any rule, regulation, or order made under this Act. Violation is punishable by a fine of up to $10,000 or imprisonment for up to 1 year, or both.

notwithstanding any other provision of law. Does this language really mean what it says? On its face, it purports to override constitutions, treaties, and later-enacted statutes. It is ill-advised.

NOT THIS:	BUT THIS:
Notwithstanding any other provision of law, the hearing examiner presiding at a hearing may order such protective measures as are necessary to protect the trade secrets of parties to the hearing. **Wis. Stat. § 227.46(7)(a).**	The presiding hearing examiner may order protective measures necessary to protect the trade secrets of a party to the hearing.
§ 23396.5. On-sale licensee; eating place; removal of partially consumed bottle of wine upon departure Notwithstanding any other law, any on-sale licensee that maintains a bona fide eating place in conjunction with such license, any on-sale beer and wine public premises licensee, or any winegrower that is exercising a privilege pursuant to Section 23358 or 23390 may allow any person who has purchased and partially consumed a bottle of wine to remove the partially consumed bottle from the premises upon departure. **Cal. Bus. & Prof. Code § 23396.5.**	**§ 23396.5. On-sale licensee; eating place; removal of partly consumed bottle of wine.** The following may allow a person who has purchased and partly consumed a bottle of wine to take that bottle off the premises: (A) an on-sale licensee that in good faith maintains an eating place under that license; (B) an on-sale beer-and-wine public-premises licensee; or (C) a winegrower exercising a privilege under § 23358 or 23390.

Note the singular wording. See § 2.4.

This type of omnibus override is unnecessary given that a particular law, especially one containing an exception, always controls over a more general one.

notwithstanding the fact that. Use *even if* or *even though.* Instead of *notwithstanding* alone, try *despite.*

NOT THIS:	BUT THIS:
Notwithstanding the fact that a public depository is required to pledge eligible securities in certain amounts to secure deposits of public moneys, a trustee shall have no duty or obligation to determine the eligibility, market value, or face value of any securities deposited with the trustee by a public depository. This applies in all situations including, without limitation, a substitution or exchange of securities. **Ohio Rev. Code § 131.15(D).**	A trustee has no duty to determine the eligibility, market value, or face value of any securities deposited with the trustee by a public depository—even if: (1) a public depository is required to pledge eligible securities in certain amounts to secure deposits of public money; or (2) the securities have been substituted or exchanged.

on and after. Use *after* or *from*—or some simpler formulation.

NOT THIS:	BUT THIS:
(c) A minor has the same capacity as an adult to consent to: . . . (8) Initial medical screening and physical examination on and after admission of the minor into a detention center. **Md. Code, Health—Gen. § 20-102(c)(8).**	(3) ***Consent of minor.*** A minor has the same capacity as an adult to consent to: . . . (h) an initial medical screening and physical examination after the minor has been admitted to a detention center.

partially. Use *partly.* Although few readers will seriously read *partially* as an antonym of *impartially*, the term is simplifiable to *partly.*

NOT THIS:	BUT THIS:
In the event that the deceased is a minor with no persons either wholly or partially dependent upon the deceased, the employer or the employer's insurance carrier, if any, shall pay to the parents of the deceased the sum of fifteen thousand dollars, not to exceed one hundred percent of the death benefit. . . . In the event that there are persons only partially dependent upon the deceased, the employer or the employer's insurance carrier, if any, shall first pay such benefits to such partially dependent persons and shall pay the balance to the surviving parents of the deceased . . . . **Colo. Rev. Stat. § 8-46-102(1)(b).**	If the deceased is a minor with no dependents, the employer or the employer's insurance carrier will pay the deceased's parents $15,000 or 100% of the death benefit, whichever is less. . . . If there are persons only partly dependent on the deceased, the employer or the employer's insurance carrier will first pay the benefits to the partly dependent persons and then pay the balance to the deceased's surviving parents . . . .

portion. Try *part* instead.

NOT THIS:	BUT THIS:
If the claimant is the grantor of a trust holding title to real or tangible personal property on which a credit is claimed, the claimant may claim the portion of the credit and be treated as the owner of that portion of the property held in trust for which the claimant proves to the satisfaction of the county that . . . . **Utah Code § 59-2-1203(3).**	If the claimant is the grantor of a trust holding title to real or tangible personal property on which a credit is claimed, the claimant may claim that part of the credit and be treated as owner of that part of the property held in trust for which the claimant proves to the county's satisfaction that . . . .
If land is held by a debtor in joint tenancy or as a tenant in common, the share thereof belonging to the debtor may be taken on execution, and shall thereafter be held in common with the co-tenant. If the whole share of the debtor is more than sufficient to satisfy the execution, the levy shall be made upon such undivided portion of such share as will, in the opinion of the appraisers, satisfy the execution, and such undivided portion shall be held in common with the debtor and the other co-tenant. **Mass. Gen. Laws ch. 236, § 12.**	If land is held by a debtor in joint tenancy or a tenancy in common, the debtor's share may be taken on execution. It will then be held in common with the cotenant. If the debtor's whole share is more than sufficient to satisfy the execution, levy may be made only on as much of the undivided part of the share as will, in the appraiser's opinion, satisfy the execution. The undivided part will then be held in common with the debtor and the other cotenant.

NOT THIS:	BUT THIS:
Whenever the owner or occupant desires to pasture livestock on land adjacent to the railroad not then used for pasturing livestock and desires the railroad to erect the portion of the fence next to the tracks, he shall fence the portion of that land which is not adjacent to the railroad, and the railroad shall construct the portion of the fence adjacent to its tracks within five days of notice to it from the owner or occupant that his portion of the fence has been completed, and shall maintain that fence so long as the adjacent land is used for pasturing livestock. **Vt. Stat. tit. 5, § 3642(b).**	An owner or occupant who wants to pasture livestock on land adjacent to the railroad and not then used for pasturing livestock, and who wants the railroad to build a fence next to the tracks, must fence the part of the land not adjacent to the railroad. When the owner or occupant completes his or her part of the fence and notifies the railroad of completion, the railroad must build the part of the fence adjacent to its tracks within 5 days and must maintain that fence as long as the adjacent land is used for pasturing livestock.

prior to. Use *before* or *more than.* Especially avoid *prior to the time when.*

NOT THIS:	BUT THIS:
No petition may be circulated prior to 60 days before the date required for filing. **Wis. Stat. § 125.05(1)(b)(2).**	No petition may be circulated more than 60 days before the date required for filing.
Not less than 10 days prior to doing business in this state, a telephonic seller shall register with the department . . . . **Cal. Bus. & Prof. Code § 17511.3.**	At least 10 days before doing business in this state, a telephone seller must register with the department . . . .
Prior to the issuance or renewal of a hospice program license, the department shall inspect the hospice program for compliance with the standards established pursuant to this chapter. **N.D. Cent. Code § 23-17.4-05.**	Before issuing or renewing a hospice-program license, the department must inspect the program for compliance with the standards established in this Act.
§ 780-A. Use of blank write-in absentee ballot. Prior to the time when regular absentee ballots are available, if an applicant requests a blank write-in absentee ballot or indicates that it takes more than 6 weeks to receive and return mail to the applicant's location, the Secretary of State shall send a blank write-in absentee ballot to the voter or shall transmit the regular absentee ballot by an authorized electronic means if the voter has designated that the voter wishes to receive that ballot by that means. **Me. Rev. Stat. tit. 21-A, § 780-A.**	**§ 780-A. Use of blank write-in absentee ballot.** Before regular absentee ballots are available, if an applicant requests a blank write-in absentee ballot or indicates that it takes more than 6 weeks to receive and return mail to the applicant's location, the Secretary of State must send a blank write-in absentee ballot to the voter or must send the regular absentee ballot by an authorized electronic means if the voter states that he or she wishes to receive the ballot by that means.

NOT THIS:	BUT THIS:
§ 17-17-10. Payment of toll prior to passage; demand of excessive toll; evading payment of toll. The proprietor of any toll bridge may require lawful toll to be paid previous to a passage thereover. But if there be demanded at any such bridge more than is lawful, the proprietor shall forfeit to the party aggrieved so much as is illegally demanded and a further sum of not less than two nor more than fifteen dollars. Whoever shall knowingly or intentionally defraud, or attempt to defraud, the proprietor of any toll bridge by evading, or attempting to evade, the payment of lawful toll for crossing such bridge, or whoever shall aid another to evade, or attempt to evade, the payment of such toll, shall be guilty of a misdemeanor, and for every such offense shall, upon conviction thereof, be fined not in excess of ten dollars. W.V. Code § 17-17-10.	**§ 17-17-10. Payment of toll before passage; demand of excessive toll; evading payment of toll.** (A) **Tolls.** A toll-bridge proprietor may require a lawful toll to be paid before crossing over the bridge. But if the proprietor demands more than a lawful toll, the proprietor forfeits to the aggrieved party the illegally demanded amount and a further sum of $2 to $15. (B) **Evading toll.** It is unlawful to knowingly or intentionally defraud, or attempt to defraud, a toll-bridge proprietor by evading, or attempting to evade, paying a lawful toll for crossing the bridge. Violation of this provision is a misdemeanor punishable by a fine up to $10. (C) **Aiding evasion.** It is unlawful to help another evade, or attempt to evade, paying a lawful toll to cross a toll bridge. Violation of this provision is a misdemeanor punishable by a fine up to $10.

provided that; provided however that. Reword using more specific language. See § 4.5.

NOT THIS:	BUT THIS:
Upon proof being made, at any hearing on a complaint under this section, that there has been discrimination in price or services or facilities furnished, the burden of rebutting the prima-facie case thus made by showing justification shall be upon the person charged with a violation of this section, and unless justification shall be affirmatively shown, the Commission is authorized to issue an order terminating the discrimination: Provided, however, that nothing herein contained shall prevent a seller rebutting the prima-facie case thus made by showing that his lower price or the furnishing of services or facilities to any purchaser or purchasers was made in good faith to meet an equally low price of a competitor, or the services or facilities furnished by a competitor. 15 U.S.C. § 13(b).	The burden of rebutting the prima facie case of discrimination in price, services, or facilities provided is on the person charged with violating this section. Unless the seller affirmatively shows justification for the discrimination, the Commission may issue an order terminating the discrimination. The seller may rebut the prima facie case by showing that the seller offered the lower price or provided services or facilities to a purchaser in good faith to match a competitor's prices, services, or facilities.

> "[R]ight law must be intelligible, intellectually accessible to the people whom that law is to serve, whose law it is, the law-consumers and the citizen 'makers' of the law."
>
> —Karl Llewellyn, *On the Good, the True, the Beautiful in Law*, 9 U. Chi. L. Rev. 224, 249 (1942).

provisions of. Avoid *the provisions of*—invariably a filler phrase.

NOT THIS:	BUT THIS:
Sec. 301. Land grant aid of colleges. There is granted to the several States, for the purposes hereinafter mentioned in this subchapter, an amount of public land, to be apportioned to each State a quantity equal to thirty thousand acres for each Senator and Representative in Congress to which the States are respectively entitled by the apportionment under the census of 1860: Provided, That no mineral lands shall be selected or purchased under the provisions of said sections. **7 U.S.C. § 301.**	**§ 301. Land-grant aid of colleges.** (A) **State allocations.** To carry out this Act's purposes, each state is granted 30,000 acres of public land to be apportioned for each senator and representative in Congress as determined according to the census of 1860. No mineral lands may be selected or purchased under this Act.
10/6. Exclusive methods of disposal. In accordance with the provisions set forth in Section 11-19-7 of the Illinois Municipal Code and Section 5-1047 of the Counties Code, units of local government may provide by ordinance, license, contract or other means that the methods of disposal of solid waste shall be the exclusive methods of disposal to be allowed within their respective jurisdictions, notwithstanding the fact that competition may be displaced or that such ordinance, license, contract or other measure may have an anti-competitive effect. **415 Ill. Comp. Stat. 10/6.**	**§ 10.6. Designation of exclusive disposal methods.** In accordance with § 11-19-7 of the Illinois Municipal Code and § 5-1047 of the Counties Code, a local-government unit may provide by ordinance, license, contract, or other means that the methods of disposal of solid waste must be the exclusive methods allowed within its jurisdiction, even if competition may be displaced and even if the ordinance, license, contract, or other means may have an anticompetitive effect.
The provisions of this chapter [22 U.S.C. §§ 1971 et seq.] shall not apply with respect to a seizure made by a country at war with the United States or a seizure made in accordance with the provisions of any applicable convention or treaty, if that treaty or convention was made with advice and consent [of] the Senate and was in force and effect for the United States and the seizing country at the time of the seizure. **22 U.S.C. § 1974.**	This chapter [22 U.S.C. §§ 1971–1980b] does not apply to a seizure made: (A) by a country at war with the United States; or (B) in accordance with any applicable convention or treaty, if that treaty or convention was made with the advice and consent of the Senate and was in effect for the United States and the seizing country at the time of the seizure.

pursuant to. Use *under* or *in accordance with.* Write *under § 3,* not *pursuant to § 3*; *in accordance with 26 U.S.C. § 1333,* not *pursuant to 26 U.S.C. § 1333.*

NOT THIS:	BUT THIS:
A prescription drug or medical device is one that may be legally sold or otherwise distributed only pursuant to a health care provider's prescription. **Restatement (Third) of Torts: Products Liability § 8(a) (Tentative Draft No. 2, 1995).**	A prescription drug or medical device is one that may be legally sold or distributed only in accordance with a healthcare* provider's prescription.

*On the preferred one-word spelling of *healthcare*, see n.* at p. 11.

NOT THIS:	BUT THIS:
If the person presumed to be dead pursuant to section 14-701* is found to be living, a person injured by the presumption shall be restored to the rights of which he was deprived by reason of the presumption. **D.C. Code § 14-702.**	If a person presumed under § 14-701 to be dead is found alive, anyone who has lost rights because of the presumption must be restored to those rights.

said, *adj.* Use *the*, *this*, or *that*. Like its siblings, *the said* and *the aforesaid*, *said* used as an article imparts no greater specificity than the definite article *the*.

NOT THIS:	BUT THIS:
[T]he establishment of the aforesaid national seashore recreational area may, in the discretion of the said Secretary, be abandoned, and that, in the event of such abandonment, the said State will accept a reconveyance of title to all lands conveyed by it to the United States for said national seashore recreational area. The lands donated to the United States for the purposes of sections 459 to 459a–3 of this title by parties other than said State shall revert in the event of the aforesaid abandonment to the donors, or their heirs, or other persons entitled thereto by law. **16 U.S.C. § 459a-2.**	At the Secretary's discretion, the establishment of the national seashore recreational area may be abandoned. If abandoned, the State is entitled to the reconveyance of title to all land that it originally conveyed to the United States for that area. If a party other than the State donated the land to the United States under §§ 459–459a-3, the land reverts upon abandonment to the donors, their heirs, or those lawfully entitled to it.
Beginning November 1, 1984, all individuals, firms, corporations, or other entities engaging in the business of abstracting, shall have available for use or commence compilation of an abstract plant and thereafter shall maintain in a current condition said plant. Failure to do so shall render its certificates of authority subject to revocation. An abstract plant shall be deemed in a current condition if it reflects all documents or other matters that are filed in said county except those filed within the preceding fifteen (15) days. Holders of a certificate of authority issued pursuant to law who were engaged in the business of abstracting on November 1, 1984, shall not be required to construct or maintain an abstract plant of documents filed or recorded prior to November 1, 1984. If any such holder allows said certificate of authority to lapse after November 1, 1984, he shall be required to apply for a new certificate of authority before resuming the business of abstracting. **Okla. Stat. tit. 1, § 31.**	Beginning November 1, 1984, all entities engaged in the business of abstracting must have an abstract plant available for use and keep it up to date. Failure to maintain the plant renders its certificates of authority subject to revocation. An abstract plant is up to date if it reflects all documents or other matters filed in the county, except those filed within the preceding 15 days. Holders of a lawfully issued certificate of authority who were engaged in the business of abstracting on November 1, 1984, are not required to construct or maintain an abstract plant of documents filed or recorded before that date. If a holder allows a certificate of authority to lapse after November 1, 1984, the holder must apply for a new certificate of authority before resuming the business of abstracting.

*Note the misplaced modifier: how can someone be "dead pursuant to section 14-701"?

NOT THIS:	BUT THIS:
Upon the written application of 10 percent of the registered voters in any city, presented to the city clerk prior to the municipal election, the city clerk shall insert on the ballot to be used at said election the following question: "Shall fluoride be used in the public water system?" Beside this question shall be printed the word "yes" and the word "no" with the proper boxes for the voter to indicate his or her choice. If a majority of those voting in a water system that serves one municipality at said election does not approve the use of fluoride in the public water system for said city, no fluoride shall be introduced into the public water system. If fluoride has, prior to said vote, been so introduced, such use shall be discontinued until such time as the majority of those voting in the town approve the use of such fluoride. After such popular referendum, the city clerk shall not insert the aforementioned question relative to the use of fluoride in the public water system on the ballot to be used at the municipal election for a minimum period of 3 years from the date of the last popular referendum, and only upon written application at that time of not less than 10 percent of the registered voters of said city. The procedure for a referendum on the use of fluoride in a city that is part of a water system serving more than one municipality shall be the procedure in RSA 485:14-a. **N.H. Rev. Stat. § 44:16.**	Upon the written application of 10% of a city's registered voters, presented to the city clerk before the municipal election, the city clerk will put on the ballot for the election the following question: "Do you want fluoride to be used in the public water system?" The words "yes" and "no" must be printed with boxes beside this question for the voter to indicate his or her choice. If a majority of those voting are in a water system serving 1 municipality and do not approve using fluoride in the city's public water system, no fluoride will be used. If fluoride has been added before the vote, its use must be discontinued until the majority of those voting in the city approve it. After the popular referendum, the city clerk must not put on a ballot any similar question about fluoride for 3 years after that election. If after those 3 years at least 10% of the city's registered voters again make a written application for the question, the city clerk will put it on the ballot as before. The procedure for a referendum on using fluoride in a city that is part of a water system serving more than 1 municipality is the procedure in RSA 485:14-a.

"In writing as lawyers, we should be driven by a zeal to increase respect for the law and by a humane goal to help our citizens understand and appreciate its benefits for them, to make available to them the fruits of our knowledge and skill. This is the mark of the true professional. It can be achieved only if we write plainly in a way that can be understood."

—Robert D. Eagleson, *What Is Plain English?*, Address at the Singapore Acad. of Law 19 (27 Jan. 1996).

same, *pron.* Use the relevant noun or *it*, *they*, or *them*. When used as a pronoun, *same* imparts faux precision that can actually mask an ambiguity.

NOT THIS:	BUT THIS:
That in those instances in which the amount of capital available for industrial financing in the State of Oklahoma tends to be reduced by reason of reduction in the volume of tax-exempt industrial bonds issued or issuable by cities or counties in Oklahoma, or by reason of federal statutes or United States Treasury Department rulings limiting or adversely affecting this method of financing said industrial projects in this state, the Oklahoma Industrial Finance Authority is hereby authorized, within its sole discretion, to accept applications and make loans to industrial development agencies, as the same are defined by law. As security therefor the Authority shall take a mortgage upon the industrial facility from such industrial development agency holding legal title to the same, and shall take a promissory note or notes for the amount of such loan from an approved industrial tenant . . . . **Okla. Stat. tit. 74, § 878.**	If the amount of capital available for industrial financing in Oklahoma is reduced because the volume of tax-exempt industrial bonds issued or issuable by Oklahoma's cities or counties has been reduced, or because federal statutes or U.S. Treasury rulings limit or adversely affect this method of financing industrial projects in Oklahoma, the Oklahoma Industrial Finance Authority may accept applications and make loans to industrial-development agencies (as they are defined by law). As security, the Authority may take a mortgage on the industrial facility from the industrial-development agency holding legal title to the facility; if it does so, the Authority must* take promissory notes for the loan amount from an approved industrial tenant . . . .

so [*verb +ed*] **as to.** Use [*verb +ed*] *to*.

NOT THIS:	BUT THIS:
All such bonds may be registered as to principal alone or both principal and interest, shall be payable as to principal within not to exceed 30 years from the date thereof, shall be in such denominations, shall be executed in such manner, and shall be payable in such medium and at such place or places as the Board may determine, and the face amount thereof shall be so calculated as to produce, at the price of their sale, the cost of the Stadium constructed pursuant to this subchapter. **D.C. Code § 3-323(a).**	The face amount of the bonds must be calculated to produce, at their sale, the cost of the stadium. The bonds may be registered for principal alone or for both principal and interest. The principal must be payable within 30 years from the registration date.

*This is a guess at the original's meaning, which is unclear.

> "Even in a legislative environment in which drafting standards are relatively low, [the drafter] can materially sharpen the tools of language by being scrupulously consistent in arranging his materials and in selecting his words, phrases, and punctuation."
>
> —Reed Dickerson, *The Interpretation and Application of Statutes* 225 (1975).

NOT THIS:	BUT THIS:
All owners of real estate or agents thereof, before constructing any artificial drain, storm sewer, conduit or culvert across private property shall submit plans and specifications therefor and receive the approval of the municipal authorities before doing the work, in order that the artificial drain, culvert, storm sewer, or conduit may be made of sufficient size and so designed as to care for the drainage water flowing from the water shed above the property. The municipal government, through its engineer, or other proper department may inspect all work to the end that the same may comply with the plans and specifications as approved for same. **La. Rev. Stat. § 33:5060.**	Before constructing an artificial drain, storm sewer, conduit, or culvert across private property, a real-estate owner must submit plans and specifications and receive the municipal authorities' approval. The project must be designed to handle the drainage water flowing from the watershed above the property. The municipal government, through its engineer or other proper department, may inspect all work to ensure that it complies with the approved plans and specifications.

subsequent to. Use *after.*

NOT THIS:	BUT THIS:
Upon retirement subsequent to a cancellation of a disability benefit under 19-3-1104, a member must receive a recalculated benefit . . . . **Mont. Code § 19-3-1105(2).**	Upon retiring after a disability benefit has been canceled under 19-3-1104, a member will receive a recalculated benefit . . . .
Those persons identified in subsection (b) of this section need not be joined as necessary parties in a mortgage foreclosure action when their interest arises subsequent to the filing of the mortgage foreclosure action. Any person acquiring an interest defined in subsection (b) of this section subsequent to the filing of the foreclosure action and at least 30 days prior to the sheriff's sale scheduled in the cause shall be given written notice in accordance with the rules of the Superior Court. Any person acquiring a property interest in real estate within 30 days prior to the sheriff's sale scheduled in the cause shall not be entitled to receive written notice of the sale, the public records of the foreclosure being sufficient notice. **Del. Code tit. 10, § 5061(e).**	A person identified in (b) need not be joined as a necessary party in a mortgage-foreclosure lawsuit when the person's interest arises after the lawsuit has been filed. Such a person must be given written notice of the sheriff's sale at least 30 days before the sale in accordance with the Superior Court's rules. But no notice need be given to a person who acquires an interest in the real estate less than 30 days before the sale; in this instance, the public records of the foreclosure are sufficient notice.

such, *adj.* Use *the, this,* or *that*—unless *such* is used in the literate nonlawyer's sense "of that general type" (e.g., *such auctions* means "auctions of that kind").

NOT THIS:	BUT THIS:
The corporation shall . . . [r]epresent and protect the interests of the residential utility consumers of this state. All actions by the corporation under this chapter shall be directed toward such duty. **Wis. Stat. § 199.05(1)(a).**	The corporation must . . . represent and protect the interests of this state's residential utility consumers. All the corporation's actions must be directed to this duty.

Perhaps *will*: The statute is establishing the Citizens Utility Board. Its duties could be stated at its creation as a policy (*will*) or as a duty (*must*).

NOT THIS:	BUT THIS:
If the Administrator intends to provide written comments to such State with respect to such permit application or such proposed general permit, he shall so notify such State not later than the thirtieth day after the date of the receipt of such application or such proposed general permit and provide such written comments to such State, after consideration of any comments made in writing with respect to such application or such proposed general permit by the Secretary and the Secretary of the Interior, acting through the Director of the United States Fish and Wildlife Service, not later than the ninetieth day after the date of such receipt. **33 U.S.C. § 1344(j).**	If the Administrator intends to give the State written comments regarding the permit application or proposed general permit, the Administrator must notify the State within 30 days after receiving it. The Administrator must then give the State comments within 90 days after receiving the application or proposed permit. The Administrator should consider any written comments made by the Secretary and Secretary of Interior, acting through the Director of the United States Fish and Wildlife Service.

such [*noun +s*] **as.** Use *any* [*noun*] (*that*) or *a* [*noun*] (*that*).

NOT THIS:	BUT THIS:
The Banking Board may take evidence and examine witnesses with respect to the propriety and justice vel non of said refusal and may make such findings and orders as may be necessary either to confirm said refusal or to permit the incorporation of such bank . . . . **Ala. Code § 5-5A-8.**	The Banking Board may take evidence and examine witnesses about the propriety and justice of the refusal and may make any finding or order necessary either to confirm the refusal or to permit the bank's incorporation . . . .
A party may appeal from a judgment by filing with the clerk of the district court a notice of appeal. Failure of the appellant to take any of the further steps to secure the review of the judgment appealed from does not affect the validity of the appeal, but is ground only for such remedies as are specified in this chapter, or when no remedy is specified, for such action as the appellate court having jurisdiction over the appeal deems appropriate, which may include dismissal of the appeal . . . . **Kan. Stat. § 60-2103(a).**	A party may appeal from a judgment by filing a notice of appeal with the district clerk. The appellant's failure to take any further steps to secure the review of the judgment appealed from does not affect the appeal's validity, but limits the grounds to any remedy specified in this Act. When no remedy is specified, the appellate court having jurisdiction over the appeal may determine whether any action is appropriate, including dismissing the appeal . . . .

therefor. Avoid altogether, often merely by deleting it, sometimes by writing *for it* or *for them.*

NOT THIS:	BUT THIS:
After the resolution authorizing an improvement shall become effective, such improvement may be made and contracts therefor may be let in the manner provided in section one hundred ninety-seven of this chapter. **N.Y. Town Law § 54(7).**	Once the resolution authorizing an improvement becomes effective, the improvement may be made. Contracts for the work may be awarded in the manner provided in § 197.

NOT THIS:	BUT THIS:
The commissioner shall, at the request of the chief of any regular or volunteer fire department or the person in charge of any organized civil preparedness auxiliary fire company, register, without charge, any motor vehicle used as fire apparatus by such department or company and shall issue a certificate of registration and number plates bearing the words "fire apparatus" therefor. **Conn. Gen. Stat. § 14-19.**	If the chief of any regular or volunteer fire department or the person in charge of any organized civil-preparedness auxiliary fire company so requests, the commissioner must: (A) register, without charge, any motor vehicle used as fire apparatus by the department or company; and (B) issue a certificate of registration and number plates bearing the words "fire apparatus."

there is, there are. Generally avoid. Use only if you must refer to the existence of something.

NOT THIS:	BUT THIS:
There is established a juvenile board in Ellis County. **Tex. Rev. Civ. Stat. art. 5139HHHH (repealed in 1989).**	This Act establishes a juvenile board in Ellis County.
There is authorized to be appropriated to the Commission such sums as may be necessary to carry out this section through fiscal year 2016. **15 U.S.C. § 8004(e).**	This Act authorizes the appropriation of funds to the Commission necessary to carry out this section through fiscal year 2016.
There is established in the treasury of the state a trust fund to be known as the Hawaiian home lands trust fund, into which shall be deposited all appropriations by the state legislature specified to be deposited therein. **Haw. Homes Comm'n Act § 213.6.**	This Act establishes a trust fund to be known as the Hawaiian Home Lands Trust Fund. The state legislature will specify appropriations to be deposited in the trust fund.
If requested by the deponent or a party before completion of the deposition, the deponent shall have 30 days after being notified by the officer that the transcript or recording is available in which to review the transcript or recording and, if there are changes in form or substance, to sign a statement reciting such changes and the reasons given by the deponent for making them. **Ga. Code § 9-11-30(e).**	Before the deposition ends, the deponent or a party may ask to receive a transcript or recording. Once the officer notifies the deponent that the transcript or recording is available, the deponent has 30 days to review it. A deponent who wishes to make changes in form or substance to the deposition must sign a statement reciting the changes and the reasons for making them.

transmit. Use *send.*

NOT THIS:	BUT THIS:
If an employer transmits the earnings to the commissioner, the employer has no liability to the prisoner for the earnings. **Alaska Stat. § 33.30.131(b).**	If an employer sends the earnings to the commissioner, the employer has no liability to the prisoner for them.

NOT THIS:	BUT THIS:
After receipt of a protest, the State Auditor and Inspector shall transmit by certified mail one copy of each protest to the district, and one copy of each protest to the county treasurer of each county in which the district is located. **Okla. Stat. tit. 19, § 901.44.**	After receiving a protest, the State Auditor and Inspector must send by certified mail 1 copy of each protest both to the district and to the county treasurer of each county in which the district is located.
Not later than 18 months after March 6, 2014, the Under Secretary shall transmit to the Committee on Science, Space, and Technology of the House of Representatives and the Committee on Commerce, Science, and Transportation of the Senate a report . . . . **15 U.S.C. § 313d(e)(1).**	By September 6, 2015, the Under Secretary must send to the House's Committee on Science, Space, and Technology and to the Senate's Committee on Commerce, Science, and Transportation a report . . . .
§ 3508. Transmission of unvoted ballots. . . . (c) **Method of transmission.**—A covered voter may request that a ballot and balloting materials be sent to the voter by mail or by Internet delivery. The county election board shall transmit the ballot and balloting materials to the voter using the means of transmission chosen by the voter. **25 Pa. Cons. Stat. § 3508(c).**	**§ 3508. Transmission of unvoted ballots.** . . . (C) **Method of transmission.** A covered voter may request that a ballot and all balloting materials be sent by mail or Internet. The county election board must send the materials using the voter's selected means.

Note that this version violates consistent usage (§ 1.1(D)).

upon. Prefer *on*. Thus, *service on a defendant*, not *service upon a defendant*. But use *upon* when introducing a condition or event—e.g., "Upon being served with a request, a party must . . . ."

NOT THIS:	BUT THIS:
(d) **Personal service of summons.** The summons shall be served by delivering a copy thereof. Service in the following manner shall constitute personal service: . . . (2) If the action is against a public corporation within this state, service may be made as follows: (i) Upon a county, by serving upon any county commissioner; (ii) Upon a first or second class municipality, by serving upon the mayor or any alderman or commissioner; (iii) Upon a third class municipality, by serving upon any trustee; (iv) Upon an organized township, by serving upon any supervisor; (v) Upon any school district, by serving upon any member of the school board or board of education; and (vi) Upon a consumers power district, by serving upon any member of the board of directors; **S.D. Codified Laws § 15-6-4(d)(2).**	(B) **Personal service of summons.** Summons must be served by personal delivery as this Act specifies: . . . (2) ***Public corporations.*** If the lawsuit is against a public corporation within this state, service may be made as follows: (a) on a county, by serving on a county commissioner; (b) on a first- or second-class municipality, by serving on the mayor or an alderman or commissioner; (c) on a third-class municipality, by serving on a trustee; (d) on an organized township, by serving on a supervisor; (e) on a school district, by serving on a member of the school board or board of education; or (f) on a consumers power district, by serving on a member of the board of directors.

NOT THIS:	BUT THIS:
[P]rovided, that the 10 hours shall be the time embraced from the leaving to the return of the prisoner to his or her place of detention. **Fla. Stat. § 951.08.**	The 10 hours begin when the prisoner leaves the place of detention and end upon return to the place of detention.

utilize. Try the verb *use* instead. Also, instead of *utilization*, try the noun *use*.

NOT THIS:	BUT THIS:
A person seeking to adopt a minor shall utilize an agency or attorney to arrange the adoption. **Ohio Rev. Code § 3107.011.**	A person seeking to adopt a minor must use an agency or attorney to arrange the adoption.

whenever. Use *if* or *when*.

NOT THIS:	BUT THIS:
Whenever the holder of any certificate issued by the board of education has been convicted of any sex offense or narcotics offense as defined in this Section, the board of education shall forthwith suspend the certificate. **105 Ill. Comp. Stat. 5/34-84b(a).**	If the holder of a certificate issued by the board of education has been convicted of a sex offense or narcotics offense as defined in this section, the board of education must promptly suspend the certificate.
Whenever a child has a catastrophic illness and is eligible for the program, the child, through his parent or guardian, may receive financial assistance from monies in the fund subject to the rules and regulations established by the commission and the availability of monies in the fund . . . . **Mass. Gen. Laws ch. 111K, § 8.**	If a child has a catastrophic illness and is eligible for the program, the child may, through a parent or guardian, receive financial assistance from the fund subject to availability and the rules established by the commission . . . .
§ 784.4. Lieutenant governor; declaration of disability; discharge of powers and duties by president pro tempore of the Senate Whenever the Lieutenant Governor transmits to the General Assembly a written declaration that he is unable to discharge the powers and duties of his office, and until he transmits to them a written declaration to the contrary, such powers and duties shall be discharged by the President pro tempore of the Senate as Acting Lieutenant Governor as provided in Article IV, section fourteen of the Constitution. **71 Pa. Cons. Stat. § 784.4.**	**§ 784.4. Lieutenant Governor; declaration of disability; discharge of powers and duties by Senate President pro tempore.** If the Lieutenant Governor sends the General Assembly a written declaration of inability to discharge the powers and duties of office, the Senate President must discharge those powers and duties as Acting Lieutenant Governor under state Constitutional Article IV, § 14, until the Lieutenant Governor sends the General Assembly a contrary written declaration.

5.5 Other wordings requiring attention.

each. This word is often replaceable with a simple indefinite pronoun (*a*, *an*). But it sometimes usefully emphasizes that a provision relates to every single instance of a thing specified.

NOT THIS:	BUT THIS:
22-1202. POTATO COMMISSION CREATED. There is hereby created and established in the department of self-governing agencies the "Idaho potato commission" to be composed of nine (9) practical potato persons, resident citizens of the state of Idaho for a period of three (3) years prior to their appointment each of whom has had active experience in growing, or shipping, or processing of potatoes produced in the state of Idaho. . . . Three (3) growers shall be nominated for each grower vacancy that occurs, from which the governor shall appoint one (1). . . . **Idaho Code § 22-1202.**	**22-1202. Potato Commission created.** The Idaho Potato Commission is a self-governing agency comprising 9 people having practical experience with the Idaho potato industry. A member must be a 3-year Idaho resident at the time of appointment with active experience growing, shipping, or processing potatoes in this state. . . . (B) **Vacancy.** The governor must fill a commission vacancy with 1 of 3 people nominated to represent the industry sector that the vacating commissioner represented.

may . . . only. This is an alternative to *must not . . . except* for a conditional prohibition—e.g., "A request *may* be served *only* after . . . ."

NOT THIS:	BUT THIS:
(a) The board must not hire a substitute teacher except: (1) For a duration of time of less than one school year to replace a regular teacher who is absent; or (2) For a duration of time equal to or greater than one school year to replace a regular teacher on a leave of absence. **Minn. Stat. § 122A.44 subd. 2(a).**	(A) The board may hire a substitute teacher only: (1) for less than 1 school year to replace a regular teacher who is absent; or (2) for 1 school year or longer to replace a regular teacher who is on a leave of absence.
The rights of a consumer enumerated in this chapter must not be denied except to protect the consumer's health and safety or to protect the health and safety of others, or both. Any denial of those rights in any facility must be entered in the consumer's record of treatment, and notice of the denial must be forwarded to the administrative officer of the facility. Failure to report denial of rights by an employee may be grounds for dismissal. **Nev. Rev. Stat. § 435.610(1).**	The consumer rights enumerated in this Act may be denied only to protect consumers' or others' health and safety. The denial of an enumerated right in any facility must be entered in the consumer's treatment record, and notice of the denial must be sent to the facility's administrative officer. An employee's failure to report the denial of a right may be grounds for dismissal.

only. Place this word carefully before the correct word.

NOT THIS:	BUT THIS:
§ 39-13-108. Enforcement. . . . (iii) Pursuant to an order of sale under paragraph (ii) of this subsection, the sheriff shall advertise the property for sale, and sell the property at public auction, without appraisal, to the highest bidder for cash. The lienholder pursuant to a certificate of purchase or tax deed may bid on the property and if he is the highest bidder, he shall only pay to the sheriff the amount by which his bid exceeds the amount due him under the court's decree. Upon confirmation of the sale by the court, the sheriff shall execute a deed conveying title to the real property to the purchaser in fee simple subject only to the rights of lienholders from junior tax sales. . . . **Wyo. Stat. § 39-13-108(d)(iii).**	**§ 39-13-108. Enforcement.** . . . (C) **Sheriff's sale.** If an order of sale is issued under paragraph (2), the sheriff must advertise the property for sale and sell it, without appraisal, for cash at public auction to the highest bidder. A lienholder who has a certificate of purchase or tax deed may bid. If the lienholder is the highest bidder, then the lienholder must pay to the sheriff only the amount by which the bid exceeds the amount due under the court's decree. If the court confirms the sale, the sheriff must execute a deed conveying the property's title to the purchaser in fee simple, subject to only the rights of lienholders from junior tax sales. . . .
(14) The term "veteran" means a person who served in the active military, naval, or air service and who was discharged or released under honorable conditions only or who later received an upgraded discharge under honorable conditions, notwithstanding any action by the United States Department of Veterans Affairs on individuals discharged or released with other than honorable discharges. **Fla. Stat. § 1.01.**	(14) The term "veteran" means a person who served in the active military, naval, or air service and who was discharged or released under only honorable conditions or who later received an upgraded discharge under honorable conditions, regardless of any action by the United States Department of Veterans Affairs on individuals discharged or released with other than honorable discharges.
Vacancies shall be filled in the same manner as the original appointment, but for the unexpired term only. **N.J. Stat. § 1:14-12(c).**	Vacancies are filled in the same manner as the original appointment, but only for the unexpired term.

on or before. Try *within* or *no later than*, whichever is more accurate (both include the last day). Avoid *by*, which also includes the last day but is arguably ambiguous.

NOT THIS:	BUT THIS:
On or before the fifteenth day after the completion of its ginning season, and in no event later than January 15 of each year, every ginner shall remit all assessments collected pursuant to this article during the ginning season to the Commissioner of Agriculture and Industries. **Ala. Code § 2-8-201(c).**	Within 15 days after the ginning season ends and in no event later than January 15 of each year, a ginner must remit all assessments collected under this article during the ginning season to the Commissioner of Agriculture and Industries.

otherwise. For emphasis, this adverb should usually end a clause—e.g., "Unless this court *directs otherwise* . . . ," not "Unless this court *otherwise directs.*" But sometimes, for the sake of parallel phrasing, this term should precede the verb—e.g., "Unless otherwise directed by the court or stipulated by the parties . . . ."

NOT THIS:	BUT THIS:
Except as otherwise provided in this part or as otherwise ordered by the court, a supervised personal representative has the same duties and powers as a personal representative who is not supervised. **Mich. Comp. Laws § 700.3501(3).**	Unless this part provides or a court order provides otherwise, a supervised personal representative has the same duties and powers as an unsupervised personal representative.
Except as otherwise provided with respect to damages liquidated in the lease agreement or otherwise determined pursuant to agreement of the parties, if the disposition is by lease agreement substantially similar to the original lease agreement and the new lease agreement is made in good faith and in a commercially reasonable manner, the lessor may recover from the lessee as damages accrued and unpaid rent as of the date of the commencement of the term of the new lease agreement, the present value, as of the same date, of the total rent for the then remaining lease term of the original lease agreement minus the present value, as of the same date, of rent under the new lease agreement applicable to that period of the new lease term which is comparable to the then remaining term of the original lease agreement, and any incidental damages allowed under s. 411.530, less expenses saved in consequence of the lessee's default. **Wis. Stat. § 411.527(2).**	(A) **Disposition by new lease.** Except as the lease provides otherwise regarding liquidated damages, a disposition by a new lease must: (1) be made in good faith; (2) be made in a commercially reasonable manner; and (3) be substantially similar to the original lease agreement. (B) **Recovery of lessor's expenses.** The lessor may recover from the lessee as damages accrued the unpaid rent due and any incidental damages allowed under § 411.530, less expenses saved because of the lessee's default. The unpaid rent due is calculated as the present value of the total rent for the remaining original-lease term minus the present value of the total rent under the new lease that now covers the same period. The present values are calculated from the new lease's effective date.

whenever. This word is often replaceable with a simple *if.* But it contains an important nuance: "each time and from time to time." Used well, it suggests recurrence—e.g.: "The flag of the District of Columbia shall be displayed inside all public buildings whenever and wherever the flag of the United States is displayed." (D.C. Code § 1-144).

NOT THIS:	BUT THIS:
A constable may execute process from any court whenever there is at the time neither sheriff nor coroner, or whenever both the sheriff and the coroner are incompetent,* or one (1) of those offices is vacant and the person holding the other office is incompetent in the particular case. **Tenn. Code § 8-10-113.**	A constable may execute process from a court if: (A) at the time there is neither a sheriff nor a coroner; (B) both the sheriff and the coroner are disqualified; or (C) either of those offices is vacant and the person holding the other office is disqualified in the particular case.

*This use of *incompetent* is troubling. It seems to mean "lacking legal ability in some respect." *See Black's Law Dictionary* 883 (10th ed. 2014). Wigmore counseled against using it. John H. Wigmore, *A Student's Textbook of the Law of Evidence* 36 (1935).

will. Use for the future tense and otherwise as the word is normally used in idiomatic English.

NOT THIS:	BUT THIS:
Every person pensioned or retired under any general or special law for disability, including accidental disability, shall in each year on or before April fifteenth subscribe, under the penalties of perjury, and file with the commission a statement, in such form as the commission shall prescribe, certifying the full amount of his earnings from earned income during the preceding year. Such pensioned or retired person shall annually submit to the commission all pertinent W-2 forms, 1099 forms, other requested tax forms and proof of income, and any other documentation requested by the commission; provided, however, that the commission may waive such filing by a member, if said member shall have been retired for more than 20 years, has not reported any earnings for the prior 10 years and signs an affidavit under the pains and penalties of perjury indicating that should the member realize any earned income in the future the member will forthwith notify the commission of that fact and again report under this section. **Mass. Gen. Laws ch. 32, § 91A.**	No later than April 15 each year, a person pensioned or retired under any general or special law for disability, including accidental disability, must file with the commission a sworn statement, in the form the commission prescribes, certifying the full amount of the person's earnings from earned income during the preceding year. The statement must be made under the penalties of perjury. The pensioned or retired person must annually submit to the commission all pertinent W-2 forms, 1099 forms, other requested tax forms and proof of income, and any other documentation that the commission requests. The commission may waive a member's filing if the member has been retired for more than 20 years, has not reported any earnings for the preceding 10 years, and signs an affidavit under the penalties of perjury indicating that if the member has any earned income in the future, the member will promptly notify the commission of that fact and again report under this section.
Should the buyer move to a community in which the cemetery does not accept transfers of outer enclosures from the cemetery which the buyer has entered into a cemetery merchandise contract, the selling organization will refund sixty-five percent (65%) of the retail price plus interest equal to the annual interest computed from the date that the contract was paid in full based on the passbook interest rate of the financial institution at the time that the refund is requested. **Okla. Stat. tit. 36, § 7126(I).**	If the buyer moves to a community where the cemetery does not accept transfers of outer enclosures from the cemetery with which the buyer has entered into a cemetery-merchandise contract, the selling organization must refund 65% of the retail price plus interest. The interest is the annual interest computed from the date when the contract was fully paid, based on the passbook interest rate of the financial institution when the refund is requested.

5.6 Matters not covered here.

For matters not covered in these guidelines, please refer to the works listed in the Select Bibliography. On matters of word usage, see especially the current version of *The Redbook: A Manual on Legal Style*; *Garner's Dictionary of Legal Usage*; and *The Chicago Manual of Style.*

On matters of capitalization, compounding, hyphenation, and other mechanical matters, legislation should follow the modern style used by mainstream works of nonfiction. For example, *Congress* is preferable to *the Congress*, *Congress's* to *Congress'*, and *congressional* to *Congressional.* Stay within the bounds of refined English usage of the day—avoiding gratuitous capitalization and other frequent quirks of statutory prose.

APPENDIX A

A Note on Prohibitions, Pains, and Penalties

American criminal statutes, both state and federal, use various wordings to prohibit certain conduct and to impose punishments. It is therefore natural for the legislative drafter to be concerned with knowing what the prevailing methods are, and which ones might be best for most circumstances. If a standard is possible, using it consistently would be highly desirable.

My recommendation—and the convention used throughout these guidelines—is to follow this format:

> It is unlawful to [adverbial mens rea] [actus reus]. Violation of this provision is [class/grade of offense] [punishable by penalty].

As a default for expressing criminal-law prohibitions, this convention has many advantages over other possibilities by avoiding: (1) overlong sentences, (2) subject-verb separation, (3) sexist language (or the ungainly avoidance of it), and (4) circumlocutions in which unlawfulness is only implied. It also allows the prohibition to be divided from the penalty—where desirable, in a separate subpart. Again and again, this approach's clarity and consistent utility will be evident.

The Wild Variability Across the Land

American legislatures now express criminal prohibitions and punishments in eight primary ways. In each of these formulations, a mens rea (the requisite mental state, such as *knowingly*) is optional before the actus reus (the prohibited conduct):

(1) Whoever [actus reus] shall be [penalty].
(2) Any person who [actus reus] is guilty of [class/grade of offense].
(3) If a person engages in [actus reus], such person is guilty of [class/grade of offense].
(4) A person commits an offense if the person [actus reus]. An offense under this provision is [penalty].
(5) No person shall [actus reus]. Violation of this act shall be [penalty].
(6) A person may not [actus reus]. A person who violates this provision is subject to [penalty].
(7) [Name of offense] is [actus reus]. [Name of offense] is punishable by [penalty].
(8) It is unlawful to [actus reus]. Violation of this act is punishable by [penalty].

Many slight variations are possible—*any* becomes *every*, *whoever* becomes *anyone*, etc. But these eight structures account for almost all the principal varieties.

Let's briefly consider their merits and demerits. The first three all put the actus reus—which can be quite long—in the middle of a sentence. That's a poor convention: it's syntactically undesirable, and it accounts for many an unreadable criminal statute. The fourth repeats *person* within seven words and very likely again in the actus reus. It's ungainly. The fifth misuses *shall* for *may*. (*No person shall* does not mean "no person is required to"; it means something more like "no person is permitted to.") The provision is meant to negate permission, not a requirement. That brings us to the next point. The sixth uses the undesirable collocation *may not*, which sounds as if permission to murder, pillage, etc. is being denied. It's just odd—and this objection also militates against *No person may*. Negating permission isn't what criminal prohibitions are about. The seventh wrongly assumes that every crime has an easily identifiable name. It's also undesirably repetitious. Though these objections may seem like so much nitpicking, they in fact are not facile: they pinpoint problems that emerge again and again with these faulty conventions.

The eighth method is clean. It clearly states illegality. It separates the actus reus and the penalty into discrete sentences. It avoids all sorts of *person . . . he or she* problems. And it works consistently. Consider an example:

The federal law against assault on a foreign official exemplifies option #1 above. Notice the huge subject-verb separation—62 words intervening:

> **Federal Assault on Foreign Official**
>
> (a) **Whoever** assaults, strikes, wounds, imprisons, or offers violence to a foreign official, official guest, or internationally protected person or makes any other violent attack upon the person or liberty of such person, or, if likely to endanger his person or liberty, makes a violent attack upon his official premises, private accommodation, or means of transport or attempts to commit any of the foregoing **shall be fined under this title or imprisoned not more than three years, or both.**

Notice also that the statute sets out the illegal conduct without any words of prohibition. Nowhere does it say that it is unlawful to assault a foreign official. The statute is greatly improved if the actus reus is moved to the predicate and unlawfulness is made explicit:

> **Federal Assault on Foreign Official**
>
> (a) It is unlawful to assault, strike, wound, imprison, or offer violence to a foreign official, official guest, or internationally protected person or to make any other violent attack on the person or liberty of such a person, or, if likely to endanger his person or liberty, to make a violent attack on his official premises, private accommodation, or means of transport or to attempt to commit any of these acts. Violation of this provision is a Class X felony [punishable by fine under this title or imprisonment of up to three years in federal prison, or both].

We now have two sentences, one for the actus reus and one for the penalty. Subjects and verbs are kept together. The bracketed language is optional—*Class X felony* might say all that needs saying. It depends on the context. More might be done, of course, but the demonstration here shows merely how a minor adjustment in syntax leads to a more workable statute.

For many more examples, see § 2.2 of the main text of these *Guidelines* at pp. 49–54. There and elsewhere in the main text, you'll find more than 50 revisions using the technique.

Critical Commentary

While few scholars have discussed the appropriate way to express criminal prohibitions and criminal punishments, some legislative-drafting manuals contain recommendations.[1] The Texas Legislative Council Drafting Manual[2] touts option #4 from the list above: "A person commits an offense if the person [verb] [the prohibited act]." The Council and other legislative-drafting organizations[3] say this formula accomplishes at least two goals. First, it neatly separates the actus reus from the penalty. That is true, and it's an advantage. Second, it uses language that expressly makes the prohibited act criminal.[4] But as we have seen, it leads to often grotesque subject–verb separations—and therefore unreadable sentences. Hence it is less than ideal.

But there is another potential problem with this formula. Like many recent American-style criminal statutes, it may blur the distinction between tort and crime. A criminal prohibition appears to be a balancing test in which a would-be criminal might weigh the consequences of punishment versus the benefit of committing the crime. The trend, so this argument goes, has been away from condemning behavior that society generally considers unacceptable. This trend has been lamented.[5]

Perhaps the most common wording of criminal prohibitions in American law takes the form of "whoever [actus reus] shall be [penalty]." This language is weak. The reader of such a statute appears to be analyzing a trade-off. The act merely comes with a price tag. At the very least, that's a rhetorical oddity given the subject matter.

For criminal sanctions to be effective, they must do three essential things: (1) identify the prohibited conduct, (2) signify that it is disapproved,[6] and (3) specify the penalty for engaging in the prohibited conduct.

In the early development of criminal law, statutes had few words of prohibition. For example, many Roman statutes read this way:

- Libels and insulting songs to be punished by death.
- Breaking a limb, unless settled for, to be punished by retaliation.
- A man who wrongfully cuts another's trees must pay twenty-five asses for each tree.

---

1 *See, e.g.,* Office of Code Revision Legislative Services Agency, *Drafting Manual for the Indiana General Assembly* (19 Dec. 2012), http://iga.in.gov/static-documents/a/e/6/c/ae6c0119/DRAFTMAN.pdf (providing examples of "properly drafted" criminal prohibition statutes).

2 Texas Legislative Council, *Texas Legislative Council Drafting Manual* (Jan. 2015), http://www.tlc.state.tx.us/legal/dm/draftingmanual.pdf.

3 *See, e.g.,* Tennessee Office of Legal Services, *Legislative Drafting Guide* (Oct. 2013), http://www.capitol.tn.gov/joint/staff/legal/2013-Drafting-Guide-WebsiteVersion-10-28-13.pdf (explaining that it prefers this formula because another Tennessee statute provides that an act is not an offense unless it is clearly defined as such).

4 Texas Legislative Council, *supra* note 2 ("[Commits an offense] phrase signals clearly the creation of a criminal offense as opposed to a mere civil rule of conduct.").

5 *See* John C. Coffee Jr., *Does "Unlawful" Mean "Criminal"?: Reflections on the Disappearing Tort/Crime Distinction in American Law*, 71 B.U. L. Rev. 193, 193 (1991) ("Characteristically, tort law prices, while criminal law prohibits.").

6 *See* William Lawrence Clark & William Lawrence Marshall, *A Treatise on the Law of Crimes* 8 (Marian Quinn Barnes ed., 7th ed. 1967) ("Criminal law remains a static blend and blur of religious concepts of sin and legal notions of liability.").

- If a man is killed whilst committing theft by night he is lawfully killed.
- Whoever gives false evidence must be thrown from the Tarpeian rock.[7]

The "excessive curtness" of these provisions, according to the eminent English lawyer and judge James Fitzjames Stephen, "implies the existence of an all but unlimited discretion in those who had to administer the law."[8] Some of these laws blur the distinction between tortious and criminal conduct. For instance, the breaking of a limb provides for either settlement between the parties, or instead retaliation, reminiscent of an "eye for an eye" from the Hammurabi Code. But at no point do these laws specifically prohibit the illegal conduct, but instead only provide punishment. Yet considering the broad discretion of those administering the law, it is no surprise that the wording of the laws was laconic.

Although murder and rape and other crimes *malum in se* are immediately understood to be morally reprehensible, that is not necessarily true of crimes *malum prohibitum*, such as insider trading and other types of white-collar crime. The language expressing unlawfulness may have a significant impact on a jury. For instance, the California law prohibiting insider trading states:

> It is unlawful for an issuer or any person who is an officer, director or controlling person of an issuer or any other person whose relationship to the issuer gives him access, directly or indirectly, to material information about the issuer not generally available to the public, to purchase or sell any security of the issuer in this state at a time when he knows material information about the issuer gained from such relationship which would significantly affect the market price of that security and which is not generally available to the public, and which he knows is not intended to be so available, unless he has reason to believe that the person selling to or buying from him is also in possession of the information.[9]

In this statute, stating *it is unlawful* is a good start. The follow-on sentence might state: "Any person who violates this statute is guilty of insider trading and must be punished by a fine amounting to treble restitution[10] or imprisonment for up to X years in the California State Penitentiary, or both." This kind of reprehending language can be helpful to a jury who might not otherwise see what particular harm has been done. Insider trading is a complex matter, and providing some deprecating language in the statute may help signal to the jury the seriousness of the crime. In close cases, the strong language may prove persuasive to a jury that is otherwise unsure about legal matters that do not affect their everyday lives.

---

7 1 James Fitzjames Stephen, *A History of the Criminal Law of England* 9–11 (1883).

8 *Id.* at 11.

9 Cal. Corp. Code § 25402 (West 2015).

10 *Id.* § 25502.5 (providing treble damages for insider trading).

Unlawful the Best Word?

Does *It is unlawful*... amount to an express prohibition? Commentators have long recognized that "[p]rohibition ... is essential."[11] Is it necessary to say *No person may*..., *You must not*..., or *Each person is prohibited*...? In the ordinary understanding, *Spitting on the sidewalk is not allowed* amounts to a prohibition. So does a declaration of illegality: *It is unlawful*.... We need not worry about the recommended formulation on grounds that "[i]n the absence of prohibition by the law, no act is a crime."[12] Further, we recommend the heading "X prohibited," which gives context to the first full sentence of a criminal provision even if it isn't an official part of the statute.

Why not say *It is a crime to*...? That formulation has some appeal. But remember, we're announcing not just felonies but also misdemeanors and lesser infractions. Is running a stop sign a crime? Yes, technically—but the popular mind doesn't think of traffic infractions as creating criminals. So *crime* is probably too extreme a word for many prohibitions. Further, seemingly no jurisdiction uses this formulation, whereas *It is unlawful*... is prevalent in many jurisdictions.

But does *unlawful* carry enough moral condemnation for serious crimes? One could argue that the more serious the crime—the more it is seen as *malum in se*—the more naturally opprobrium automatically arises in the reader's mind. *Unlawful* is a broad word intended to fit misdemeanors as well as felonies. Some have claimed that it might even suggest mere civil violations to the ordinary reader, such as breaches of contract. This seems far-fetched. When English speakers use the phrase *against the law*, they almost invariably mean "against the criminal laws." And the most concise equivalent of that idea is *unlawful*—not its near-synonyms *illegal* and *illicit*.[13]

Among those three possibilities—*illegal*, *illicit*, and *unlawful*—the last is best-suited for criminal prohibitions. *Illegal* has the greatest breadth and is the most common term. Many things are said to be illegal, from wrestling holds to flight crews who have put in the maximum hours within a day. The adjective is a little too all-purpose. The Latin derivative *illicit* has strong connotations of salaciousness and lubricity—and in the popular mind, too, it's often confused with *elicit*.[14] It's unsatisfactory. But *unlawful* is pure Anglo-Saxon that is immediately comprehensible to English speakers. Yet it's unusual enough to carry with it some solemnity and gravity. And because *It is unlawful to*... is already a widespread convention, it requires little by way of reacculturation.

One last point. The word *unlawful* is astonishingly broad. It attaches with almost equal aptness to murder and to tearing the tag off a mattress. So it is particularly versatile. You might at first fear that readers will turn numb to the introductory words *It is unlawful to*. Experience will probably dissipate the fear, as you will see when glancing through the dozens of criminal prohibitions presented throughout this book. There remains enough variety in the other parts of criminal prohibitions that you're unlikely ever to feel that you're reading one monotonous prohibition after another. More likely, you'll conclude that the drafter simply has a systematic technique that works.

---

11 William L. Clark, *Hand-book of Criminal Law* 3 (Francis B. Tiffany ed., 2d ed. 1902).

12 *Id.*

13 *See Garner's Dictionary of Legal Usage* 422–23, 915 (3d ed. 2011).

14 *Id.* at 423.

A Grammatical Note on Mens Rea Adverbs

The statement of mens rea has created recurrent problems in criminal law. Take the sentence "Whoever knowingly pushes, shoves, or otherwise touches another in an offensive manner commits a Class B misdemeanor." Must the shoving and offensive touching be committed knowingly? Yes—probably—under the series-qualifier canon of construction.[15] But the rule of lenity might suggest otherwise.[16] Judicial decisions will vary.

One advantage of the *It is unlawful*... formula is that the best placement of the state-of-mind adverb—after the *to* in the infinitive—more clearly keeps it modifying each of the infinitives: "It is unlawful to knowingly push, shove, or otherwise touch another person in an offensive manner. Violation of this provision is a Class B misdemeanor." Both the shoving and the offensive touching must be done knowingly, in a fair reading.

But what ho! We've split an infinitive. No matter, say the most respected grammatical authorities: doing so is often necessary, and especially in this particular context. Let the authorities set your mind at ease:

- **(19th c.):** "There is a busybody on your staff who devotes a lot of his time to chasing split infinitives. Every good literary craftsman splits his infinitives when the sense demands it. I call for the immediate dismissal of this pedant. It is of no consequence whether he decides to go quickly or quickly to go or to quickly go. The important thing is that he should go at once." George Bernard Shaw, Letter to *The Times* (19th c.) (as quoted in *Best Advice on How to Write* 259–60 (Gorham Munson ed., 1952)).
- **1898:** "Anybody who doesn't wish to see too wide a division between the spoken and the written speech will not be too severe against the split infinitive. A man may write 'to tell really' or 'really to tell,' but he will probably say 'to really tell.' It seems to us that there are phrases in which the split infinitive is the more direct and instinctive form." "The Split Infinitive" (1898), in *Casual Essays of the Sun* 238, 240 (1905).
- **1932:** "The evidence in favor of the judiciously split infinitive is sufficiently clear to make it obvious that teachers who condemn it arbitrarily are wasting their time and that of their pupils." Sterling A. Leonard, *Current English Usage* 124 (1932).
- **1940:** "Let the breeze of common sense blow away the mists of a presumptuous authority, dispel the heavy fog of pedantry. The split infinitive is not a violation of literary morality. It is not even a blemish until it is grossly overdone." Edward T. Teall, *Putting Words to Work* 184 (1940).
- **1947:** "The split infinitive is in full accord with the spirit of modern English and is now widely used by our best writers." George O. Curme, *English Grammar* § 70.B, at 148 (1947).
- **1952:** "A split infinitive will sometimes give a meaning that is destroyed if the intruding word is moved." R.G. Ralph, *Put It Plainly* 41 (1952).
- **1957:** "The notion that it is a grammatical mistake to place a word between *to* and the simple form of a verb, as in *to quietly walk away*, is responsible for a great deal of bad writing by people who are trying to write well. Actually the rule against 'splitting an infinitive' contradicts the principles of English grammar and the practice of

15 *See* Antonin Scalia & Bryan A. Garner, *Reading Law: The Interpretation of Legal Texts* 147–51 (2012).

16 *Id.* at 296–302.

our best writers." Bergen Evans & Cornelia Evans, *A Dictionary of Contemporary American Usage* 469 (1957).

- **1961:** "To deliberately split an infinitive, puristic teaching to the contrary notwithstanding, is correct and acceptable English." Norman Lewis, *Better English* 287 (rev. ed. 1961).
- **2000:** "Splitting an infinitive is preferable both to jamming an adverb between two verbs, where everyone must puzzle out which verb it modifies ('They *refused* boldly *to go* so far away'), and to 'correcting' a split in a way that gives an artificial result ('They wanted *to shorten greatly* the length of the trip')." Barbara Wallraff, *Word Court* 99 (2000).
- **2010:** "Although from about 1850 to 1925 many grammarians stated otherwise, it is now widely acknowledged that adverbs sometimes justifiably separate an infinitive's *to* from its principal verb." *The Chicago Manual of Style* § 5.106, at 233 (16th ed. 2010).

Similar statements from equally august sources could be easily multiplied.

The alternative—the highly undesirable unsplit infinitive—actually creates more semantic uncertainty than the *Whoever*... formulation. The unsplit version would say: *It is unlawful knowingly to push, shove, or otherwise touch another person.* The adverb now looks almost like a squinting modifier that could look in either direction. In any event, it's less closely tied to the follow-on verbs *shove* and *touch*. If you're using the convention recommended here, you must eradicate any hangups you might have about the split infinitive (that is, at least when you're using an *-ly* adverb to specify the mens rea). And you may well have to be prepared to enlighten a legislator who raises an objection. (Keep this page handy.) Even if the split infinitive were a blemish—and it never has been—it would be the smallest of the many blemishes found on every page of the statute books. Here, though, it definitely helps make the prohibition unambiguous.

Consider a typical rewrite. The federal "Smokey Bear" statute reads as follows:

> **§ 711. "Smokey Bear" character or name.**
> Whoever, except as authorized under rules and regulations issued by the Secretary of Agriculture after consultation with the Association of State Foresters and the Advertising Council, knowingly and for profit manufactures, reproduces, or uses the character "Smokey Bear", originated by the Forest Service, United States Department of Agriculture, in cooperation with the Association of State Foresters and the Advertising Council for use in public information concerning the prevention of forest fires, or any facsimile thereof, or the name "Smokey Bear" shall be fined under this title or imprisoned not more than six months, or both.
>
> 18 U.S.C. § 711.

With the recommended format, a split infinitive now appears in § 711(A)—and the manifold improvements in structure are immediately apparent:

> **§ 711. Unlawful use of "Smokey Bear" character or name prohibited.**
>
> (A) **Unlawful use.** It is unlawful to knowingly and for profit manufacture, reproduce, or use the character Smokey Bear or any facsimile of it, or the name Smokey Bear without authorization.

(B) **Character identified.** "Smokey Bear" refers to the character originated by the Forest Service, United States Department of Agriculture, in cooperation with the Association of State Foresters and the Advertising Council for use in public information concerning the prevention of forest fires.

(C) **Authorization.** Authorization to use Smokey Bear may be given only under the rules and regulations issued by the Secretary of Agriculture after consultation with the Association of State Foresters and the Advertising Council.

(D) **Penalty.** Violation of this title is punishable by fine or imprisonment of up to 6 months, or both.

Note that the prohibition in (A) is separated from the penalty in (D) by two subparts. The syntactic flexibility afforded by the method here advocated makes the use of subparts possible and enhances readability.

Expressing the Penalty

For the penalty provision of a criminal statute, when made into its own sentence, two methods are prevalent: "[actus reus] is punishable by [penalty]"[17] and "[actus reus] constitutes [classification of offense]." The latter, which is perhaps a little more common, lends tidiness to the criminal code in three ways. First, it standardizes penalties. All felonies of a certain degree or class are generally subject to the same punishments under a classification scheme. Second, it enables legislative counsel to draft concise criminal-prohibition statutes. To illustrate, California's aggravated-mayhem statute provides: "Aggravated mayhem is a felony punishable by imprisonment in the state prison for life with the possibility of parole." If California adopted a classification system and cross-referenced the criminal prohibition with a general punishment statute explaining the offense levels, it might communicate the same concept more concisely: "A person who commits aggravated mayhem is guilty of a first-degree felony." Third, drafting the criminal-penalty statute this way may reduce later challenges to the statute. Several jurisdictions have the equivalent of gap-fillers when criminal statutes do not specify whether the offense is a felony or misdemeanor.[18] In those jurisdictions, failure to so specify may attach a criminal sanction that the legislator did not intend.[19] Hence this iteration may well be the best way to express a criminal penalty.

---

17 Mass. Gen. Laws Ann. ch. 266, § 15 (West 2015) ("shall be punished by imprisonment in the state prison for not more than twenty years and, if he shall have been previously convicted of any crime named in this or the preceding section, for not less than five years").

18 *See, e.g.,* Legislative Council Division of Research, *Delaware Legislative Drafting Manual* (Nov. 2013), http://legis.delaware.gov/Legislature.nsf/1688f230b96d580f85256ae20071717e/eb5bfd31cbf3cbe5852572490052c342/$FILE/Delaware%20Legislative%20Drafting%20Manual%20%282013%20Update%20%29.pdf (explaining that "A drafter should keep in mind that when crimes are created by legislation, any offense not specifically designated by statute to be a felony, a class A or class B misdemeanor, or a violation is an unclassified misdemeanor or an environmental misdemeanor. . . . Any felony not specified in a class is a class G felony.").

19 Legislative Council, *Maine Legislative Drafting Manual* (2009), http://www.maine.gov/legis/ros/manual/Draftman2009.pdf (instructing legislative drafters to use this format rather than "punishable by" because failure to do so "may operate to provide a fine or term of imprisonment that was not intended").

Conclusion

Every legislative body should work toward systematizing its criminal prohibitions and penalties. The question is how to do that. The American trend away from words declaring unlawfulness is unfortunate. The most desirable language for statutory prohibitions makes it clear that the conduct is both disallowed and to some degree morally objectionable. The formulation *It is unlawful to . . .* followed by a sentence expressing the penalty, perhaps through simply stating the classification of the crime, is the optimal wording—not just for expressing content clearly but for making the syntax manageable.

APPENDIX B

Two Model Acts Using These Guidelines

The two statutes that follow are not as adopted by the Uniform Law Commission. Instead, they have been edited to reflect the principles embodied in this book. The better the statute to begin with, the easier it is to edit effectively. Because the originals are architecturally sound, editing them was a comparatively straightforward exercise. Even so, constant practice is the only means of maintaining the skill to achieve satisfactory editorial results.

If you're highly motivated in studying legislative drafting, you might want to print the actual model acts and compare them against these revisions to see what might be learned from comparing and contrasting.

Uniform Premarital Agreement Act

1. **Definitions.**
   1.1 "Premarital agreement" means an agreement between prospective spouses made in contemplation of marriage and intended to be effective upon marriage.
   1.2 "Property" means an interest—present or future, legal or equitable, vested or contingent—in real or personal property, including income and earnings.
2. **Formalities.** A premarital agreement must be in writing and signed by both parties. It is enforceable without consideration.
3. **Content.**
   3.1 **Permissible coverage.** Parties to a premarital agreement may contract with respect to any of the following as long as doing so does not violate public policy or a statute imposing a criminal penalty:
      (A) the rights and obligations of each party in any of the property of either or both of them whenever and wherever acquired or located;
      (B) the right to buy, sell, use, transfer, exchange, abandon, lease, consume, expend, assign, create a security interest in, mortgage, encumber, dispose of, or otherwise manage and control property;
      (C) the disposition of property upon separation, marital dissolution, death, or the occurrence or nonoccurrence of a specified event;
      (D) the modification or elimination of spousal support;
      (E) the making of a will, trust, or other arrangement to carry out the agreement's provisions;
      (F) the ownership rights in and disposition of the death benefit from a life-insurance policy;
      (G) the choice of law governing the agreement's interpretation; and
      (H) any other matter, including the parties' personal rights and obligations.
   3.2 **Exclusion of child support.** A child's right to support cannot be adversely affected by a premarital agreement.
4. **Time of taking effect.** A premarital agreement becomes effective upon marriage.
5. **Amendment; revocation.** After marriage, a premarital agreement may be amended or revoked only by a written agreement signed by both parties. The amended agreement or the revocation is enforceable without consideration.
6. **Enforcement.**
   6.1 **Proving unenforceability.** A premarital agreement is not enforceable if the party against whom enforcement is sought proves that:
      (A) that party did not execute the agreement voluntarily;
      (B) the agreement was unconscionable when executed and, before execution, that party:

(1) was not provided a fair and reasonable disclosure of the other party's property or financial obligations;

(2) did not voluntarily and expressly waive, in writing, any right to disclosure of the other party's property or financial obligations beyond the disclosure provided; and

(3) did not have, or could not reasonably have had, an adequate knowledge of the other party's property or financial obligations.

6.2 **Public-assistance override.** If a provision within a premarital agreement modifies or eliminates spousal support and that modification or elimination causes one party to the agreement to be eligible for support under a program of public assistance at the time of separation or marital dissolution, a court may, despite the agreement's terms, require the other party to provide support to the extent necessary to avoid that eligibility.

6.3 **Unconscionability as matter of law.** An issue of a premarital agreement's unconscionability must be decided by the court as a matter of law.

7. **Void marriage.** If a court determines that a marriage is void, an agreement that would otherwise have been a premarital agreement is enforceable only to the extent necessary to avoid an inequitable result.

8. **Limitation of actions.** Any statute of limitations applicable to a lawsuit asserting a claim for relief under a premarital agreement is tolled during the parties' marriage. But equitable defenses limiting the time for enforcement, including laches and estoppel, are available to both parties.

9. **Interpretation and application.** This Act must be interpreted and applied to give effect to its general purpose to make uniform the law relating to its subject matter among the states enacting it.

10. **Severability.** If any provision of this Act or its application to any person or circumstances is held invalid, the invalidity does not affect the Act's other provisions or applications that can be given effect without the invalid provision or application. To this end, the provisions of this Act are severable.

Uniform Anatomical Gift Act

1. **Definitions.**

 1.1 "Body part" means an organ, tissue, eye, bone, artery, blood, fluid, or other portion of a human body.

 1.2 "Decedent" means a deceased person and includes a stillborn infant or fetus.

 1.3 "Donee" means a person who is the recipient of a gift.

 1.4 "Donor" means a person who makes a gift.

 1.5 "Enucleator" means a person who is licensed by the State Board of Medical Examiners to remove or process eyes or parts of eyes.

 1.6 "Gift" means a donation of all or part of a human body to take effect upon or after death.

 1.7 "Gift document" means a card, a statement attached to or imprinted on a motor-vehicle operator's or chauffeur's license, a will, or other writing used to make a gift.

 1.8 "Hospital" means a facility licensed, accredited, or approved as such under the law of any state or a facility operated as such by the United States government, a state, or a subdivision of a state.

 1.9 "Person" means an individual, corporation, business trust, estate, trust, partnership, joint venture, association, government, governmental subdivision or agency, or any other legal or commercial entity.

 1.10 "Physician" or "surgeon" means a person licensed or otherwise authorized to practice medicine and surgery or osteopathy and surgery under the laws of any state.

 1.11 "Procurer" means a person or organization licensed, accredited, or approved under the laws of any state to procure, distribute, or store human bodies or body parts.

 1.12 "State" means any state, territory, or possession of the United States, the District of Columbia, or the Commonwealth of Puerto Rico.

 1.13 "Technician" means a person who is licensed by the State Board of Medical Examiners to remove or process a body part.

2. **Making, Amending, Revoking, and Refusing to Make Anatomical Gifts by Person.**

 2.1 **Capacity.** A person who is at least 18 years of age may:

 (A) make a gift for any purpose stated in § 6.1(A);

 (B) limit a gift to one or more of those purposes; or

 (C) refuse to make a gift.

 2.2 **Attestation.** A gift may be made only by a gift document signed by the donor. If the donor cannot sign, the gift document must be signed by another person and by two witnesses, all of whom have signed at the direction and in the presence of the donor and of each other, and state that it has been so signed.

2.3 **Durability of driver's license gift document.** A gift document attached to or imprinted on a donor's motor vehicle operator's or chauffeur's license must comply with § 2.2. Revocation, suspension, expiration, or cancellation of the license does not invalidate the gift.

2.4 **Durability of testamentary gift.** A gift by will takes effect upon the testator's death, whether or not the will is probated. If, after death, the will is declared invalid for testamentary purposes, the validity of the gift is unaffected.

2.5 **Designation of doctor.** A gift document may designate a particular physician or surgeon to carry out the appropriate procedures. In the absence of a designation or if the designee is not available, the donee or other surgeon authorized to accept the gift may employ or authorize any physician, surgeon, technician, or enucleator to carry out the appropriate procedures.

2.6 **Amendment or revocation.**

(A) **Gift not made by will.** A donor may amend or revoke a gift not made by will only by:

(1) a signed statement;

(2) an oral statement made in the presence of two persons;

(3) any form of communication during a terminal illness or injury addressed to a physician or surgeon; or

(4) the delivery of a signed statement to a specified donee to whom a gift document has already been delivered.

(B) **Gift made by will.** A donor by will may amend or revoke the gift in the manner provided for amendment or revocation of wills, or as provided in § 2.6.

(C) **Lack of revocation.** A gift that the donor does not revoke before death is irrevocable and does not require the consent or concurrence of any person after the donor's death.

(D) **Effect of amendment or revocation.** Unless the donor indicates otherwise, an amendment or revocation of a gift is not a refusal to make another gift. If the donor intends a revocation to be a refusal to make a gift, the donor must make the refusal under § 2.7.

2.7 **Refusal to make gift.** A person may refuse to make a gift of the person's body or body part by:

(A) a writing signed in the same manner as a gift document;

(B) a statement attached to or imprinted on a donor's motor-vehicle operator's or chauffeur's license; or

(C) any other writing used to identify the person as refusing to make a gift; or

(D) if the person is suffering from a terminal illness or injury, an oral statement or any other form of communication.

2.8 **No negative implication.** Unless the donor indicates otherwise, a gift of a body part is neither a refusal to give other body parts nor a limitation on a gift under § 3. Nor is it a removal or release of other body parts under § 4.

3. **Making, Revoking, and Objecting to Gifts, by Others.**

3.1 **Classes of authorized decision-makers.** Any member of the following classes of persons, in the order of priority listed, may make a gift of all or a part of the decedent's body for an authorized purpose, unless the decedent, at the time of death, has made an unrevoked refusal to make that gift:

(A) the decedent's spouse;

(B) an adult son or daughter of the decedent;

(C) a parent of the decedent;

(D) an adult brother or sister of the decedent;

(E) a grandparent of the decedent; and

(F) a guardian of the decedent's person at death.

3.2 **Conditions of lacking authority.** A gift cannot be made by a person in § 3.1 if:

(A) a person in a prior class is available at the time of death to make a gift;

(B) the person proposing to make a gift knows of a refusal or contrary indication by the decedent; or

(C) the person proposing to make a gift knows of any objection to making a gift by a member of the person's class or a prior class.

3.3 **Means of making gift by authorized decision-maker.** A gift by a person authorized under § 3.1 must be made by:

(A) a gift document signed by the person; or

(B) the person's telegraphic, recorded telephonic, or other recorded message, or other form of communication from the person that is contemporaneously reduced to writing and signed by the recipient.

3.4 **Revocation by decision-maker with authority.** A gift by a person authorized under § 3.1 may be revoked by any member of the same or a prior class if, before procedures have begun for the removal of a body part from the decedent, the physician, surgeon, technician, or enucleator removing the body part knows of the revocation.

3.5 **Distinction between failure and objection.** A failure to make a gift under § 3.1 is not an objection to the making of a gift.

4. **Authorization by Medical Examiner or Local Health Official.**

4.1 **Grant of authority.** The medical examiner may release and permit the removal of any part from a body within that official's custody, for transportation or therapy, if:

(A) the official has received a request for the body part from a hospital, physician, surgeon, or procurer;

(B) the official has made a reasonable effort, taking into account the useful life of the body part, to locate and examine the decedent's medical records and inform persons listed in § 3.1 of their option to make, or object to making, a gift;

(C) the official does not know of a refusal or contrary indication by the decedent or objection by a person having priority to act as listed in § 3.1;

(D) the removal will be by a physician, surgeon, or technician—but in the case of eyes, by one of them or by an enucleator;

(E) the removal will not interfere with any autopsy or investigation;

(F) the removal will be in accordance with accepted medical standards; and

(G) cosmetic restoration will be done, if appropriate.

4.2 **Health officer in default of medical examiner.** If the body is not within the medical examiner's custody, the local public-health officer may release and permit the removal of any part from a body in the officer's custody for transportation or therapy if the requirements of § 4.1 are met.

4.3 **Record-keeping requirement.** An official releasing and permitting the removal of a body part must maintain a permanent record of the decedent's name, the person making the request, the date and purpose of the request, the body part requested, and the person to whom it was released.

5. **Routine Inquiry and Required Request; Search and Notification.**

5.1 **Question required of hospital patients.** On or before admission to a hospital, or as soon as possible thereafter, a person designated by the hospital must ask each patient who is at least 18 years of age: "Are you an organ or tissue donor?" If the answer is affirmative, the person must request a copy of the gift document. If the answer is negative or there is no answer and the attending physician consents, the person designated must discuss with the patient the option to make or refuse to make a gift. The answer to the question, an available copy of the gift document or refusal to make a gift, and any other relevant information, must be placed in the patient's medical record.

5.2 **If no record, hospital representative to inquire of authorized decision-maker.** If, at or near the time of a patient's death, there is no medical record that the patient has made or refused to make a gift, the hospital administrator or a representative designated by the administrator must discuss the option to make or refuse to make a gift and request the making of a gift under § 3.1. The request should be made with reasonable discretion and sensitivity to the family's circumstances. A request is not required if the gift is not suitable. An entry must be made in the patient's medical record, stating the name and affiliation of the person making the request, and of the name, response, and relationship to the patient of the person to whom the request was made. The Commissioner of Health must adopt regulations to implement this § 5.2.

5.3 **Required search for gift document.** The following persons must make a reasonable search for a gift document or other information identifying the bearer as a donor or as someone who has refused to make a gift:

(A) a law-enforcement officer, firefighter, paramedic, or other emergency rescuer finding a person who the searcher believes is dead or near death; and

(B) a hospital, upon the admission of a patient at or near the time of death, if there is not immediately available any other source of that information.

5.4 Notification of hospital upon locating gift document. If a gift document or evidence of refusal to make a gift is located by the search required in § 5.3(A), and the person or body to whom it relates is taken to a hospital, the hospital must be notified of the contents and the document or other evidence must be sent to the hospital.

5.5 Notification of donee. If, at or near the time of a patient's death, a hospital knows that a gift has been made under § 3.1 or a release and removal of a body part has been permitted under § 4, or that a patient or a person identified as in transit to the hospital is a donor, the hospital must notify the donee if one is named and known to the hospital. If not, the hospital must notify an appropriate procurer. The hospital must cooperate in the implementation of the gift or release and removal of a body part.

5.6 Immunities. A person who fails to discharge the duties imposed within § 5 is not subject to criminal or civil liability but is subject to appropriate administrative sanctions.

6. Persons Who May Become Donees; Purposes for Which Gifts May Be Made.

6.1 Permissible donees. The following persons may become donees of gifts for the purposes stated:

(A) a hospital, physician, surgeon, or procurer, for transplantation, therapy, medical or dental education, research, or advancement of medical or dental science;

(B) an accredited medical or dental school, college, or university for education, research, advancement of medical or dental science; or

(C) a designated person for transplantation or therapy needed by that person.

6.2 Lack of donee designation. A gift may be made to a designated donee or without designating a donee. If a donee is not designated or if the donee is not available or rejects the gift, the gift may be accepted by any hospital.

6.3 Conditions requiring declination. If the donee knows of a decedent's refusal or contrary indications to make a gift or that a gift by a member of a class having priority to act is opposed by a member of the same class or a prior class under § 3.1, the donee must not accept the gift.

7. Delivery of Gift Document.

7.1 No delivery required. Delivery of a gift document during the donor's lifetime is not required for the validity of a gift.

7.2 Optional delivery for expediting gift. If a gift is made to a designated donee, the gift document, or a copy, may be delivered to the donee to expedite the appropriate procedures after death. The gift document, or a copy, may be deposited with any hospital, procurer, or registry office that accepts it for safekeeping or for facilitation of procedures after death. Upon request of an interested person after the donor's death, the person in possession must allow the interested person to examine or copy the gift document.

8. **Rights and Duties at Death.**

8.1 **Generally.** A donee's rights created by a gift are superior to others' rights except with respect to an autopsy under § 11.2. A donee may accept or reject a gift. If a donee accepts a gift of an entire body, the donee may, subject to the terms of the gift, allow embalming and use of the body in funeral services. If the gift is of a body part, the donee must, upon the donor's death and before embalming, cause the body part to be removed without unnecessary mutilation. After removal of the body part, custody of the remainder of the body vests in the person under obligation to dispose of the body.

8.2 **Determination of death; disability of doctor who determines death.** The time of death must be determined by a physician or surgeon who attends the donor at death or, if none, by the physician or surgeon who certifies the death. Neither the physician or surgeon who attends the donor at death nor the physician or surgeon who determines the time of death may participate in the procedures for removing or transplanting a body part unless the gift document designates a particular physician or surgeon under § 2.4.

8.3 **General procedure to be followed.** If there has been a gift and a physician or surgeon has made a determination of death, a technician may remove any donated body part and an enucleator may remove any donated eyes or parts of eyes.

9. **Coordination of Procurement and Use.** After consulting with other hospitals and with procurers, each hospital in this State must establish agreements or affiliations for coordinating the procurement and use of human bodies and body parts.

10. **Sale and Purchase of Body Parts Prohibited.**

10.1 **Prohibition.** It is unlawful to knowingly, for valuable consideration, purchase or sell a body part for transplantation or therapy, if removal of the body part is intended to occur after the decedent's death.

10.2 **Exclusion from "valuable consideration."** Valuable consideration does not include reasonable payment for a body part's removal, processing, disposal, preservation, quality control, storage, transportation, or implantation.

10.3 **Penalty for violation.** A person who violates this § 10 is guilty of a felony punishable by a fine of up to $50,000 or imprisonment of up to 5 years, or both.

11. **Examination, Autopsy, Liability.**

11.1 **Examination for acceptability.** A gift authorizes any reasonable examination necessary to ensure medical acceptability of the gift for the purposes intended.

11.2 **Autopsy laws still in effect.** The provisions of this Act are subject to the laws of this State governing autopsies.

11.3 **Immunity for good-faith actions.** A hospital, physician, surgeon, medical examiner, local public-health officer, enucleator, technician, or other person who acts in accordance with this Act or with the applicable anatomical-gift law of another state, or attempts in good faith to do so, is not liable for that act in a civil lawsuit or criminal proceeding.

11.4 **Immunity for donor and estate.** A person who makes a gift under § 2 or § 3 and the person's estate are not liable for any injury or damage that may result from the making or the use of the gift.

12. **Transitional Provisions.** This Act applies to a gift document, revocation, or refusal to make a gift signed by the donor or a person authorized to make or object making a gift before, on, or after the Act's effective date.

13. **Uniformity of Application and Construction.** This Act must be construed and applied to effectuate its general purpose to make uniform the law with respect to its subject matter among the states enacting it.

14. **Severability.** The provisions of this Act are severable: if any provision of this Act or its application to any person or circumstance is held invalid, the invalidity does not affect other provisions or applications that can be given effect without the invalid provision or application.

15. **Short Title.** This Act is to be cited as the "Uniform Anatomical Gift Act (1987)."

16. **Repeals.** The following acts and parts of acts are repealed:

    16.1 [name & citation].

    16.2 [name & citation].

    16.3 [name & citation].

    16.4 [name & citation].

17. **Effective Date.** This Act takes effect [date].

APPENDIX C

A Typical Statute in Need of an Overhaul, with Annotations

A Typical Statute in Need of an Overhaul, with Annotations

The comment boxes are merely illustrative—hardly exhaustive. If every edit necessary were accompanied by a comment box, all the text would be obscured. Hence not every problem is highlighted, but only those considered most illuminating.

Contrast the very look of this statute with what you see on pages 181–89. Note how much the lack of headings, together with the quirky numbering system, impairs your ability to read the statute with ease. Try reading it through the eyes of an ordinary citizen with child-support problems. That kind of empathy is precisely what everyone needs who aspires to draft or edit statutes with skill.

Serial comma needed: § 4.9(D).

Hanging indents and headings needed for all subparts: §§ 1.3.

Shall appears 23 times in this section. It usually means *must*, but in at least 11 instances it means *will*. See § 2.1(B).

Phrasal adjectives require hyphens: See § 4.9(G).

Avoid passive voice (*be entered* and *kept*): see § 2.6(A).

767.29 Maintenance, child support and family support payments, receipt and disbursement; circuit court commissioner, fees and compensation. (1) (a) All orders or judgments providing for temporary or permanent maintenance, child support or family support payments shall direct the payment of all such sums to the department or its designee for the use of the person for whom the same has been awarded. A party securing an order for temporary maintenance, child support or family support payments shall forthwith file the order, together with all pleadings in the action, with the clerk of court.

(b) Upon request, after the filing of an order or judgment or the receipt of an interim disbursement order, the clerk of court shall advise the county child support agency under s. 59.53(5) of the terms of the order or judgment within 2 business days after the filing or receipt. The county child support agency shall, within the time required by federal law, enter the terms of the order or judgment into the statewide support data system, as required by s. 59.53(5)(b).

(c) Except as provided in sub. (1m), the department or its designee shall disburse the money received under the judgment or order in the manner required by federal regulations and take receipts therefor, unless the department or its designee is unable to disburse the moneys because they were paid by check or other draft drawn upon an account containing insufficient funds. All moneys received or disbursed under this section shall be entered in a record kept by the department or its designee, whichever is appropriate, which shall be open to inspection by the parties to the action, their attorneys and the circuit court commissioner.

Phrasal adjectives require hyphens. See § 4.9(G).

(d) For receiving and disbursing maintenance, child support, or family support payments, including arrears in any of those payments, and for maintaining the records required under par. (c), the department or its designee shall collect an annual fee of $35. The court or circuit court commissioner shall order each party ordered to make payments to pay the annual fee under this paragraph in each year for which payments are ordered or in which an arrearage in any of those payments is owed. In directing the manner of payment of the annual fee, the court or circuit court commissioner shall order that the annual fee be withheld from income and sent to the department or its designee, as provided under s. 767.265. All fees collected under this paragraph shall be deposited in the appropriation account under s. 20.445(3)(ja). At the time of ordering the payment of an annual fee under this paragraph, the court or circuit court commissioner shall notify each party ordered to make payments of the requirement to pay the annual fee and of the amount of the annual fee. If the annual fee under this paragraph is not paid when due, the department or its designee may not deduct the annual fee from any maintenance, child or family support, or arrearage payment, but may move the court for a remedial sanction under ch. 785.

Prefer singular over plural: see § 2.4.

Section symbol (§) would be better: see § 2.9(C).

Don't use three words when one will do (Instead of *At the time of* try *When*): see § 1.2(C).

Avoid the ambiguous *may not*; try *cannot*: see § 2.1(A).

Avoid double-negative constructions: see § 2.7(A).

For how to handle subsequent inserts, see § 3.3.

(dm) 1m. The department or its designee may collect any unpaid fees under s. 814.61(12)(b), 1997 stats., that are shown on the department's automated payment and collection system on December 31, 1998, and shall deposit all fees collected under this subdivision in the appropriation account under s. 20.445(3)(ja). The department or its designee may collect unpaid fees under this subdivision through income withholding under s. 767.265(2m). If the department or its designee determines that income withholding is inapplicable, ineffective, or insufficient for the collection of any unpaid fees under this subdivision, the department or its designee may move the court for a remedial sanction under ch. 785. The department or its designee may contract with or employ a collection agency or other person for the collection of any unpaid fees under this subdivision and, notwithstanding s. 20.930, may contract with or employ an attorney to appear in any action in state or federal court to enforce the payment obligation. The department or its designee may not deduct the amount of unpaid fees from any maintenance, child or family support, or arrearage payment.

A list would eliminate redundancy and improve readability: see § 3.4(D).

Avoid vague internal references: see § 3.2(C).

For the problems of *notwithstanding*, see § 5.4.

2m. A clerk of court may collect any unpaid fees under s. 814.61(12)(b), 1997 stats., that are owed to the clerk of court, or to his or her predecessor, and that were not shown on the department's automated payment and collection system on December 31, 1998, through income withholding under s. 767.265(2m). If the clerk of court determines that income withholding is inapplicable, ineffective or insufficient for the collection of any unpaid fees under this subdivision, the clerk of court may move the court for a remedial sanction under ch. 785.

Court clerk would be shorter (by removing *of*): see § 4.8(A).

This would be better at the outset of the sentence (*Using income-withholding under. . . .*).

First sentence here is seven lines long (79 words). Shorten sentence length: § 1.1(B).

(e) If the maintenance, child support or family support payments adjudged or ordered to be paid are not paid to the department or its designee at the time provided in the judgment or order, the county child support agency under s. 59.53(5) or a circuit court commissioner of the county shall take such proceedings as he or she considers advisable to secure the payment of the sum including enforcement by contempt proceedings under ch. 785 or by other means. Copies of any order issued to compel the payment shall be mailed to counsel who represented each party when the maintenance, child support or family support payments were awarded. In case any fees of officers in any of the proceedings, including the compensation of the circuit court commissioner at the rate of $50 per day unless the commissioner is on a salaried basis, is not collected from the person proceeded against, the fees shall be paid out of the county treasury upon the order of the presiding judge and the certificate of the department.

A weak *shall*: not a duty but discretionary ("as considers advisable"): see § 2.1(B).

The plural subject *fees* is widely separated from its verb (*is*), which is singular: see § 4.1.

(f) If the department determines that the statewide automated support and maintenance receipt and disbursement system will be operational before October 1, 1999, the department shall publish a notice in the Wisconsin Administrative Register that states the date on which the system will begin operating. Before that date or October 1, 1999, whichever is earlier, the circuit courts, county child support agencies under s. 59.53(5), clerks of court and employers shall cooperate with the department in any measures taken to ensure an efficient and orderly transition from the countywide system of support receipt and disbursement to the statewide system.

Use consistent terms unless a different meaning is intended (*be operational* vs. *begin operating*): see § 1.1(D).

Serial comma needed: see § 4.9(D).

(1m) Notwithstanding ss. 767.25(6) and 767.261, if the department or its designee receives support or maintenance money that exceeds the amount due in the month in which it is received and that the department or its designee determines is for support or maintenance due in a succeeding month, the department or its designee may hold the amount of overpayment that does not exceed the amount due in the next month

Note the quirky numbering: see §3.3(A), (B).

A *succeeding* month could be any month in the future, but the sense seems to be that this applies to the next month, as stated below; see 1.1(A).

for disbursement in the next month if any of the following applies:

(a) The payee or the payer requests that the overpayment be held until the month when it is due.

This provision seems to largely repeat the introductory matter, rendering it surplusage: see § 1.2(D).

(b) The court or circuit court commissioner has ordered that overpayments of child support, family support or maintenance that do not exceed the amount of support or maintenance due in the next month may be held for disbursement in the next month.

Be consistent with terms. Use the same phrase unless the meaning changes: see § 1.1(D).

(c) The party entitled to the support or maintenance money has applied for or is receiving aid to families with dependent children and there is an assignment to the state under s. 49.19(4)(h)1.b. of the party's right to the support or maintenance money.

Formatting this as a list could remove a lot of redundancy: see § 3.4(D).

(cm) A kinship care relative or a long-term kinship care relative of the child who is entitled to the support money has applied for or is receiving kinship care payments or long-term kinship care payments for that child and there is an assignment to the state under s. 48.57(3m)(b)2. or (3n)(b)2. of the child's right to the support money.

This quirky use of full stops is distracting.

(d) The department or its designee determines that the overpayment should be held until the month when it is due.

Avoid the word *any*—replace it with *a*: see § 5.4.

(2) If any party entitled to maintenance payments or support money, or both, is receiving public assistance under ch. 49, the party may assign the party's right thereto to the county department under s. 46.215, 46.22 or 46.23 granting such assistance. Such assignment shall be approved by order of the court granting the maintenance payments or support money, and may be terminated in like manner; except that it shall not be terminated in cases where there is any delinquency in the amount of maintenance payments and support money previously ordered or adjudged to be paid to the assignee without the written consent of the assignee or upon notice to the assignee and hearing. When an assignment of maintenance payments or support money, or both, has been approved by the order, the assignee shall be deemed a real party in interest within s. 803.01 but solely for the purpose of securing payment of unpaid maintenance payments or support money adjudged or ordered to be paid, by participating in proceedings to secure the payment thereof. Notwithstanding assignment under this

Superfluous comma separates parts of a compound predicate (*shall be approved* and *may be terminated*): see § 5.6.

Watch for troublesome words, such as *deem*, *notwithstanding*, *such*, *thereof*, and *thereto*: see § 5.4.

subsection, and without further order of the court, the department or its designee, upon receiving notice that a party or a minor child of the parties is receiving public assistance under ch. 49 or that a kinship care relative or long-term kinship care relative of the minor child is receiving kinship care payments or long-term kinship care payments for the minor child, shall forward all support assigned under s. 48.57(3m)(b)2. or (3n)(b)2., 49.19(4)(h)1. or 49.45(19) to the assignee under s. 48.57(3m)(b)2. or (3n)(b)2., 49.19(4)(h)1. or 49.45(19).

Subject (*department or designee*) is separated from its verb (*shall forward*) by 49 words: see § 4.1.

Poor lack of headings: see § 1.1(F).

Subject-verb agreement error.

(3) (a) If maintenance payments or support money, or both, is ordered to be paid for the benefit of any person, who is committed by court order to an institution or is in confinement, or whose legal custody is vested by court order under ch. 48 or 938 in an agency, department or relative, the court or a circuit court commissioner may order such maintenance payments or support money to be paid to the relative or agency, institution, welfare department or other entity having the legal or actual custody of said person, and to be used for the latter's care and maintenance, without the appointment of a guardian under ch. 880.

Prefer singular, and always ensure that the subject and verb agree in number (they don't in this 109-word sentence): see § 1.1(B).

Avoid legalese: see § 1.1(C).

Passive voice: see § 2.6.

(b) If a child who is the beneficiary of support under a judgment or order is placed by court order in a residential care center for children and youth, juvenile correctional institution, or state mental institution, the right of the child to support during the period of the child's confinement, including any right to unpaid support accruing during that period, is assigned to the state. If the judgment or order providing for the support of a child who is placed in a residential care center for children and youth, juvenile correctional institution, or state mental institution includes support for one or more other children, the support that is assigned to the state shall be the proportionate share of the child placed in the center or institution, except as otherwise ordered by the court or circuit court commissioner on the motion of a party.

Subject-verb separation: see § 4.1

Exceedingly repetitive: see § 1.2(D).

(4) If an order or judgment providing for the support of one or more children not receiving aid under s. 48.57(3m) or (3n) or 49.19 includes support for a minor who is the beneficiary of aid under s. 48.57(3m) or (3n) or 49.19, any support payment made under the order or judgment is assigned to the state under s. 48.57(3m)(b)2. or (3n)(b)2. or 49.19(4)(h)1.b. in the amount that is the proportionate share of the minor receiving aid under s. 48.57(3m) or (3n) or 49.19, except as otherwise ordered by the court on the motion of a party.

Ending with unemphatic exceptions decreases comprehensibility: see § 4.4(B).

A list could make this dense material more understandable: see § 3.4.

Select Bibliography

Books

Adler, Mark. *Clarity for Lawyers: The Use of Plain English in Legal Writing.* London: Law Soc'y, 1990. 2d ed. *Clarity for Lawyers: Effective Legal Writing.* London: Law Soc'y, 2007.

Allen, Carleton Kemp. *Law in the Making.* 7th ed. Oxford: Oxford Univ. Press, 1964.

Asprey, Michele M. *Plain Language for Lawyers.* Annandale, Aus.: Federation Press, 1991. 4th ed. Leichhart, Aus.: Federation Press, 2010.

Beccaria, Cesare. *An Essay on Crimes and Punishments.* Anon. trans. Rev. ed. Edinburgh: Alexander Donaldson, 1778.

Bell, John A. *Prose of Law: Congress As a Stylist of Statutory English.* Ellicott City, Md.: Paper Tiger, 1981.

Bentham, Jeremy. *The Works of Jeremy Bentham.* 11 vols. John Bowring, ed. Edinburgh: William Tait, 1843.

Butt, Peter. *Modern Legal Drafting: A Guide to Using Clearer Language.* Cambridge: Cambridge Univ. Press, 2001. 2d ed. 2006. 3d ed. 2013.

Child, Barbara. *Drafting Legal Documents: Principles and Practices.* 2d ed. St. Paul: West, 1992.

Coode, George. *On Legislative Expression; or, the Language of Written Law.* 2d ed. London: Thomas Turpin, 1852.

Cook, Robert N. *Legal Drafting.* Rev. ed. Brooklyn: Foundation Press, 1951.

Cross, Rupert. *Statutory Interpretation.* London: Butterworths, 1976.

Cutts, Martin. *Clarifying Eurolaw.* Stockport, England: Plain Language Commission, 2001.

Cutts, Martin. *Lucid Law.* Whaley Bridge, U.K.: Plain Language Commission, 1994. 2d ed. 2000.

Cutts, Martin. *Unspeakable Acts?: Clarifying the Language and Typography of an Act of Parliament.* Stockport: Words at Work, 1993.

Cutts, Martin; and Emma Wagner. *Clarifying EC Regulations.* U.K.: Plain Language Comm'n, 2002.

Dale, William. *Legislative Drafting: A New Approach.* London: Butterworths, 1977.

Darmstadter, Howard H. *Hereof, Thereof, and Everywhereof: A Contrarian Guide to Legal Drafting.* Chicago: Am. Bar Ass'n, 2002.

Davies, Jack. *Legislative Law and Process in a Nutshell.* 2d ed. St. Paul: West, 1986.

Dick, Robert C. *Legal Drafting.* 2d ed. Toronto: Carswell, 1985.

Dickerson, Reed. *The Fundamentals of Legal Drafting.* 2d ed. Boston: Little, Brown & Co., 1986.

Dickerson, Reed. *The Interpretation and Application of Statutes.* Boston: Little, Brown & Co., 1975.

Dickerson, Reed. *Legislative Drafting.* Boston: Little, Brown & Co., 1954.

Dickerson, Reed. *Materials on Legal Drafting.* St. Paul: West, 1981.

Dickerson, Reed (ed.). *Professionalizing Legislative Drafting—The Federal Experience.* Chicago: American Bar Ass'n, 1973.

Doonan, Elmer. *Drafting.* Julie MacFarland, ed. London: Cavendish, 1995.

Driedger, Elmer A. *The Composition of Legislation*. Ottawa: E. Cloutier, Queen's Printer & Controller of Stationery, 1957. 2d ed. Ottawa: Dep't of Justice, 1976.

Duxbury, Neil. *Elements of Legislation*. Cambridge: Cambridge Univ. Press, 2013.

Eagleson, Robert D. *Writing in Plain English*. Canberra: Australian Gov't Pub. Serv., 1990.

Eagleson, Robert D. *What Is Plain English?* Address at the Singapore Acad. of Law, 27 January 1996.

Evans, B. Ifor. *The Use of English: Being a Primer of Direct English*. London: Staples Press, 1949.

Filson, Lawrence E. *The Legislative Drafter's Desk Reference*. Washington, D.C.: Congressional Quarterly, 1992.

Flesch, Rudolf. *How to Write Plain English: A Book for Lawyers and Consumers*. N.Y.: Harper & Row, 1979.

Freund, Ernst. *Legislative Regulation: A Study of the Ways and Means of Written Law*. N.Y.: Commonwealth Fund, 1932.

Freund, Ernst. *Standards of American Legislation*. Chicago: Univ. of Chicago Press, 1917.

Garner, Bryan A. *Garner's Dictionary of Legal Usage*. 3d ed. N.Y. & Oxford: Oxford Univ. Press, 2011.

Garner, Bryan A. *Garner's Modern English Usage*. 4th ed. N.Y. & Oxford: Oxford Univ. Press, 2016.

Garner, Bryan A. *Guidelines for Drafting and Editing Court Rules*. Wash., D.C.: Administrative Office of the U.S. Courts, 1996. [Available in downloadable PDF at www.lawprose.org.]

Garner, Bryan A. *Legal Writing in Plain English*. 2d ed. Chicago: Univ. of Chicago Press, 2013.

Garner, Bryan A. *The Redbook: A Manual on Legal Style*. 3d ed. St. Paul: West Academic Publishing, 2013.

Haggard, Thomas R. *Legal Drafting in a Nutshell*. St. Paul: West, 1996.

Haggard, Thomas R.; and George W. Kuney. *Legal Drafting: Process, Techniques, and Exercises*. 2d ed. St. Paul: West, 2007.

Ilbert, Courtenay. *Legislative Methods and Forms*. London: Henry Frowde and Steven & Sons, 1901.

Ilbert, Courtenay. *The Mechanics of Law Making*. N.Y.: Columbia Univ. Press, 1914.

Jones, Chester Lloyd. *Statute Law Making in the United States*. Boston: Boston Book Co., 1912.

Kelly, David St. Leger (ed.). *Essays on Legislative Drafting: in Honour of J.Q. Ewens CMG, CBE, QC*. Adelaide: Adelaide L. Rev. Ass'n, 1988.

Kennedy, Duncan L. *Drafting Bills for the Minnesota Legislature*. St. Paul: West, 1946.

Kimble, Joseph. *Lifting the Fog of Legalese*. Durham, N.C.: Carolina Academic Press, 2006.

Law Reform Comm'n of Victoria. *Access to the Law: The Structure and Format of Legislation*. [Report 33.] Melbourne: The Comm'n, 1990.

Light, Paul. *Forging Legislation*. N.Y.: W.W. Norton & Co., 1992.

Martineau, Robert J.; and Michael B. Salerno. *Legal, Legislative, and Rule Drafting in Plain English*. St. Paul: Thomson West, 2005.

Mellinkoff, David. *The Language of the Law*. Boston: Little, Brown & Co., 1963.

Mellinkoff, David. *Legal Writing: Sense and Nonsense*. N.Y.: Scribner, 1982.

Montesquieu, Charles Louis, II [Baron de Montesquieu]. *The Spirit of Laws* [1748]. 2 vols. Thomas Nugent trans. London: The Colonial Press, 1900.

Murawski, Thomas A. *Writing Readable Regulations*. Durham, N.C.: Carolina Academic Press, 1999.

Office of Legislative Counsel, U.S. House of Representatives. *House Legislative Counsel's Manual on Drafting Style*. Wash., D.C.: U.S. Gov't Printing Office, 1995.

Office of Parliamentary Counsel (Canberra). *Plain English Manual*. Canberra: Office of Parliamentary Counsel, 1993.

O'Hayre, John. *Gobbledygook Has Gotta Go*. Washington, D.C.: U.S. Gov't Printing Office, 1966.

Piesse, E.L. *The Elements of Legal Drafting*. J.K. Aitken & Peter Butt, eds. 10th ed. Sydney: Lawbook Co., 2004.

Pigeon, Louis-Philippe. *Drafting and Interpreting Legislation*. Toronto: Carswell, 1988.

Plain Language Action & Information Network. *Federal Plain Language Guidelines*. May 2011.

Plain Language Inst. *Editorial and Design Stylebook*. Plain Language Report. Vancouver: Plain Language Inst., 1993.

Read, Horace E.; John W. McDonald; and Jefferson B. Fordham. *Cases and Other Materials on Legislation*. 2d ed. Brooklyn: Foundation Press, 1959.

Redish, Janice C. *How to Write Regulations and Other Legal Documents in Clear English*. Wash., D.C.: American Institutes for Research, 1991.

Redman, Eric. *The Dance of Legislation*. Seattle: Univ. Wash. Press, 2001.

Renton, Lord (ed.). *The Preparation of Legislation*. London: Her Majesty's Stationery Office Pubs., 1975.

Russell, Alison. *Legislative Drafting and Forms*. 4th ed. London: Butterworth & Co., 1938.

Russell, Bertrand. *The Basic Writings of Bertrand Russell*. Robert E. Egner & Lester E. Denonn, eds. N.Y.: Simon & Schuster, 1961.

Scalia, Antonin; and Bryan A. Garner. *Reading Law: The Interpretation of Legal Texts*. St. Paul: Thomson Reuters, 2012.

Solan, Lawrence. *The Language of Statutes: Laws and Their Interpretation*. Chicago: Univ. of Chicago Press, 2010.

Solan, Lawrence; and Peter M. Tiersma (eds.). *The Oxford Handbook of Language and Law*. Oxford: Oxford Univ. Press, 2012.

Statsky, William P. *Legislative Analysis and Drafting*. 2d ed. St. Paul: West, 1984.

Stephen, James Fitzjames. *A Digest of the Criminal Law*. Herbert Stephen & Harry Lushington Stephen eds. 5th ed. London: Macmillan & Co., 1894.

Stephen, James Fitzjames. *A Digest of the Law of Evidence*. 4th ed. London: Macmillan & Co., 1893.

Stephen, James Fitzjames. *A General View of the Criminal Law of England*. London: Macmillan & Co., 1890.

Stephen, James Fitzjames. *A History of the Criminal Law of England*. 3 vols. [1883] Repr. N.Y.: Burt Franklin, 1973.

Sterne, Simon. *The Prevention of Defective and Slipshod Legislation.* Philadelphia: G.S. Harris & Sons, 1884.

Stimson, Frederic Jesup. *Popular Law-Making: A Study of the Origin, History, and Present Tendencies of Law-Making by Statute.* N.Y.: Charles Scribner's Sons, 1910.

Thornton, G.C. *Legislative Drafting.* 4th ed. London: Butterworths, 1996.

Thring, Henry. *Practical Legislation.* 2d ed. Toronto: George N. Morang & Co., 1902.

Tiersma, Peter M. *Legal Language.* Chicago: Univ. Chicago Press, 1999.

Williams, Glanville. *Criminal Law: The General Part.* 2d ed. London: Stevens, 1961.

Wydick, Richard C. *Plain English for Lawyers.* 5th ed. Durham, N.C.: Carolina Academic Press, 2005.

Xanthaki, Helen. *Drafting Legislation: Art and Technology of Rules for Regulation.* Oxford: Hart Pub., 2014.

Zander, Michael. *The Law-Making Process.* 2d ed. London: Weidenfeld & Nicolson, 1985.

Articles

Cavers, David. *The Simplification of Government Regulations.* 8 Fed. B.J. 339 (1947).

Conard, Alfred F. *New Ways to Write Laws.* 56 Yale L.J. 458 (1947).

Cullen, Robert K. *Mechanics of Statutory Revision.* 24 Or. L. Rev. 1 (1944).

Dickerson, Reed. *Clear Legal Drafting: What's Holding Us Back?* 11 ALI-ABA CLE Rev. 3 (1980).

Dickerson, Reed. *The Diseases of Legislative Language.* 1 Harv. J. on Legis. 5 (1964).

Eagleson, Robert D. "Efficiency in Legal Drafting," in *Essays on Legislative Drafting: in Honour of J.Q. Ewens.* David St. Leger Kelly, ed. Adelaide: Adelaide L. Rev. Ass'n, 1988.

Eagleson, Robert D.; and Michele Asprey. *Must We Continue with "Shall"?* 63 Austl. L.J. 75 (1989).

Elliott, David C. *Plain Language: A Global Perspective.* 70 Mich. B.J. 562 (1991).

Elliott, David C. *Tools for Simplifying Complex Legislation.* 3 N.Z.J. Tax'n L. & Pol'y 153 (1997).

Jaworski, Leon. "The American Bar Association's Concern with Legislative Drafting," in *Professionalizing Legislative Drafting—The Federal Experience.* Reed Dickerson, ed. Chicago: American Bar Ass'n, 1973.

Kerr, Edward. *Plain Language: Is It Legal?* 52 Law Soc'y J. 52 (1991).

Kimble, Joseph. *Drafting Examples from the Proposed New Federal Rules of Evidence* (pts. 1–4). Mich. B.J., Aug. 2009, at 52; Sept. 2009, at 46; Oct. 2009, at 54; Nov. 2009, at 50.

Kimble, Joseph. *Guiding Principles for Restyling the Federal Rules of Civil Procedure* (pts. 1–2). Mich. B.J., Sept. 2005, at 56; Oct. 2005, at 52.

Kimble, Joseph. *How to Mangle Court Rules and Jury Instructions.* 8 Scribes J. Legal Writing 39 (2001–2002).

Kimble, Joseph. *Lessons in Drafting from the New Federal Rules of Civil Procedure.* 12 Scribes J. Legal Writing 25 (2008–2009).

Kimble, Joseph. *Plain English: A Charter for Clear Writing.* 9 Thomas M. Cooley L. Rev. 1 (1992).

Kimble, Joseph. *You Think Lawyers Are Good Drafters?* 17 Green Bag 2d 41 (2014).

Kirk, Maurice B. *Legal Drafting: Curing Unexpressive Language.* 3 Tex. Tech. L. Rev. 23 (1971).

Krongold, Susan. *Writing Laws: Making Them Easier to Understand.* 24 Ottawa L. Rev. 495 (1992).

Llewellyn, Karl. *On the Good, the True, the Beautiful in Law.* 9 U. Chi. L. Rev. 224 (1942).

Mackay, J.G. *Introduction to an Essay on the Art of Legal Composition Commonly Called Drafting.* 3 L.Q. Rev. 326 (1887).

Oliver, Lord, of Aylmerton. *A Judicial View of Modern Legislation.* 14 Statute L. Rev. 1 (1993).

Russell, Bertrand. "How I Write," in *The Basic Writings of Bertrand Russell.* Robert E. Egner & Lester E. Denonn, eds. N.Y.: Simon & Schuster, 1961.

Samuels, Alec. *Stalking Defined.* 18 Statute L. Rev. 244 (1997).

Siegel, Alan. "Language Follows Logic: Practical Lessons in Legal Drafting," Remarks at Conference of Experts in Clear Legal Drafting, Nat'l Ctr. for Admin. Justice, June 2, 1978, in Reed Dickerson, *Materials on Legal Drafting.* St. Paul: West, 1981.

Smith, J.A. Clarence. *Legislative Drafting: English and Continental.* 1 Statute L. Rev. 14 (1980).

Strylowski, John. *Using Tables to Present Complex Ideas.* Mich. B.J., Feb. 2013, at 44.

Williams, Glanville. *Language and the Law* (pts. 1–5). 61 L.Q. Rev. 71, 179, 293, 384 (1945), 62 L.Q. Rev. 387 (1946).

Index

A

Access to the Law (Law Reform Commission of Victoria), 200
action, 138
active voice, 58–59
actus reus, 49, 169–71, 176
adjectives. *See also* modifiers.
  as antecedents, 131
  changing prepositional phrases to, 124
  passive voice, to replace, 59
  phrasal adjectives, hyphenating, 129
Adler, Mark, xii, 132, 140, 199
adverbs. *See also* modifiers.
  adverbial interruptive phrases, 119–20
  adverbial modifiers, 107, 121–22
  phrasal adjectives, with, 129
  mens rea adverbs, 169–70, 174–76
aforesaid, 157
after, 146, 151, 153, 160–61
agreement, nouns and pronouns, 132
Alabama Code
  commencing in, 142
  displays of complex information, 70
  dollar amounts, zeros in, 69
  interpolated information, and dashes, 128
  on or before in, 166
  plain English and, 1
  such in, 161
Alaska Statutes
  headings, lack of, 24
  limitation for *limit,* 150
  related items separated, 77
  transmit for *send,* 162
  which used as restrictive, 133
Allen, Carleton Kemp, 77, 199
all of, 139
ambiguity
  active voice to avoid, 58
  by to indicate ending times, 166
  commaless *which,* 133
  cost of, Jaworski on, 61
  distinguished from vagueness, 93
  double dashes to avoid, 127
  misplaced modifiers, 121–22
  preventing, 14–18
  provisos causing, 116–17
  serial comma and semicolon to avoid, 127
and, 136
and/or, 16, 136, 138, 139–40
antecedents, of pronouns, 64, 131–32
any, 141, 148
a person commits (criminal prohibition formula), 169–71
appositives, for foreshadowing in lists, 90
archaic style. *See also* plain English.
  Beccaria on, 55
  Conard on, 11
  Dick on, 66
  generally, 1–13
  Kimble on, 31
  masking errors, 146
Arizona Revised Statutes
  except as used, 144
  except when used, 146
  numbers spelled out, 65
Arkansas Code
  ambiguity in, 15
  stilted language in, 3
  word-numeral doublets in, 67
Armstrong, Walter P., Jr., vii
Asprey, Michele, 43 199, 202
assault, federal law on, 170
audiences, and comprehension, 15

B

Bankruptcy Code, 96
Barnes, Marian Quinn, 171
Basic Writings of Bertrand Russell, The (Egner & Denonn eds.), 45, 201, 203
Beccaria, Cesare, 55, 199
before, 154–55
begin, 142–43
Bell, John A., 139, 199
Bentham, Jeremy
  on grammatical skill in drafting, x
  on sentence length, 28
  on simplicity in drafting, 74
  on singular and plural, 56
  on word choice, 99
  works, in bibliography, 199
Best Advice on How to Write (Munson ed.), 174
Better English (Lewis), 175
blocks of text, 85
Bowring, John, x, 28, 56, 74, 99, 199
brevity. *See* conciseness.
building and safety codes, 58
bullets, in lists, 98
Burchfield, R.W., 114
Burke, Edmund, 29
but, 136, 137
Butt, Peter, xii, 64, 100, 146, 199, 201
by, 166

C

calculations, 70
California Business and Professions Code, 143, 152, 154
California Civil Procedures Code, 56
California Constitution, 86
California Corporations Code, 172
California Education Code, 57, 59
California Government Code, 123
California Harbors and Navigation Code, 19
California Penal Code, 134
California Public Utilities Code, 33, 150
California Revenue and Taxation Code, 45
California Streets and Highway Code, 20

California Vehicle Code, 15
California Water Code, 144
can, 43
cannot, 43
capitalization
  in lists, 99–101
  style of, 168
cascading indents, 5, 38–42, 82
  colon before, 126
  romanettes with, 83–84
  semicolons with, 126
Cases and Other Materials on Legislation (Read, McDonald, & Fordham), 201
Castle, Richard, 64, 100, 146
Casual Essays of the Sun, 174
cataphora, 131
Cavers, David, 36, 202
charts, 70
Chicago Manual of Style, The, 126, 133, 168, 175
Child, Barbara, 199
chronological order, 73
circumlocution, 33, 47, 169
Clarifying EC Regulations (Cutts), 199
Clarifying Eurolaw (Cutts), 199
clarity
  as basic principle, 1–13
  as drafter's noblest goal, x
  campaign for, Evans on, 15
  citizens as readers, 155, 158
  Coode on, 109
  Cutts on, 21
  direct statement, Jones on, 135
  general terms and, 55
  Lord Thring on, 88
  phrasal adjectives, and, 129
  prejudice against simplicity, Stephen on, 137
  structural division, and references to, 19
  substantive defects and, 115
  syntax and, 107
Clarity for Lawyers: The Use of Plain English in Legal Writing (Adler), 132, 140, 199
Clark, William L., 171, 173
clauses, converting to phrases, 32
"Clear Legal Drafting: What's Holding Us Back?" (Dickerson), 115, 202
Coffee, John C., Jr., 171
colons, before indented enumerations, 126
Colorado Revised Statutes
  partially for *partly*, 153
  shall have the duty to for *must*, 47
commas, 114, 120, 127–28, 133, 134, 137
comma splices, 137
commence, 142
commencing . . ., 142–43
complexity
  Lord Renton on, 53
  O'Hayre on, 9
Composition of Legislation, The (Driedger), 95, 107, 200
compound sentences, breaking of, 5
compound words, style of, 168
Conard, Alfred F., 11, 13, 50, 97, 202
conciseness, 28–37
  Ilbert on, 129
  needless words, Adler on, 132, 140
conditions, 110–14
conditions precedent, 57
Congress, 6, 139, 168
conjunctions, 124, 136–37
Connecticut General Statutes
  doublet used in, 34
  therefor used in, 162
consequentialist school, ix
considered, 143–44
consistency
  Dickerson on, 159
  Kennedy on, 4
  in numbering, 79
  in usage, 13, 28
  Mackay on, 2
  of form, in parallels, 91–95
Coode, George, 109, 120, 199
Cook, Robert N., 199
counterintuitive definitions, 106
Criminal Law: The General Part (Williams), 49, 202
criminal prohibitions, 46, 49–54, 169–77
Cross, Rupert, 199
cross-references, 79, 80
Cullen, Robert K., 89, 202
Curme, George O., 174
Current English Usage (Leonard), 174
Cutts, Martin, xii, 21, 150, 199

D

Dale, William, 7, 27, 199
Dance of Legislation, The (Redman), 201
"dangling" flush text, 96–97, 98
Darmstadter, Howard H., 199
dashes, for interruptive phrases, 70, 120, 126, 127–28, 133
Davies, Jack, 199
deadlines, 73, 147
decimals, 78, 81
deem, 143–44
definitions
  generally, 103–06
  glossary, in, 106
  justifying, Ilbert on, 102
  overdefining, Butt and Castle on, 100
  placement of, 104–05
  problems with, Samuels on, 101
  shall mean, avoiding, 106
  words of authority, 43
defuse, 65
Delaware Code
  improved by enumeration, 86
  subsequently for *after,* 160
  triplet used in, 35
Delaware Legislative Drafting Manual (Legislative Council Division of Research), 176
Denonn, Lester E., 45, 201, 203

despite, 152
detail
  degree of, 55
  Kennedy on, 4
  Lord Renton on, 53
diagrams, 70–71
Dick, Robert C., 66, 199
Dickerson, Reed, iii
  as editor, 61
  on active voice, 58
  on ambiguity as distinguished from vagueness, 93
  on consistency, 159
  on the price of clarity, 115
  works in bibliography, 199, 202, 203
dictionaries
  Garner's. *See Garner's Dictionary of Legal Usage* and *Garner's Modern English Usage.*
  Merriam-Webster, 114
Dictionary of Contemporary American Usage (Evans & Evans), 174–75
diffuse, 65
Digest of the Criminal Law, A (Stephen), 201
Digest of the Law of Evidence, A (Stephen), 137, 201
"Diseases of Legislative Language, The" (Dickerson), 93, 202
disjunction, 136–37
District of Columbia Code
  except that in, 145
  hidden conditions in, 113
  of-phrases in, 124
  passive voice in, 59
  pursuant to in, 157
  semicolons, in nonterminal parts, 126
  singular and plural, mixing, 56
  so as to in, 159
  verbosity in, 28
  whenever used well in, 167
does not include, 90, 93, 105, 106
Does "Unlawful" Mean "Criminal"? (Coffee), 171
dollar amounts, 69
Doonan, Elmer, 71, 199
double-dash construction. *See* dashes.
double negatives, 60–62
doublets
  avoiding, 34–36
  words and numerals, 65–67
Drafting (Doonan ed.), 71, 199
Drafting and Interpreting Legislation (Pigeon), 201
Drafting Bills for the Minnesota Legislature (Kennedy), 4, 200
Drafting Legal Documents (Child), 199
Drafting Legislation (Xanthaki), 202
Drafting Manual for the Indiana General Assembly (Office of Code Revision Legislative Services Agency), 171
Driedger, Elmer A., 95, 107, 200
duties, generally, 47–48
Duxbury, Neil, 200

E

each, 165
Eagleson, Robert D., 22, 43, 158, 200, 202
Editorial and Design Stylebook (Plain Language Institute), 57, 201
Edward III, iii
"Efficiency in Legal Drafting" (Eagleson), 22, 202
Egner, Robert E., 45, 201, 203
ejusdem generis, 147
elegant variation, 13
Elements of Legal Drafting, The (Piesse), 201
Elements of Legislation (Duxbury), 200
Elliott, David C., 82, 121, 202
end, 142
end weight, principle of, 109
English Grammar (Curme), 174
enumerations, 85–102
  colons before, 126
  commas in, 127
  semicolons in, 126
  errors, preventing, 14
Essay on Crimes and Punishments, An (Beccaria), 55, 199
Essays on Legislative Drafting in Honour of J.Q. Ewens (Kelly ed.), 22, 200, 202
Evans, Bergen, 174–75
Evans, B. Ifor, 15, 200
Evans, Cornelia, 174–75
even if, 152
even though, 152
every, 144
except as, 144–45
exceptions, 23, 27, 39, 73, 112, 113, 115, 117
except that, 145
except when, 145–46
except with, 146
expire, 142
expressing duties, ix, 43–48

F

Federal Rules of Appellate Procedure, x
Federal Rules of Civil Procedure, x
Federal Rules of Criminal Procedure, x
figures. *See* numbers.
Filson, Lawrence E., 24, 65, 69, 200
Flesch, Rudolf, 200
Florida Statutes
  adverbial interruptive phrases, 119
  ambiguity in, 17
  gender neutral language, 63
  hanging indents, 38
  jargon in, 11
  only, placement, 166
  prepositional phrases, rewriting as adjectives, 124
  provided that in, 116
  remote relative pronouns in, 135
  romanettes, 84
  section, subsection, and other divisions, 78, 84, 87
  that vs. *which* in, 133
  upon introducing conditions or events, 164
flush left text, 96–98
following, 146

Fordham, Jefferson B., 201
foreshadowing, 90, 112
Forging Legislation (Light), 200
for it, 161
formatting
  Elliott on, 82
  with hanging indents, 38–42, 78–81
formulas
  for calculations, 70
  Elliot on, 121
for them, 161
forthwith, 147
fractions, 70
Freund, Ernst, 200
from, 153
"front-loading," Murawski on, 75
Fundamentals of Legal Drafting, The (Dickerson), 199
future perfect tense, 57

G

gaps in numbering, 83
Garner, Bryan A., vii, viii, ix, 5, 62, 147, 174, 200, 201
Garner's Dictionary of Legal Usage
  on *Congress,* 6, 68
  on doublets and triplets, 34
  on *lienholder* and *lienor,* 91
  on *unlawful,* 173
  on words of authority, 43
  on word usage, 168
Garner's Modern English Usage, 57, 101, 114, 119, 133, 134, 137
gender-neutral language, 63–64
general terms, 55
General View of the Criminal Law of England, A (Stephen), 201
Georgia Code
  conditions, placement in sentence, 110–11
  definitions in, 103
  except with in, 146
  expressing duties, 47
  hyphens in words with prefixes, 128
  no person shall in, 54
  organization of a section, 74
  singular and plural in, 56
  there are in, 162
Ginsburg, Ruth Bader, vii
glossaries, 106
Gobbledygook Has Gotta Go (O'Hayre), 9, 201
grammatical divisions, Coode on, 109
graphics, 70–71
Gray, John Chipman, 141
Guam Code
  benefits from parallel construction, 94
  which used as restrictive, 133
Guidelines for Drafting and Editing Court Rules (Garner), x, 200

H

Haggard, Thomas R., 91, 200
Hammurabi Code, 172
Hand-book of Criminal Law (Clark), 173
hanging indents, formatting with, 38–42, 78–81
Hart, Henry M., ix
Hawaiian Homes Commission Act, 160
Hawaii Revised Statutes
  past tense use in, 57
  multiple disjunctive conjunctions used in, 136
headings
  abundant use, 19–27
  grouping related items, 76
healthcare, 11, 54, 146, 156
he or she, 63, 64, 170
hereby, herein and similar words, 147
  Adler on, 140
  Krongold on, 124
  Tiersma on, 76
Hereof, Thereof, and Everywhereof (Darmstadter), 199
History of the Criminal Law of England, A (Stephen), 172, 201
House Legislative Counsel's Manual on Drafting Style (Office of Legislative Counsel), 201
however, 135
"How I Write" (B. Russell), 45, 203
How to Mangle Court Rules and Jury Instructions (Kimble), 202
How to Write Plain English (Flesch), 200
How to Write Regulations and Other Legal Documents in Clear English (Redish), 201
hyphens
  phrasal adjectives, 11, 129
  rules generally, 168
  words with prefixes, 128

I

Idaho Code
  ambiguity in, 15
  circular language in, 15
  commence and *expire* in, 142
  criminal prohibitions in, 50
  each in, 165
  end weight, principle of, 109
  hidden conditions in, 114
  word-numeral doublets in, 66
if, 110–14, 116–17, 149, 164
if any, 141, 148
Ilbert, Courtenay, 102, 105, 129, 200
Illinois Compiled Statutes
  capitalization, in lists, 101
  dollar amounts, 69
  hanging indents, 38
  numbering systems in, and consistency, 82
  provisions of in, 156
  remote relatives, 134
  verbosity in, 28
  whenever in, 164
includes, 106
including but not limited to, 149
including without limitation, 149
inclusive, 65
inconsistency. *See* consistency.

indents, hanging, 5, 38–42, 78–81
Indiana Code
  misplaced modifier in, 121
  parallelism, economy of 92
  wordy clause in, 32
individual, 114
infinitives, splitting, 174–75
internal references, 79–80
Internet access to law, xi
interpolations, 127–28
interpretation
  bad drafting and, 77
  Dickerson on, 159
  Evans on, 15
  generally, ix
  judges reading law, Gray on, 141
  Samuels on, 101
  Scalia and Garner on, 147
  Williams on, 125
Interpretation and Application of Statutes, The (Dickerson), 159, 199
interruptive phrases, 118–20
in the event of, 149
in the event that, 150
Introduction to an Essay on the Art of Legal Composition Commonly Called Drafting (Mackay), 2, 203
introductory phrases, 91, 127
invisibility, as goal of gender-neutral language, 63–64
Iowa Code, 14, 106, 113, 118, 141
  ambiguity in, 14
  any, using, 14
  counterintuitive definition in, 6
  hidden condition in, 113
  interruptive phrase in, 118
is entitled to, 43
it is unlawful, 46–54, 169–77

J

jargon, 10–12
Jaworski, Leon, 61, 202
Jones, Chester Lloyd, 135, 200
judges, reading law. *See* interpretation.
Judicial Opinions and Appellate Advocacy in Federal Courts—One Judge's Views (Posner), ix
"Judicial View of Modern Legislation, A" (Oliver), 29, 203
Justinian I, iii

K

Kansas Statutes
  romanettes in, 83
  such in, 161
Kelly, David St. Leger, 22, 200, 202
Kennedy, Duncan L., 4, 200
Kentucky Revised Statutes
  and/or causing ambiguity in, 16
  negative phrasing in, 61
kernel sentence parts, 107–08, 118
Kerr, Edward, 113, 202
Kimble, Joseph, x, xii, 31, 200, 202–03
Kirk, Maurice B., 17, 203
knowingly, 169, 174–75
Krongold, Susan, 39, 124, 203
Kuney, George W., 200

L

"Language and the Law" (Williams), 125, 203
Language of the Law, The (Mellinkoff), 30, 201
Lansing, Harriet, viii, x, xii
Latinisms. *See* plain English.
Law in the Making (Allen), 77, 199
Law-Making Process, The (Zander), 202
Law Reform Commission of Victoria, 200
lawsuit, 138
Legal Drafting (Cook), 199
Legal Drafting (Dick), 66, 199
"Legal Drafting: Curing Unexpressive Language" (Kirk), 17, 203
Legal Drafting in a Nutshell (Haggard), 91, 200
Legal Drafting: Process, Techniques, and Exercises (Haggard), 200
legalese. *See* archaic style.
Legal Language (Tiersma), 76, 202
Legal, Legislative, and Rule Drafting in Plain English (Martineau), 200
Legal Process: Basic Problems in the Making and Application of Law, The (Hart & Sacks), ix
Legal Writing in Plain English (Garner), 5, 200
Legal Writing: Sense and Nonsense (Mellinkoff), 136, 201
Legislative Council, 176
Legislative Council Division of Research, 176
Legislative Drafter's Desk Reference, The (Filson), 24, 65, 69, 200
legislative drafting, ix–xii
  art of, Driedger on, 107
  as individual talent, 17
  improvement, by change of habits, 116
Legislative Drafting (Dickerson), 199
Legislative Drafting (Thornton), 201
Legislative Drafting and Forms (A. Russell), 123, 138, 201
Legislative Drafting: A New Approach (Dale), 7, 27, 199
Legislative Drafting: English and Continental (Smith), 203
Legislative Drafting Guide (Tennessee Office of Legal Services), 171
Legislative Law and Process in a Nutshell (Davies), 199
Legislative Methods and Forms (Ilbert), 102, 105, 129, 200
Legislative Regulation (Freund), 200
Leonard, Sterling A., 174
Lewis, Norman, 175
lienholder, 91
lienor, 91
Lifting the Fog of Legalese (Kimble), 200

Light, Paul, 200
limitation, 150
lists, numbered. *See* enumerations.
Llewellyn, Karl, iii, 155, 203
logical arrangement, 73
Louisiana Children's Code, 47
Louisiana Revised Statutes
  negative phrasing used in, 60
  so as to for *to,* 160
  then and in that event used in, 36
Lucid Law (Cutts), 21, 199

M

MacFarland, Julie, 71, 199
Mackay, J.G., 2, 203
Maine Legislative Drafting Manual (Legislative Council), 176
Maine Revised Statutes
  ambiguous *shall,* 43
  forthwith used in, 147
  prior to used for *before,* 154
  related items not grouped, 76
  weak sentence ending, 109
malum in se crimes, 172–73
malum prohibitum crimes, 172
Marshall, William Lawrence, 171
Martineau, Robert J., 200
Maryland Code, Business Regulations, 59
Maryland Code, Health—General, 153
Massachusetts General Laws, 176
  commence used for *begin,* 142
  forthwith used for *promptly,* 168
  portion used for *part,* 153
  unclear proviso, 117
  whenever used for *if,* 164
Materials on Legal Drafting (Dickerson), 58, 122, 199, 203
may, 43
may not, 43
may . . . only, 165
McDonald, John W., 201
means, 106
Mechanics of Law Making (Ilbert), 200
"Mechanics of Statutory Revision" (Cullen), 89, 202
mechanics of style, 168
Mellinkoff, David, 30, 136, 201
mens rea, 169, 174–75
Merriam-Webster's Concise Dictionary of English Usage, 114
Michigan Compiled Laws
  headings and formatting, improved by, 26
  limitation used for *limit,* 150
  otherwise, placement of, 167
  tightening in, 32
Micklethwait, Sir Robert, 80
Minnesota Statutes
  negative phrasing used in, 60
  and-or used in, 139
  must not . . . except used for *may . . . only,* 165
misplaced modifiers, 121–22
Mississippi Code
  headings, would benefit from, 27
  word-numeral doublets used in, 65, 66
Missouri Revised Statutes, 5
misstatements, preventing, 14–18
model acts, 179–89
Modern Legal Drafting (Butt & Castle), 64, 100, 146, 199
modifiers. *See also* adjectives; adverbs.
  placement, 121–22
  relative clauses, 133–34
money, dollar amounts, 69
Montesquieu, Charles Louis, II (Baron de Montesquieu), 142, 201
more than, 154
Morris, Gouverneur, iii
Munson, Gorham, 174
Murawski, Thomas A., 44, 75, 201
must, 43
must not, 43
must not . . . except, 165
"Must We Continue with 'Shall'?" (Eagleson & Asprey), 43, 202

N

National Conference of Commissioners on Uniform State Laws, vii
Nature and Sources of the Law, The (Gray), 141
Nebraska Revised Statutes
  headings, would benefit from, 23
  interruptive adverbial phrase used in, 119
  thereof used in, 147
negative expressions, 57, 60–62
Nevada Revised Statutes
  must not . . . except used for *may . . . only,* 165
  percent spelled out in, 68
  readability problems in, 3
New Fowler's Modern English Usage, The (Burchfield), 114
New Hampshire Revised Statutes
  imprecise *shall mean* used for *means,* 106
  said used as definite article *the,* 158
New Jersey Statutes
  ambiguity in, 14
  illustration clears up convoluted text, 71
  only placed after term it affects, 166
  readability problems in, 2
New Mexico Statutes
  action used for *lawsuit,* 138
  formula clears up textual computation, 70
"New Ways to Write Laws" (Conard), 11, 13, 50, 97, 202
New York Alcoholic Beverage Control Laws, 79
New York Domestic Relations Law, 10, 41
New York Environmental Conservation Law, 100
New York Family Court Act, 40
New York General Business Law, 139
New York General Obligations Law, 149
New York Lien Law, 79, 91
New York Local Finance Law, 143

New York Public Housing Law, 7
New York Second Class Cities Law, 35
New York Town Law, 161
no later than, 166
nominal style. *See* zombie nouns.
nonproprietary, 103
nonrestrictive relative pronouns, 133
nonsexist language, 63–64
no person may, 46, 170
no person shall, 46
North Carolina General Statutes
  adverbial interruptive phrases, 119
  and/or in, 140
  criminal prohibitions in, 50
  except when in, 145
  headings in, 22
  plain English, rewriting for, 1
North Dakota Century Code
  deemed for *considered,* 144
  inconsistent use of *person, individual,* 13
  doublets used in, 34
  phrase can be trimmed, 124
  prior to for *before,* 154
not later than, 151
not less than, 151
not more than, 152
notwithstanding any other provision of law, 152
notwithstanding the fact that, 152
Nugent, Thomas, 42, 201
number, grammatical
  agreement of pronouns, 132
  singular, preference for, 56
numbering systems, 78–82
numbers
  calculations, displaying, 70
  generally, 65–69
  listed items, 85–102
  subpart numbering, 78–82

O

obligations, generally, 43–48
Office of Code Revision Legislative Services Agency, 171
Office of Legislative Counsel, U.S. House of Representatives, 201
Office of Parliamentary Counsel (Canberra), 201
of-phrases, 123–25
O'Hayre, John, 9, 201
Ohio Revised Code
  definitions, placement of, 105
  formatting, improved by, 42
  headings, improved by, 25
  notwithstanding the fact that used in, 152
  percent spelled out in, 68
  utilized used in, 164
Oklahoma Administrative Code, 85
Oklahoma Statutes
  arrangement of provisions, 75
  said used as article, 157
  such used as noun, 159
  transmit used for *send,* 163
  will used to designate a duty, 168
Oliver, Peter Raymond (Baron Oliver of Aylmerton), 29, 203
on, 163
on and after, 153
On Legislative Expression (Coode), 109, 120, 199
only, 166
on or before, 166
"On the Good, the True, the Beautiful in Law" (Llewellyn), 155, 203
or, 139
Oregon Revised Statutes
  agreement in number, 132
  not later than used in, 151
organization, 73–77
otherwise, 167
outline form, 78
Oxford Handbook of Language and Law, The (Solan & Tiersma eds.), 201

P

paragraphs, 78
parallel structure, 91–95
part, 153
partially, 153
partly, 153
Partridge, Eric, 114
parts, structural, 73–74
passive voice, 58–59
Pedestrian Safety Enhancement Act of 2010, 97
penalties, 73, 75, 176
  nonsensical expression, Thring on, 18
Pennsylvania Consolidated Statutes
  deem in, 60
  enumerations in, 85
  except in, 145
  exceptions, placement, 115
  hanging indent format, 39
  negative language in, 60
  of-phrases in, 123
  provided that in, 116
  structural divisions in, 78
  transmit in, 163
  whenever in, 164
percent signs, 68–69
phrasal adjectives, 124, 129
phrases, converting to words, 33–34
Piesse, E.L., 201
Pigeon, Louis-Philippe, 201
pilcrows, 68
placement of definitions, 104–06
plain English. *See also* readability.
  as basic principle, 1–4
  Eagleson on, 22
  Kimble on, 31
Plain English: A Charter for Clear Writing (Kimble), 203
Plain English for Lawyers (Wydick), 202
Plain English Manual (Office of Parliamentary Counsel (Canberra)), 201

Plain Language Action & Information Network, 201
"Plain Language: A Global Perspective" (Elliott), 82, 202
Plain Language for Lawyers (Asprey), 199
Plain Language Institute, 57, 201
"Plain Language: Is It Legal?" (Kerr), 113, 202
plurals, 56, 64
polysyndeton, 136
Popular Law-Making (Stimson), 202
portion, 153–54
positive expressions, 60–61
Posner, Richard A., ix
possessives, 64, 123, 125
Practical Legislation (Thring), 18, 81, 88, 112, 202
prefixes and hyphenation, 128
Preparation of Legislation, The (Renton, ed.), 53, 80, 116, 201
prepositional phrases, 37, 92, 123–25
present perfect tense, for conditions precedent, 57
present tense, preference for, 57
presumption of consistent usage, 13
Prevention of Defective and Slipshod Legislation, The (Sterne), 202
Principles of the Law of Family Dissolution, 37, 111, 131, 135
prior to, 154–55
Professionalizing Legislative Drafting—The Federal Experience (Dickerson ed.), 61, 201, 202
prohibitions
  conditional, 165
  criminal, 46, 49–54, 169–76
  generally, 43–48
  negative language, 62
pronouns
  antecedents of, 131–32
  gender-neutral language and, 64–65
  number agreement, 132
  relative pronouns, 133–35
Prose of Law: Congress as a Stylist of Statutory English (Bell), 139, 199
provided, however, that, 116–17, 155
provided that, 116–17, 155
provisions of, 156
provisos, 113, 116–17
punctuation, 126–29
purposivist school, ix
pursuant to, 156–57
Put it Plainly (Ralph), 174
Putting Words to Work (Teall), 174

R

Ralph, R.G., 174
Read, Horace E., 201
readability. *See also* plain English.
  bullets and, 98
  Dale on, 27
  format and, Siegel on, 122
  generally, 77
  Lord Renton on, 80
Reading Law: The Interpretation of Legal Texts (Scalia & Garner), ix, xi, 147, 174, 201
Redbook, The: A Manual on Legal Style (Garner), 126, 168, 200
Redish, Janice C., 201
Redman, Eric, 201
references to structural divisions, 79–80
Régis de Cambacérès, Jean-Jacques, iii
related items, grouping, 76
relative pronouns, 133–35
remote relative pronouns, 134–35
Renton, David (Baron Renton), 53, 80, 116, 201
repetition
  Cullen on, 89
  doublets, 34–36, 65–67
requirements, *See* words of authority.
"reserved" numbers, 83
residence, xi
Restatement (Third) of Property, 118
Restatement (Third) of the Law Governing Lawyers
  bullet points, rewriting with, 98
  interruptive phrases, rewriting with dashes, 120, 127
  misplaced modifiers in, 121, 122
  parallel structure in, 93
  passive voice in, 58
  zombie nouns in, 37
Restatement (Third) of Torts; Products Liability, 92
restrictive relative pronouns, 133–34
Rhode Island General Laws
  and in conjunctive lists, 136
  conditions, placement, 110
  modifiers, placement, 121
  shall in, 44
  "splintering" or unhelpful enumeration, 102
  using general terms, 55
rights. *See* words of authority.
romanettes, 83–84
Roman law, 171–72
roman numerals, small, 83–84
rule of lenity, 95, 174
Russell, Alison, 123, 138, 201
Russell, Bertrand, 45, 197, 201, 203

S

Sacks, Albert M., ix
safety codes, 58
said, 139, 157–58
Salerno, Michael B., 200
same, 159
Samuels, Alec, 101, 200
Scalia, Antonin, ix, 147, 174, 201
section signs, 68
semicolons, 126, 127
sentence length
  Bentham on, 28
  breaking up long sentences, 28–31
  computing, 5
  Conard on, 97
  Dale on, 27

generally, 5–9
sentence structure, naturalness, 1
serial commas, 127
sexism, 58, 63–64
shall
  alternative meanings, 43
  Cutts on, 150
  eliminating, 43–46
shall mean, 106
Shaw, George Bernard, 174
(s)he, 63
s/he, 63
should, 59
Siegel, Alan, 122, 203
simplicity
  Bentham on, 74
  Montesquieu on, 142
"Simplification of Government Regulations, The" (Cavers), 36, 202
singular noun, 56
singular number
  Bentham on, 56
  preference for, 56
singular *they,* 63
Smith, J.A. Clarence, 203
"Smokey Bear" statute, 175–76
so as to, 159–60
Solan, Lawrence, 201
South Carolina Code
  any used for *a, an,* or *other,* 141
  comma after introductory phrase, 127
South Dakota Codified Laws
  he used as gender-neutral in, 63
  long condition in midsentence, 112
  upon used in, 163
specificity. *See* detail.
Spirit of Laws, The (Montesquieu), 142, 201
splintering, 102
split infinitives, 174–75
"Stalking Defined" (Samuels), 101, 203
Standards of American Legislation (Freund), 200
Standing Committee on Rules of Practice and Procedure, x
Statute Law Making in the United States (Jones), 135, 200
statutory interpretation, ix. *See* interpretation.
Statutory Interpretation (Cross), 199
Stephen, James Fitzjames, iii, 137, 172, 201
Sterne, Simon, 202
Stimson, Frederic Jesup, 202
streamlining, Cavers on, 36
structure
  divisions of, 78–79
  Lord Thring on, 81
style
  Duncan Kennedy on, 4
  Mackay on, 2
subitems, 78
subject-verb separation, 118–19, 169, 170, 171
subordinate clauses, 127
subparts
  conjunctive and disjunctive, 136
  headings, 19
  indenting, 38
  numbering, 81
  structuring of, 78–80
subsequent to, 160
such, 123, 137, 160–61
surplusage. *See* verbosity.
synonym strings, 34
syntax, 99, 107–08

T

tables, 70
  Doonan on, 71
  Filson on, 69
Teall, Edward T., 174
technical terms. *See* terms of art.
Tennessee Code, 167
Tennessee Office of Legal Services, 171
tense, 57
terms of art
  confusion shown by, Bell on, 139
Texas Business Organizations Code, 58
Texas Family Code, 23
Texas Government Code
  may not used as prohibitory, 48
  not later than used in, 151
  phrasal adjective not hyphenated in, 129
  unparallel construction in, 91
Texas Legislative Council, 171
Texas Legislative Council Drafting Manual (Texas Legislative Council), 171
Texas Local Government Code, 48
Texas Revised Civil Statutes
  artificial language used in, 1
  hidden condition in, 162
  numbers spelled out in, 65
  shall used unnecessarily, 43
Texas Transportation Code, 131
text blocks, 85, 95
textualist school, ix
that, 147, 157
that (relative pronoun), 133–35
there are, 162
therefor, 161
therein, 147
there is, 162
thereof, 147
thereto, 147
they, as singular, 63
this, 147, 157
Thornton, G.C., 202
Thring, Henry (1st Baron Thring), 18, 81, 88, 112, 202
Tiersma, Peter M., 76, 201, 202
Tiffany, Francis B., 173
titles. *See* headings.

tone, 1
"Tools for Simplifying Complex Legislation" (Elliott), 121, 202
transmit, 162–63
treated as, 143
Treatise on the Law of Crimes, A (Barnes ed.), 171
triplets, 34
tyranny, bad drafting as a form of, 29

U

under, 156–57
under the following circumstances, 112
Uniform Anatomical Gift Act, 183–89
Uniform Commercial Code, vii
Uniform Law Commission, vii, viii, x, xii
Uniform Premarital Agreement Act, 181–82
United States Code
  ambiguity in, 16, 18
  any in, 141
  appositives, 90
  bullet points, 98
  conditions, placement, 110, 113
  criminal prohibitions in, 49–54
  definitions, 104
  end weight, principle of, 109
  enumerations, 85, 87–89, 126
  every in, 144
  exceptions, placement, 115
  expressing duties, 47
  foreshadowing, 90
  gender-neutral language, 63, 64
  headings, 21
  here- and *there-* compounds in, 147, 148
  hyphens, in phrasal adjectives, 129
  hyphens, in prefixed terms, 128
  interruptive phrases, 118, 119, 120
  in the event that in, 149, 150
  jargon, 10, 12
  kernel sentence parts, 107, 108
  not less than in, 151
  not more than in, 152
  number agreement of nouns and pronouns, 132
  obligations, 47
  of-phrases in, 123
  organization, 73
  parallel structure, 92, 95
  passive voice, rewriting as active, 59, 61
  plain English, 1, 4
  preference for positives, 61
  provided that in, 155
  provisions of in, 156
  remote relatives in, 135
  said in, 157
  semicolons, in lists of nonterminal parts, 126
  sentence length, 7–9, 107, 108
  shall in, 44
  such in, 161
  that vs. *which* in, 134, 135
  there is in, 162
  transmit in, 163
  unnumbered "dangling" flush text, 96
  verbosity, removing, 29, 30, 33, 37
unlawful, 46, 49, 169, 170, 171
unless, 144
unnumbered text, 96–97
Unspeakable Acts?: Clarifying the Language and Typography of an Act of Parliament (Cutts), 150, 199
upon, 163–64
up to, 152
usage
  consistency in, 13
  Redbook and, 166
Usage and Abusage: A Guide to Good English (Partridge), 114
use, 164
Use of English, The (Evans), 15, 200
usual place of abode, xi
Utah Code
  long sentence used in, 5
  portion used for *part,* 153
utilize, 164

V

vaccinate, 26
vaccine, 26
vagueness, 14, 61, 93, 147
verb–object separation, 118
verbosity, 28–34
verb phrases, splitting, 119
verbs
  subject–verb separation, 118–19, 169, 170, 171
Vermont Statutes
  if any used in, 148
  portion used for *part,* 154
  related items not grouped in, 76
  unhelpful enumeration in, 102
  unnecessary detail in, 55
Virginia Code
  and used as disjunctive, 136
  doublets used in, 35
  per centum spelled out, 68
Virgin Islands Code, 138
voice, 58–61

W

Wagner, Emma, 199
Wallraff, Barbara, 175
Washington Revised Code, 49, 137
West Virginia Code
  appositives, 90
  following in, 146
  foreshadowing, 90
  headings in, 20
  interruptive phrases, 118
  negatives, 62
  phrases into words, 34
  possessives, 125
  previous to in, 155
  provided in, 117
  references to structural divisions in, 80
  shall in, 45
  verbosity in, 28, 29
"What Is Plain English?" (Eagleson), 158, 200
when, 110, 164
whenever, 57, 164, 167

where, 110
which (relative pronoun), 133–35
Whitcut, Janet, 114
will, 43, 168
Williams, Glanville, 49, 125, 202, 203
Wisconsin Statutes
  all of in, 139
  ambiguity in, 14
  capitalization in lists, 99
  comma splices with *however,* 137
  conditions, placement, 112
  deem in, 143
  except as in, 145
  expressing duties, 47
  false future in, 57
  headings and levels of indent in, 26
  not less than in, 151
  notwithstanding any other provision of law in, 152
  of-phrases in, 125
  otherwise in, 167
  parallel structure in, 93
  plain English, 2
  prior to in, 154
  pronouns, when antecedents are clear, 131
  sentence length, breaking up, 5
  serial commas and serial semicolons, 127
  shall in, 45–47
  such in, 160
  tense, 57
within, 166
word choice
  Bentham on, 99
  Bertrand Russell on, 45
  Krongold on, 39
  naturalness, 1
  needless words, Adler on, 132
  precise terminology, in definitions, 103
  straightforwardness in, 47
  terms of art, Mellinkoff on, 30
Word Court (Wallraff), 175
wordiness. *See* verbosity.
word-numeral doublets, 65–67
words of authority, definitions for, 43
Works of Jeremy Bentham, The (Bowring ed.), x, 28, 56, 74, 98, 199
World War I American Veterans Centennial Commemorative Coin Act, 31
Wright, Charles Alan, iii, 62
Writing in Plain English (Eagleson), 200
"Writing Laws: Making Them Easier to Understand" (Krongold), 39, 124, 203
Writing Readable Regulations (Murawski), 44, 75, 201
"Wrong—Again—About Plain Language" (Kimble), 31
Wydick, Richard C., 202
Wyoming Statutes
  (a) without (b) used in, 79
  doublets used in, 35
  only misplaced in, 166
  shall used in various senses in, 46

X

Xanthaki, Helen, 202

Z

Zander, Michael, 202
zeros, 69
zombie nouns, 37, 149

CPSIA information can be obtained
at www.ICGtesting.com
Printed in the USA
BVHW011012120719
552996BV00012B/5/P